Trade in Services:
A Theoretical Analysis

Trade in Services:
A Theoretical Analysis

by

James R. Melvin

**The Institute for Research on Public Policy/
L'Institut de recherches politiques**

Printed in Canada

Legal Deposit Fourth Quarter
Bibliothèque nationale du Québec

Canadian Cataloguing in Publication Data

Melvin, James R.

Trade in services

Prefatory material in English and French
Includes bibliographical references.
ISBN 0-88645-090-X

1. Service industries.   2. International
trade.   3. Economic policy.   I. Institute
for Research on Public Policy.   II. Title.

HD9980.5.M45   1989   382'.45   C90-097512-1

Camera-ready copy and publication management by
PDS Research Publishing Services Limited
P.O. Box 3296
Halifax, Nova Scotia   B3J 3H7

Published by
The Institute for Research on Public Policy
L'Institut de recherches politiques
P.O. Box 3670 South
Halifax, Nova Scotia   B3J 3K6

Table of Contents

Foreword

It is becoming widely recognized that many consumer services previously generated within the household have migrated into the marketplace. Similarly many activities which might best be viewed as personal and social investment, and previously were undertaken within the family unit, now show up in our social accounts as health care, education, and social services provided through the public sector. And many services previously offered as internal activities within the hierarchy of organizations in primary or secondary industries now are marketed formally by service enterprises whose revenues therefore appear as part of the output of a formal service sector.

Thus the measured scale of the service sector grows, and many new activities come within the scope of public policies affecting market transactions.

Moreover, technological change increasingly makes possible a process of intermediation in service activities—a separation in space or time of the ultimate recipient of services from the original producer of those services. "Value-added" services along the way introduce new actors into the process of service provision, and the possibility of trade in such services across national boundaries brings within the scope of international negotiations and rules a vast range of activities previously missing from the trade policy arena.

Further, the nature of service activities moves trade away from a model of separated individual transactions and toward a structure of sustained relationships. The analysis of economic decisions, and of the possible impacts of public policy upon those decisions, becomes a very different and challenging exercise in these circumstances.

The growth of service activities based on such new technologies and more diverse, flexible organizational structures also introduces dramatically different approaches to competition and comparative advantage in international trade.

In place of strategies based on standardized products exploiting economies of scale in a settled organization of production, service-intensive, flexible production systems open up possibilities for global competition on the basis of custom services offered by flexible and adaptive organizations exploiting economies of scope in the utilization of a knowledge base and management skills.

Thus social investment in the creation and diffusion of knowledge, in education and training, is seen as a fruitful and productive investment—not just frivolous public consumption—and human capital is recognized as a durable asset on which longer term relationships in the organization of labour must be built. Comparative advantage in the international trading system is likely to reflect the extent of this knowledge base, the growth of human capital endowments, and the effectiveness of these organizational arrangements with the labour force.

Comparative advantage and competitive position in these circumstances are therefore likely to be ephemeral and heavily dependent on continued social investment in learning and adaptation, as well as in the maintenance of the renewable resource base and a healthy ecological system.

Anticipating the need for greater analysis of these developments, Industry, Science and Technology Canada (formerly the Department of Regional Industrial Expansion) in 1984 initiated discussions with the Institute for Research on Public Policy. Following some preliminary work undertaken by the Institute, the Department launched in May 1986 the Service Industries Studies Program (SISP) aimed at investigating the structure and dynamics of the service sector and its component industries. The Institute contributed to that program by focusing its research on Canada's international trade in services, while the Fraser Institute was asked to undertake a comprehensive examination of the growth of the service sector in the Canadian economy, and Statistics Canada was commissioned to review and develop the relevant underlying database. Industry, Science and Technology Canada will continue to work to develop a better understanding of the role of the service sector in the economy and to promote policies and programs in support of the international competitiveness of Canada's service industries.

The research program set up by IRPP was organized under four research modules, each dealing with a different aspect of the overall problem.

The first module, Trade in Services: A Theoretical Perspective, explored the various branches of economic theory to determine the positive and normative aspects of trade in services. Since the neo-classical trade and investment model was originally developed for analyzing goods trade, the research under this module was directed at identifying and exploring the various economic characteristics of services trade that must be incorporated into theoretical analysis of trade in services.

The second module, The Service Sector and Regional Balance, recognized that the extension of marketed services into broader inter-regional trade is a step—conceptually, if not chronologically—in the process leading to international trade, and therefore explored the role played by the service sector in the growth of regional economies.

The third module consisted of a series of case studies and dealt with the statistical and empirical issues encountered in analyzing trade in specific services. Transportation, financial services, computer and telecommunications, engineering services and real estate develop-ment and management were studied to explore the determinants of competitive position. These analyses were complemented by an exploration of the data already available on trade in services and foreign investment.

The fourth and last research module examined legal, institu-tional and negotiating issues particular to trade in services.

The present volume is the centrepiece of the first component of this work program. Starting from traditional theories of international trade, it extends the reasoning to reflect particular features of trade in services, and explores the extent to which traditional conclusions as to the welfare gains from trade remain valid. Possible increasing returns to scale, or so-called economies of scope, arising from fixed costs of investment in human resources or unique information underlying business or professional services are central concerns. The results suggest a number of new features with significant policy implications, but also confirm the impression that existing trade theory can possibly be extended to deal effectively with questions of the sort mentioned earlier.

As the Uruguay Round of multilateral trade negotiations enters its final year, efforts to develop a general framework agreement governing international trade in services seem likely to establish an effective basis for later, more detailed sectoral negotiations. The Institute hopes that results from this present volume on the theory underlying production and trade in services can contribute both to greater understanding of current developments in services trade, and to greater appreciation of the potential for significant further developments arising from future trade negotiations on a sectoral basis.

The financial support of the Government of Canada for the initiation and conduct of this research program is gratefully acknowledged. Related publications from the program are listed at the back of this volume.

Rod Dobell
President
November 1989

Avant-propos

On se rend de plus en plus compte qu'un grand nombre de services aux consommateurs, qui autrefois étaient l'affaire des ménages, sont en train de devenir un des éléments de l'économie de marché. Similairement, beaucoup d'activités qu'on aurait pu qualifier d'investissement personnel et social, et qui comme tel relevaient de la responsabilité de la cellule familiale, apparaissent maintenant dans les dépenses publiques aux chapitres de la santé, de l'éducation et des autres services sociaux. Et beaucoup d'autres services, auparavant considérés comme partie intégrante des activités de fonctionnement des industries primaires et secondaires, sont actuellement l'objet du commerce d'entreprises de services dont les revenus apparaissent, par conséquent, comme inclus dans la production d'un secteur officiel des services.

Ainsi la dimension quantifiable du secteur des services est en pleine croissance, et de nombreuses activités nouvelles entrent dans le domaine de compétence de la législation relative aux transactions de l'économie de marché.

Les changements technologiques, qui plus est, facilitent de plus en plus le processus de médiation dans les activités de services et par conséquent la séparation dans l'espace et dans le temps entre celui qui fournit originellement le service et celui qui en est le bénéficiaire final. Les services avec "valeur ajoutée" introduisent tout au long de la chaîne de nouveaux participants dans le processus de prestation de services, et la possibilité du commerce de ces services entre les pays ouvre la voie aux négociations internationales et régit un vaste éventail d'activités inconnues jusqu'ici dans ce domaine.

La nature particulière des activités de services contribue à éloigner le commerce d'un modèle de transactions individuelles indépendantes pour le rapprocher d'une structure relationnelle consolidée. L'analyse des décisions économiques et des conséquences possibles d'une politique officielle sur ces décisions devient, dans ces circonstances, un exercice très différent et qui demande une nouvelle approche.

La croissance des activités de services dérivant de ces nouvelles technologies et de structures organisationnelles plus différenciées et plus souples entraîne un changement considérable dans les attitudes vis-à-vis de la concurrence et de l'avantage comparatif en commerce international.

En remplacement des stratégies de standardisation de produits mettant à profit des économies d'échelle au sein d'une organisation de production bien établie, les systèmes axés principalement sur les services et sur une production adaptée aux circonstances ouvrent de nouvelles possibilités sur le plan mondial. Les entreprises innovatrices et prêtes à s'adapter au marché peuvent offrir des services sur mesure, employant les économies d'échelle qui mettent a profit leur base de connaissances solide et les compétences administratives de leur personnel de direction.

Ainsi, les investissements sociaux en matière de création et de diffusion des connaissances, dans les domaines de l'enseignement et de la formation professionnelle, peuvent-ils être considérés comme des investissements productifs et non pas simplement comme des dépenses publiques sans signification. Le capital humain est reconnu comme un bien durable à partir duquel doit s'élaborer, dans l'organisation du travail, un système de relations à plus long terme. L'avantage relatif sur le plan du commerce international a toutes les chances d'être fonction de cette base de connaissances, de la croissance de ces ressources humaines et de l'efficacité des rapports d'organisation avec le monde du travail.

Dans ces circonstances, l'avantage relatif et la position avantageuse d'une économie face à la concurrence seront vraisemblablement de courte durée et dépendront largement du renouvellement des investissements sociaux dans les domaines de l'apprentissage, de l'adaptation et de l'entretien des ressources renouvelables et d'un système écologique équilibré.

Dès 1984, prévoyant qu'il serait bientôt nécessaire de procéder à une analyse plus approfondie de ces nouvelles tendances, Industrie, Sciences et Technologie Canada (anciennement le ministère de l'Expansion industrielle régionale) prenait contact avec l'IRP pour discuter de cette question. À la suite de quelques travaux préliminaires entrepris par l'Institut, le ministère inaugurait en mai 1986 le Programme d'études sur les industries de services, dont le but était d'étudier la structure et la dynamique de ce secteur et des industries qui le composent. L'Institut a collaboré à ce programme en orientant plus particulièrement ses recherches sur le commerce international des services du Canada, alors que l'Institut Fraser entreprenait, de son côté, l'examen complet de la croissance du secteur des services dans l'économie canadienne et que Statistique Canada était chargé de revoir et d'améliorer la base de données fondamentale. Industrie, Sciences et Technologie Canada persévérera dans ses efforts pour améliorer la compréhension du rôle du secteur des services dans l'économie et pour promouvoir les politiques et les programmes afin d'appuyer la compétitivité internationale des industries de services canadiennes.

Le programme de recherches mis sur pied par l'IRP a été réparti en quatre modules portant chacun sur un aspect particulier du problème général.

Le premier, intitulé "Commerce des services : une perspective théorique", a été consacré à l'exploration des diverses branches de la théorie économique, afin de déterminer les aspects positifs et normatifs du commerce des services. Étant donné que le modèle néo-classique pour le commerce et les investissements était, à l'origine, destiné à l'étude du commerce des biens, les recherches dans le cadre de ce module ont visé à préciser et à identifier les diverses caractéristiques économiques du commerce des services qui pourraient être incorporées à l'analyse théorique de celui-ci.

Le second module, intitulé "Le secteur des services et l'équilibre régional", est parti de l'idée que la commercialisation des services à l'échelon interrégional était un premier pas, théoriquement sinon chronologiquement, vers l'internationalisation de ce commerce. Les recherches ont donc porté sur le rôle joué par le secteur des services dans la croissance des économies régionales.

Le troisième module a eu pour objectif l'étude d'une série de cas particuliers et des questions statistiques et empiriques qui se posaient au cours de l'analyse du commerce dans certains secteurs de services. Les transports, les services financiers, l'informatique et les télé-communications, l'ingénierie, l'expansion et la gestion de l'immobilier ont été examinés afin d'identifier quels facteurs déterminants permettaient l'accès à une situation concurrentielle. Ces analyses ont été complétées par une révision des données préalablement disponibles en matière de commerce des services et d'investissements étrangers.

Le quatrième et dernier module a été consacré à l'examen de questions particulières au commerce des services relativement à la législation, aux institutions et aux négociations.

Le présent volume constitue l'essentiel du premier constituant de ce programme de travail. Les théories traditionnelles en matière de commerce international y sont d'abord examinées; elles sont suivies de l'examen des aspects particuliers du commerce des services. Enfin, l'auteur se demande dans quelle mesure les conclusions traditionnelles, relativement à l'importance du commerce pour le bien-être, demeurent valides. L'accroissement possible des rendements d'échelle, ou de ce qu'on appelle les économies d'envergure, dû aux coûts fixes des investissements en ressources humaines ou à l'exceptionnelle compétence fondamentale pour les services commerciaux et professionnels, demeure une question préoccupante. Les résultats de ces recherches révèlent un certain nombre de particularités importantes pouvant avoir des conséquences politiques, mais ils confirment également notre impression que la théorie commerciale existante peut être adaptée pour répondre efficacement aux questions dont il a été fait mention ci-dessus.

Alors que les négociations commerciales multilatérales de l'Uruguay Round entrent dans leur dernière année, les efforts pour réaliser un accord en matière de commerce international des services devraient permettre d'assurer un point de départ raisonnable pour de futures négociations sectorielles plus détaillées. L'Institut espère que les résultats présentés ici, quant à la théorie relative à la production et au commerce des services, pourront contribuer à une plus grande compréhension des changements qui se produisent actuellement dans le commerce des services et à une meilleure évaluation des chances de progrès que comportent les futures négociations sur le plan sectoriel.

Nous désirons, pour finir, exprimer notre reconnaissance au Gouvernement du Canada pour l'aide financière apportée dans la mise sur pied et la conduite de ce programme de recherches. La liste des autres publications issues de ce programme est publiée au dos de ce volume.

Rod Dobell
Président
Novembre 1989

Executive Summary

1. Introduction

In the last few years economists have begun to pay more attention to the role that services play in the economy, and there is now a substantial literature describing the rise of the service sector in the industrialized nations. The service sector now accounts for some 60% of the GNP of most countries, and the importance of the sector along with the real or perceived problems associated with productivity growth are now widely discussed. The role of services has not escaped the attention of trade treaty negotiators, and services have become an important item on the upcoming GATT round of trade talks. An important feature of the free trade negotiations between Canada and the United States was liberalization of restrictions in the service area, and it seems clear that in the future service trade will form an important component of bilateral and multilateral trade talks. The policy questions have lead international trade theorists to begin investigations of to what extent trade in services differs from trade in goods, and there is now a small and growing theoretical literature that addresses these issues.

While studies on the theoretical issues associated with trade in services have begun to appear, the research is widely dispersed among books, economic journals, and volumes of conference proceedings. The present study tries to bring together the various theoretical arguments under a unifying structure. It is hoped that this study will provide a building block that will facilitate further theoretical research in this important area. The study focuses primarily on the series of research papers commissioned by the Institute for Research on Public Policy and financed by the Department of Regional Industrial Expansion, although some earlier theoretical works are reviewed in Chapter 2 and referred to throughout.

The principal issue when analyzing the consequences of trade in services is whether, in the context of traditional international trade theory, trade in services differs from trade in goods. In the final analysis it is found that, while there are fundamental similarities, there are, nevertheless, important differences. This study tries to identify both the similarities and the differences by bringing to bear on the issues of trade in services the analytical techniques and the theoretical models that would be found in a discussion of international trade in goods. The various techniques used in the chapters below are all familiar from traditional international trade theory, and the principal purpose of this analysis is to illustrate how the traditional conclusions must be modified when trade in services is considered. Of course the issue is not trade in services versus trade in goods, for it is difficult to imagine a world in which only trade in services occurs. Rather the issue is how appending trade in services to models in which trade in goods exists would be expected to change the theoretical conclusions and the policy implications.

As is true for any theoretical discussion of international trade, the final goal of this analysis is to provide a framework that will be useful for the analysis of real world problems and the formulation of economic policy. The primary motivation of the research is the question of whether the explicit introduction of services in trade models will fundamentally affect policy analysis. A variety of questions arise. For example, does the recognition that trade in services takes place require a reformulation of the effects of tariffs and other commercial policies? Can issues associated with trade in services be separated from issues concerning trade in goods or the questions associated with foreign investment? Will trade in services substitute for trade in goods, or will trade in goods and services be complements? Does the development of services facilitate or encourage the formation of multinationals, and if so, how would this be expected to affect trade patterns and the gains from international trade? All such questions have important policy implications, and these are examples of the issues that are addressed in the book.

In the few pages below I will try to provide a brief outline of the principal issues addressed in the study and will highlight some of the important propositions that are derived. Some of the principal recommendations, which are discussed in detail in Chapter 11, are also highlighted. It should be noted, however, that the study, while not high theory, is nevertheless theoretical in nature, and some of the propositions found throughout the book may not be self evident. I make no attempt to justify the results provided here but refer the reader to the relevant chapter in the book.

2. Conceptual Issues and Comparative Advantage

Chapter 2 provides a brief survey of some of the literature related to the trade in services area. While the notion of trade in services as such has not received much attention, there has been some discussion of topics which are clearly service related. First, there is quite an extensive empirical literature that focuses on the importance of services both nationally and internationally. No attempt has been made to summarize this quite extensive body of research in this study. A second body of related literature includes theoretical studies on industries that are in the service sector, such as transportation and education. Other topics include the issues of international and national factor movements. A brief outline of some of the literature in this area is provided in Chapter 2.

In Chapter 3 I turn to the conceptual issue of what distinguishes services from goods. The basic argument is that services relate to the dimensionality of economic analysis, and that it is the struggle to overcome the constraints associated with time and space that provide the activities that have come to be known as services. It is also argued that there are a variety of different kinds of services having quite different characteristics, and that such a distinction is important, particularly when the issue of tradability is considered.

In Chapter 4 the issue of comparative advantage in services is considered in more detail. The question of what gives rise to comparative advantage has a long and well-known history in the international trade literature, and indeed much of traditional trade theory is concerned with the issue of why trade takes place. Standard trade models attribute comparative advantage to such things as endowment differences, returns to scale, differences in tastes, and differences in technologies, and it seems clear that service trade, just as is true for goods trade, could be caused by any such difference among countries. But while substantial similarities between the determinants of service trade and goods trade were identified, the principal result of Chapter 3 is that sources of comparative advantage in services often do seem to differ from those of traditional trade theory. In particular, in many of the models considered, comparative advantage in services is seen to depend on human capital. Thus in Chapters 6 and 7, which addressed various aspects of trade in factor services, trade in services involved the international provision of information, engineering skills, management skills, or other special forms of human capital.

An important characteristic of comparative advantage based on human capital is the fact that the producers of these services typically are footloose. Thus the comparative advantage that a country might enjoy, and which is embodied in a group of architects, physicians, or specialized managers, could easily disappear if these individuals migrated elsewhere. Thus maintaining a comparative advantage in such activities may involve providing an economic and social climate that is attractive to the professionals involved. As the production of services becomes a more and more important component of economic activity it will become increasingly important to provide an economic, social, and physical environment that professionals and entrepreneurs find amenable.

The footloose and ephemeral nature of services emphasizes the importance of education for an economy if it is to be an active player in services trade. This leads to our first major set of recommendations, which are that higher levels of expenditure on education research and development are required, and that the provision of higher education should be substantially privatized and that whatever public funding is required should be provided by the federal government.

3.   The Transportation Sector

In Chapter 5 we concentrate on transportation and use, as the starting point, the Ricardian model. We begin by examining a model of a simple closed economy that produces two commodities, and where transportation of these commodities between production locations is required if individuals are to consume both goods. Services are shown to arise endogenously, and the allocation of labour among the three industries is found to depend on the technology used in the production of goods and services and on consumers' preferences. Changes in technology, both in services and in the production of commodities, are assumed, and the welfare consequences of such changes derived. A simple trading world is then examined where it is assumed that service technologies differ between countries. The consequences of having differences in the production function for commodities is also examined, and the distribution of gains from trade between the two countries is considered.

We then move to the consideration of a more traditional transportation model which concentrates on regional and international transportation costs (as opposed to considering the transportation costs associated with *all* trades) and consider the consequences of technological change. Because of the importance of inter-regional trade in the Canadian economy, the regional implications of transportation costs are emphasized in this section. Extensions of this model to the case where there are more than two factors is then considered briefly.

Some of the interesting results in this chapter concern the relationship between improvements in technology in the transportation sector, changes in the output of consumer goods and on the level of consumer's utility. In some circumstances an improvement in the technology for transporting goods will result in an increase in the output of all consumer goods and therefore an increase in the utility level of consumers. In other circumstances, however, while utility will increase, the actual output of all consumption goods may fall due to the increase in the demand for factors of production in the expanding transportation sector. The importance of this point is that the observation of an expanding service sector, even if production of consumer goods is declining, does not necessarily mean that welfare for consumers will fall.

When international trade in transportation services is considered, it is shown that service trade can increase the welfare of either or both countries and that, in general, differences in the efficiency of transportation industries among countries will be reflected in a merchandise trade deficit by the efficient country. When a model with both capital and labour is considered it is shown that a technological improvement in transportation will lower the real return of the factor used intensively in the import industry.

The policy recommendations from this chapter focus on the importance of providing an efficient transportation sector for any economy that wishes to engage in trade in transportation. Of course the provision of an efficient transportation sector is doubly important for a country such as Canada where distances between producers and consumers are often great. The importance of the transportation sector for Canada leads to the recommendation that deregulation of the transportation system be undertaken, and that less reliance be placed on fuel taxes as a source of general government revenue.

4. Factor Services

The analysis of factor services is taken up in Chapters 6 and 7. In Chapter 6 constant returns to scale is assumed and the traditional endowment model is used to analyze factor service trade. Chapter 7 considers the case where there is increasing returns to scale in the production of producer services, and where these services in turn enter the production of the consumer goods for the economy.

The model in which constant returns to scale is assumed uses the traditional Heckscher-Ohlin model with two factors and two goods. The analysis differs from the traditional model by assuming that only one commodity is tradable and that one of the factors, namely capital services, can be supplied by residents of one country to users in the other. Thus this model considers the case where there is trade in a producer service for a commodity. A geometric technique to analyze this case is developed and it is shown that efficient production and consumption can be achieved by trade just as is true in the more traditional model. There are important differences from the standard Heckscher-Ohlin model, however. For example, if the tradable commodity uses the mobile factor service intensively, the imported commodity is the one that was relatively cheap in autarky, and commodity trade patterns will not be as predicted as by the Heckscher-Ohlin theorem. It is also shown that in this case, trade of commodities for factor services will always result in efficient world output regardless of the initial endowment of factors. Thus service trade is more likely to lead to efficient world output than is traditional commodity trade.

Important differences are also found when commercial policy is considered. It is shown that if the imported commodity uses the mobile factor service intensively, then a tariff will reduce the price of the import relative to other commodity prices. Furthermore, the tariff will result in a relative and real reduction in the return to the factor used extensively in the import-competing industry. This result is just the opposite to what would be found in the traditional endowment model, and is shown to depend on the fact that a service is being traded for a commodity rather than a commodity for a commodity. Another important result from this chapter is that any tariff, whether applied to the capital-intensive or to the labour-intensive commodity will increase the return to labour. Thus in a model of trade for services labour will always favour a tariff.

With trade in producer services, domestic taxation is seen to play an important role in commercial policy. Indeed, for a country that imports a factor service in exchange for the exports of a good, a tariff takes the form of a tax on repatriated service income. Thus any differential treatment of foreign-earned income by domestic economy must be considered as a tariff, and the elimination of tariffs must ensure that any such differential treatment of foreign income is eliminated.

Some interesting results are also derived when the imposition of commodity taxes is considered. It is shown, for example, that when factor services are traded, differential domestic factor income taxes have the same production effects as tariffs and trade taxes. It is also shown that a domestic consumption tax combined with the tax on the factor income of the internationally-mobile service is equivalent to a tariff. Thus tariffs can be duplicated by a set of domestic taxes, but the taxes required are quite different than in the traditional model.

The analysis of Chapter 6 emphasizes the importance for national and international welfare of the unimpeded flow of factor services. The free flow of producer services is of particular importance since it has been shown that with service trade tariffs may not have the results predicted by traditional trade theory.

Chapter 7 is also concerned with trade in producer services but considers the possibility that some such services are produced under conditions of increasing returns to scale. In this chapter such production inputs as accounting, legal counsel, insurance, architecture, engineering consulting, and management consulting are considered. These are intermediate inputs to the production process, and are generally characterized by having large amounts of human capital embodied in them. The provision of human-capital intensive services such as legal advice and engineering skills can be provided only by individuals or groups of individuals who have undertaken significant periods of specialized training. The acquisition of the human capital typically involves a fairly lengthy period during which little or no returns to the individual are forthcoming, and which are typically quite costly to acquire. Once these skills have been acquired, however, they can typically be provided to firms at low marginal cost. Indeed, in many circumstances the output of such service producers may have a marginal cost approaching zero and the inputs may take on public good characteristics. Thus a skilled engineer or architect can provide sophisticated plans to many firms in many different locations simply by sending detailed blueprints and other forms of instruction.

It is the production of this human capital, and its implication as a service input to the production process, that is emphasized in Chapter 7. We assume that a factor service requires a significant fixed cost before any of the input can be provided, and assume that inputs can be produced at low and constant marginal cost. Thus the service inputs are produced under conditions of increasing returns to scale. The model assumes that there are two consumer goods, both produced under conditions of constant returns to scale. One uses labour and capital as inputs while the other uses only factor services. These factor services in turn are produced using only labour, and these production functions exhibit increasing returns to scale.

In this model there are several forms that international trade can take. As well as the traditional trade in commodities one can have trade in services, and indeed it can be shown that in simple symmetric models all the gains from trade can be achieved by trade in services only. Such trade will necessarily result in welfare improvements for both countries. Gains from trade need not be shared equally between the two countries, however, even if the countries are identical in every respect. Furthermore, if countries are not symmetric then trade in services will generally result in a change in commodity prices which would generate further trade and further gains for at least one country.

It is also found that the size of countries can be important in this model, with the smaller country generally gaining proportionally more than the larger. It is shown that while trade in goods alone will increase welfare for the large country but may reduce welfare for the small country, trade in services will unambiguously increase utility for both countries. It is therefore possible that in this model a tariff on goods can increase the welfare of a small country. These conclusions again lead to the recommendation that the free international flows of services be maintained and encouraged.

5. Multinationals and Foreign Investment

The possibility that services may give rise to the formation of multinationals and the introduction of international franchising operations is considered in Chapter 8. The principal result from this discussion is that, to some extent at least, multinationals arise because of economies of scale in the provision of some services internal to the firm. Producer services that are produced with high fixed and very low marginal cost can be provided to two or more plants almost as cheaply as to one. In particular, the average and marginal cost of producing a commodity in a two-plant firm will be less than if two independent firms existed to produce this product. The principal result is that, since the existence of multinationals lowers cost, economic welfare will generally be increased by their existence.

The fact that multinationals increase efficiency, however, is not the end of the story. Because the economies of scale are internal to the firm, one would expect some type of imperfect competition to develop. Firms can typically make pure economic profits, and in this case the distribution of welfare will very much depend on where the owners of the multinational firms reside. It is certainly possible that a substantial share of the gains associated with the high level of efficiency will be transferred to foreign countries if the multinationals are foreign owned. Even with this proviso, however, it was shown that it will generally be true that both the host and donor countries will gain from the existence of multinational firms.

Some of the same characteristics are true for franchising operations. Franchises typically arise when there are economies of scale, either in advertising, promotion, or in the purchasing of inputs. In general, the ability of such firms to capture these economies of scale will result in welfare gains, although as was the case with multinationals, it is not always clear to whom these gains will accrue. On balance, however, and particularly since multinationals are not domiciled in a single country, general welfare gains to society are to be expected from the operation of such companies.

In some circumstances economic policy makers may be faced with a choice of allowing trade in a service product, or of granting rights of establishment to foreign firms, which may require the importation of service factors. Thus, for example, we may have the choice between allowing domestics to buy banking services from foreigners, or alternatively of allowing foreign banks to bring their expertise to Canada and set up branches that will directly serve domestics. These options were addressed in Chapter 9, and it is found that an unambiguous ranking is not possible unless endowments at home are "extreme". One general result shown is that there is always a positive relationship between the size of the welfare gain and the expansion of the service industry. This provides a convenient and simple rule for policy formation. Since larger welfare gains are associated with increases in the size of the service sector in the domestic economy, policy should be formulated on the basis of how the size of the industry will be affected.

An important issue related to investment in the service industries taken up in Chapter 10 is the question of how productivity can be measured and whether technical change in services can form the basis of sustained economic growth. Methods of measuring technical change in services have proven to be elusive, due partly to the fact that new technologies in this area are often markedly different than the old, making comparisons difficult. At the same time it is clear that many of the really important technological advances throughout history have occurred in service industries, and have facilitated trade and communications. Indeed, any trade requires transportation services, and thus gains from trade are really gains from services, and this includes *all* trade, not just international trade. This suggests that technological advances in service industries, particularly in transportation and communication, can provide enormous benefits to society, and thus social policy should encourage research in these important areas.

6. Conclusions

In conclusion it seems important to recognize that the research reported here is still at a very preliminary stage, and should be thought of simply as the starting point for what will undoubtedly become a significant research area in the future. The theoretical results we have reported must be regarded as preliminary, and undoubtedly many important topics have been omitted. The lack of information on exactly which services are most important for international trade makes it difficult to be sure that we have focused attention on issues of major importance. Thus our discussion has been very general, and future research will undoubtedly show that some of the issues we have considered are not as important as others. Nevertheless, it is hoped that the theoretical research presented here will prove useful for subsequent researchers interested in the area of international trade in services.

Abrégé

1. Introduction

Au cours des dernières années, les économistes ont commencé à s'intéresser davantage au rôle joué par les services dans l'économie, et il existe aujourd'hui un grand nombre de publications qui font état de la montée du secteur des services dans les pays industrialisés. Le secteur des services représente de nos jours environ 60% du PNB de la plupart des pays, et son importance, ainsi que les problèmes associés à l'accroissement de la productivité, que ces problèmes soient réels ou perçus comme tel, font actuellement l'objet de nombreuses discussions. Le rôle joué par les services n'a pas manqué d'être remarqué par les négociateurs chargés de discuter des traités commerciaux, et ce sujet occupera une place importante lors des entretiens sur le commerce dans le cadre du GATT. L'un des points importants abordés dans les négociations commerciales entre le Canada et les États-Unis était la libéralisation des restrictions dans le secteur des services, et il semble clair qu'à l'avenir, le commerce des services constituera une composante importante des entretiens bilatéraux et multilatéraux sur le commerce. Les questions de politique générale ont mené les théoriciens du commerce international à mener des enquêtes visant à découvrir jusqu'à quel point le commerce des services différait du commerce des biens, et il existe aujourd'hui un certain nombre de publications, encore peu nombreuses mais en passe de le devenir, qui traitent de ces questions.

Alors que les études sur les questions théoriques associées au commerce des services ont commencé à faire leur apparition, les résultats des recherches sont encore publiés d'une manière dispersée (livres, revues d'économie, publications de comptes rendus de congrès). La présente étude a pour but de rassembler les différents arguments théoriques dans un seul et même volume, et il est à souhaiter qu'elle constituera une base sur laquelle pourront s'appuyer les futures recherches dans ce domaine d'importance capitale. L'étude porte principalement sur la série de documents de recherche préparés à la demande de l'Institut de recherches politiques et financés par le ministère de l'Expansion industrielle régionale, bien que certains travaux théoriques antérieurs soient examinés au chapitre 2 et mentionnés d'un bout à l'autre de l'ouvrage.

Lorsqu'on procède à l'analyse des conséquences du commerce des services, la question primordiale est de savoir si, dans le contexte de la théorie traditionnelle du commerce international, le commerce des services diffère du commerce des biens. L'analyse finale démontre que, bien qu'il existe des similarités fondamentales entre les deux, il y a malgré tout d'importantes différences. Cette étude vise à identifier à la fois ces similarités et ces différences; pour ce faire, toutes les techniques analytiques et les modèles théoriques qui pourraient apparaître dans des entretiens sur le commerce international des biens ont été appliqués aux questions de commerce des services. Les différentes techniques employées dans les chapitres décrits ci-dessous sont toutes familières, étant tirées de la théorie traditionnelle du commerce international, et le but principal de cette analyse est d'illustrer la manière dont les conclusions traditionnelles doivent être modifiées dans le cas du commerce des services. Bien entendu, l'objectif n'est pas d'opposer le commerce des services au commerce des biens, car il serait difficile d'imaginer un monde où seul existerait le commerce des services. Il s'agit plutôt de savoir comment l'annexion du commerce des services aux modèles où il existe déjà un commerce des biens pourrait changer les conclusions théoriques et les implications politiques.

Comme c'est le cas lors de n'importe quelle discussion portant sur le commerce international, le but ultime de cette analyse est de fournir un cadre qui puisse servir à l'analyse des véritables problèmes mondiaux et à la formulation de politiques en matière d'économie. Les mobiles principaux de la recherche sont de déterminer si l'introduction explicite des services dans les modèles commerciaux affectera de façon fondamentale l'analyse politique. Il en découle un certain nombre de questions, entre autres : est-ce que le fait de reconnaître que le commerce des services existe implique qu'il faille reformuler les effets des tarifs et autres politiques commerciales? Les questions relatives au commerce des services peuvent-elles être dissociées de celles relatives au commerce des biens ou encore de celles se rapportant aux investissements étrangers? Le commerce des services remplacera-t-il le commerce des biens, ou est-ce que le commerce des biens et celui des services peuvent se compléter? L'expansion du commerce des services peut-elle faciliter ou encourager la création de multinationales, et si oui, dans quelle mesure cela affectera-t-il les structures commerciales et les profits découlant du commerce international? Toutes ces questions ont des implications politiques importantes et représentent quelques uns des problèmes dont il est question dans cet ouvrage.

Dans les pages qui suivent, j'essaierai de présenter un bref aperçu des problèmes principaux dont il est question dans cette étude et je soulignerai quelques-unes des propositions importantes qui en découlent. Certaines des recommandations principales, qui sont exposées en détail au chapitre 11, y seront également mises en lumière. J'aimerais toutefois faire remarquer que l'étude, sans être hautement théorique, est néanmoins de nature théorique, et certaines des propositions qui y sont présentées ne sont pas toujours évidentes. Je n'essaierai pas de justifier les résultats présentés ici, et j'invite le lecteur à se reporter au chapitre approprié de l'ouvrage.

2. Questions conceptuelles et avantage comparatif

Le chapitre 2 présente un bref examen d'un certain nombre de publications se rapportant au secteur du commerce des services. Alors que la notion de commerce des services n'a pas été largement étudiée en tant que telle, on a passablement discuté de sujets qui sont nettement apparentés au secteur des services. Tout d'abord, il existe un grand nombre de publications empiriques consacrées à l'importance des services à la fois sur le plan national et international. Aucun effort n'a été fait, cependant, pour résumer dans cette étude les nombreuses recherches menées dans ce domaine. Il existe également un certain nombre d'autres publications, parmi lesquelles se trouvent des études théoriques sur les industries appartenant au secteur des services, telles que l'industrie des transports et l'éducation. Parmi les autres sujets traités, citons les questions traitant des mouvements dans les services des facteurs nationaux et internationaux. Un bref résumé de quelques ouvrages publiés dans ce domaine est présenté au chapitre 2.

Au chapitre 3, je me penche sur la question conceptuelle suivante : qu'est-ce qui distingue les services des biens? L'argument de base est que les services se rapportent à la caractéristique dimensionnelle de l'analyse économique, et que c'est la lutte pour surmonter les contraintes de temps et d'espace qui aboutit aux activités que l'on appelle communément services. Un des autres arguments présentés est qu'il existe toute une variété de diverses sortes de services, dont les caractéristiques sont très différentes les unes des autres, et qu'il est important de faire cette distinction, surtout lorsqu'il s'agit de déterminer la valeur commerciale des services en question.

Au chapitre 4, la question de l'avantage comparatif est examinée en détail. Le phénomène qui donne naissance à l'avantage comparatif a souvent été analysé dans différentes publications traitant de commerce international, et en fait, une grande partie de la théorie traditionnelle du commerce vise à déterminer pourquoi les échanges commerciaux ont lieu. Les modèles commerciaux courants attribuent l'avantage comparatif à des caractéristiques telles que les différences de qualité, les rendements d'échelle, les différences de goût et de technologies, et il semble évident que le commerce des services, tout comme le commerce des biens, pourrait avoir pour origine n'importe laquelle de ces différences entre les pays. Pourtant, alors qu'on a identifié des similarités appréciables entre les causes déterminantes du commerce des services et celles du commerce des biens, la conclusion principale du chapitre 3 est que les sources de l'avantage comparatif dans les services semblent souvent différer de celles de la théorie traditionnelle du commerce. En particulier, dans plusieurs des modèles examinés, l'avantage comparatif dans les services est perçu comme étant fonction du capital humain. C'est pourquoi aux chapitres 6 et 7, consacrés aux différents aspects du commerce des services des facteurs, le commerce des services est examiné sous l'angle de la fourniture d'information, des compétences en génie, des compétences en gestion ou d'autres formes de capital humain, à l'échelle internationale.

Une des caractéristiques importantes de l'avantage comparatif basé sur le capital humain est le fait que les producteurs de ces services sont en général mobiles. Ce qui fait que l'avantage comparatif qu'un pays peut avoir à son actif, concrétisé par un groupe d'architectes, de médecins ou de directeurs spécialisés, pourrait facilement disparaître si ces individus venaient à émigrer. C'est pourquoi il peut être parfois nécessaire qu'un pays, afin de maintenir son avantage comparatif, soit en mesure d'offrir à ses professionnels un climat économique et social attrayant. La production des services devient une composante de l'activité économique dont l'importance croit sans cesse, et il sera de plus en plus impératif que l'environnement économique, social et physique sache plaire aux professionnels et aux entrepreneurs.

La nature mobile et éphémère des services souligne l'importance de l'éducation pour l'économie, si celle-ci doit jouer un rôle actif dans le commerce des services. Ceci nous mène à notre première série de recommandations, à savoir : il est indispensable d'augmenter les montants consacrés à l'éducation, à la recherche et au développement; l'enseignement supérieur devrait être substantiellement privatisé; les fonds publics nécessaires devraient être fournis par le gouvernement fédéral.

3. Le secteur des transports

Au chapitre 5, nous nous intéressons plus particulièrement aux transports et nous nous servons, comme point de départ, du modèle de Ricardian. Pour commencer, nous examinons le modèle d'une simple économie fermée qui produit deux marchandises, et où le transport de ces marchandises entre les lieux de production est nécessaire pour que les particuliers puissent consommer ces deux marchandises. On observe que les services se créent d'une manière endogène, et que la répartition de la main-d'oeuvre parmi les trois industries dépend de la technologie employée dans la production des biens et services et des préférences des consommateurs. Les changements technologiques, aussi bien dans le secteur des services que dans celui de la production des marchandises, sont pris en considération et les conséquences de ces changements sur le bien-être des consommateurs sont calculées. Nous examinons ensuite un monde commercial simple, et l'on part du principe que les technologies de services diffèrent d'un pays à l'autre. Le fait qu'il existe des différences dans la production des marchandises est également pris en considération, ainsi que la répartition des profits du commerce entre les deux pays.

Nous examinons ensuite le modèle d'un secteur de transports plus traditionnel, plus particulièrement la question des coûts du transport régional et international (par opposition aux coûts du transport relatif à *tous* les échanges commerciaux) et nous étudions les conséquences des changements technologiques. Étant donné l'importance du commerce inter-régional dans l'économie canadienne, les implications à l'échelle régionale des coûts de transport sont soulignées dans ce paragraphe. Nous examinons ensuite brièvement l'application de ce modèle dans les cas où il existe plus de deux facteurs.

Parmi les résultats les plus intéressants présentés dans ce chapitre, citons les rapports qui existent entre les améliorations technologiques apportées dans le secteur des transports relativement à la distribution des biens de consommation et le niveau d'utilité des consommateurs. Dans certains cas, l'amélioration de la technologie des transports entraînera une augmentation de la production des biens de consommation, et par conséquent le niveau d'utilité des consommateurs sera lui-même augmenté. Dans d'autres cas, au contraire, malgré l'augmentation de l'utilité, la production réelle des biens de consommation risque de diminuer à cause de l'accroissement de la demande pour des facteurs de production dans le secteur des transports en expansion. Ceci est un phénomène important car, lorsque le secteur de services est en expansion, le fait que la production des biens de consommation est en baisse ne signifie pas nécessairement que le bien-être des consommateurs va décroître.

Lorsqu'on examine le secteur des services de transports dans le contexte du commerce international, on s'aperçoit que le commerce des services peut accroître la prospérité de l'un ou l'autre des pays, ou même des deux, et qu'en général, les différences d'efficacité qui existent d'un pays à l'autre dans les industries de transports auront pour conséquence un déficit de marchandises commerciales pour le pays efficace. Lorsque l'on examine un modèle avec capital et main-d'oeuvre, on constate que l'amélioration technologique dans les transports entraînera une diminution du rendement effectif du facteur utilisé intensément dans l'industrie d'importation.

Les recommandations politiques présentées en conclusion à ce chapitre insistent sur l'importance de l'efficacité dans le secteur des transports, si l'on veut que l'économie puisse jouer un rôle actif dans le commerce des transports. Il va de soi que, pour un pays comme le Canada, il est doublement important que le secteur des transports soit efficace, du fait des énormes distances qui séparent souvent les producteurs des consommateurs. L'importance du secteur des transports pour le Canada nous mène à recommander que la déréglementation du système des transports soit entreprise et que le gouvernement compte moins sur les taxes sur le carburant comme source de revenu général.

4.   Les services des facteurs

L'analyse des services des facteurs est faite aux chapitres 6 et 7. Au chapitre 6, on part du principe que le rendement d'échelle est constant et on utilise le modèle de qualité traditionnel pour analyser le commerce des services des facteurs. Au chapitre 7, on examine un cas où les rendements d'échelle dans la production des services sont en croissance et où ces services, à leur tour, entrent en jeu dans la production des biens de consommation pour l'économie.

Le modèle à rendement d'échelle constant est basé sur le modèle traditionnel de Heckscher-Ohlin, mettant en jeu deux facteurs et deux marchandises. L'analyse diffère du modèle traditionnel en ce sens que l'on suppose qu'une seule des marchandises peut faire l'objet d'une transaction commerciale et que l'un des facteurs, celui des services en capital, peut être fourni par les habitants de l'un des pays aux utilisateurs de l'autre. Ce modèle présente donc un cas où un service de production est échangé contre une marchandise. Ce cas est analysé grâce à une technique géométrique, et il en découle que la transaction commerciale peut mener à une production et à une consommation efficaces, comme c'est aussi le cas dans le modèle plus traditionnel. Il existe toutefois des différences importantes par rapport au modèle standard de Heckscher-Ohlin. Par exemple, si la marchandise qui fait l'objet du commerce dépend largement du facteur de mobilité, la marchandise importée est celle qui était relativement bon marché en autarcie, et les structures du commerce des marchandises seront différentes de celles présentées dans le théorème de Heckscher-Ohlin. On constate aussi que dans ce cas, l'échange d'une marchandise contre des services de facteurs aura toujours pour résultat une production mondiale efficace, quelle que soit la qualité initiale des facteurs. Par conséquent, le commerce des services aura plus de chances d'aboutir à une production mondiale efficace que le commerce traditionnel des marchandises.

On trouve également d'importantes différences lorsqu'on examine la politique commerciale. Il s'avère que si la marchandise importée dépend grandement du facteur de mobilité, l'application d'un tarif douanier réduira le prix de l'importation par rapport aux prix des autres marchandises. Qui plus est, ce tarif douanier aura pour résultat une réduction relative et réelle du rendement du facteur largement employé dans l'industrie compétitive d'importation. Ce résultat est exactement contraire à ce qu'on pourrait trouver dans le modèle de qualité traditionnel, et on s'aperçoit qu'il dépend du fait qu'un service est échangé contre une marchandise plutôt qu'une marchandise contre une autre marchandise. Ce chapitre met en lumière un autre résultat important : tout tarif douanier, qu'il soit appliqué à une marchandise capitalistique ou à une marchandise de main-d'oeuvre, aboutira à l'augmentation du rendement de la main d'oeuvre. Par conséquent, un modèle de commerce de services de main-d'oeuvre sera toujours plus rentable si un tarif douanier est appliqué.

Dans les cas de services de production, on constate que l'imposition intérieure joue un rôle important dans la politique commerciale. En fait, pour un pays qui importe un service de facteur en échange de l'exportation de marchandises, le tarif douanier est appliqué sous la forme d'un impôt sur le revenu pour service rapatrié. Par conséquent, tout traitement différentiel des revenus étrangers par l'économie intérieure doit être considéré comme un tarif douanier, et l'élimination des tarifs douaniers doit aboutir à l'abolition de tout traitement différentiel des revenus étrangers de cet ordre.

On aboutit également à des résultats intéressants lorsqu'on examine les taxes sur les marchandises. On constate par exemple que, lorsque les services des facteurs sont l'objet d'un échange commercial, les impôts intérieurs différentiels sur le revenu ont les mêmes effets de production que les tarifs douaniers et les taxes commerciales. On constate également qu'une taxe intérieure de consommation, combinée à la taxe sur le facteur de revenu du service mobile à l'échelle internationale, est équivalente à un tarif douanier. Par conséquent, les tarifs douaniers peuvent être reproduits par un ensemble de taxes intérieures, mais les taxes requises sont bien différentes de celles du modèle traditionnel.

L'analyse du chapitre 6 souligne l'importance de maintenir la continuité des services des facteurs, à l'échelle nationale et internationale. L'importance des services de production a été prouvée lorsqu'on a constaté qu'avec le commerce des services, les tarifs douaniers risqueraient de ne pas avoir les résultats escomptés selon la théorie commerciale traditionnelle.

Le chapitre 7 est également consacré au commerce des services de production, mais on y envisage le cas où certains de ces services sont fournis dans des conditions où le rendement d'échelle est en croissance. Dans ce chapitre, les facteurs de production tels que la comptabilité, les conseils juridiques, l'assurance, l'architecture, les ingénieurs conseils et la consultation en gestion sont pris en considération. Ces facteurs occupent une place intermédiaire dans le processus de production et comportent généralement une forte proportion de capital humain. Les services de capital humain tels que les conseils juridiques et les compétences en génie ne peuvent être fournis que par des individus ou des groupes d'individus qui ont reçu une longue formation spécialisée. En général, l'acquisition d'un capital humain implique un délai assez long et relativement coûteux, pendant lequel on doit s'attendre à un rendement individuel faible ou même inexistant. Mais une fois les compétences acquises, celles-ci peuvent servir les besoins des entreprises à des coûts marginaux peu élevés. En fait, dans de nombreux cas, la production de tels services peut atteindre un coût marginal proche de zéro, et les facteurs peuvent avoir les caractéristiques des biens publiques. Ce qui fait qu'un ingénieur ou un architecte spécialisé peut fournir des projets élaborés à de nombreuses entreprises situées dans des endroits différents en leur envoyant, tout simplement, des plans détaillés et d'autres instructions.

La production de ce capital humain, ainsi que ses implications en tant que facteur du processus de production, sont examinées en détail au chapitre 7. Nous supposons qu'un service de facteur requiert des frais indirects élevés avant qu'aucun service puisse être fourni, et que ces services peuvent être produits à un coût marginal peu élevé et constant. Ces services sont donc produits dans des conditions de rendement d'échelle en croissance. Le modèle part du principe qu'il y a deux marchandises, toutes deux produites avec un rendement d'échelle constant. L'une fait appel aux facteurs de la main-d'oeuvre et du capital, l'autre n'utilise que des facteurs de services. Ceux-ci, de leur côté, ne sont produits qu'à partir de la main-d'oeuvre, et ces fonctions de production indiquent des rendements d'échelle en croissance.

Selon ce modèle, le commerce international peut prendre plusieurs formes : le commerce traditionnel des marchandises ou le commerce des services. On peut montrer que, dans les cas de simples modèles symétriques, tous les profits commerciaux peuvent provenir uniquement du commerce des services. De tels échanges commerciaux ne pourront qu'améliorer la prospérité des deux pays. Toutefois, les profits commerciaux ne doivent pas être partagés également entre les deux pays, même si ceux-ci sont identiques à tous points de vue. De plus, si les pays ne sont pas symétriques, le commerce des services engendrera généralement une modification des prix des marchandises, qui à son tour entraînera davantage d'échanges commerciaux et davantage de profits pour au moins un des pays.

On constate également que la taille du pays peut jouer un rôle important selon ce modèle, les petits pays gagnant proportionnellement davantage que les plus grands. On constate que, si seul le commerce des marchandises est pratiqué, la prospérité des grands pays augmentera alors que celle des pays plus petits risquera de diminuer, alors que dans le cas du commerce des services, l'utilité des deux types de pays augmentera sans ambiguïté. Il est donc possible que, selon ce modèle, l'application d'un tarif douanier sur les marchandises permette d'augmenter la prospérité d'un petit pays. Ces conclusions mènent encore une fois à la recommandation que le libre commerce des services doit être maintenu et encouragé.

5. Les multinationales et les investissements étrangers

Au chapitre 0, on examine la possibilité que le commerce des services entraîne la création de multinationales et l'introduction d'opérations internationales de franchisage. Le résultat principal de cette discussion est que, dans une certaine mesure tout au moins, les multinationales sont la conséquence des économies d'échelle dans la fourniture de certains services à l'intérieur d'une même compagnie. Les services de production qui sont fournis à des coûts élevés fixes et à des coûts marginaux très bas peuvent être fournis à deux usines ou plus pratiquement au même prix qu'à une seule. En particulier, le coût moyen et marginal de production d'une marchandise par une compagnie ayant deux usines sera inférieur à celui de deux entreprises indépendantes l'une de l'autre qui existeraient pour produire cette même marchandise. Le résultat principal de ceci est que, puisque l'existence des multinationales permet de réduire les coûts, la présence de celles-ci favorisera l'accroissement de la prospérité économique.

Le fait que les multinationales permettent d'augmenter l'efficacité n'est pas tout. Du fait que les économies d'échelle sont intérieures à l'entreprise, on pourrait s'attendre à ce qu'une forme de compétition imparfaite ait lieu. Les entreprises sont à même de faire des profits purement économiques, et dans ce cas la répartition de la prospérité dépendra grandement du lieu de résidence des propriétaires de la multinationale. Il est certainement possible qu'une part considérable des profits associés au niveau élevé d'efficacité soient transférés dans des pays étrangers, si les multinationales appartiennent à des propriétaires étrangers. Toutefois, même dans ce cas, l'étude a montré qu'en général, le pays hôte aussi bien que le pays donateur profiteront de l'existence des multinationales.

Certaines des mêmes caractéristiques sont valables pour les opérations de franchisage. Les franchises naissent lorsqu'on est en présence d'économies d'échelle, dans les domaines de la publicité, de la promotion ou de l'achat de services. En général, de telles compagnies sont capables de capturer ces économies d'échelle, et leur prospérité s'en accroît, bien que, comme c'était le cas pour les multinationales, l'identité des bénéficiaires de ces profits n'est pas toujours évidente. Toutefois, l'un dans l'autre, et surtout du fait que les multinationales ne sont pas domiciliées dans un seul pays, la société a tout à gagner de l'existence de ces compagnies.

Dans certains cas, les économistes responsables des décisions politiques peuvent avoir à choisir entre permettre l'échange commercial de services ou accorder le droit à une compagnie étrangère de s'établir au pays, ce qui risque d'impliquer l'importation de services de facteurs. Nous pouvons donc, par exemple, avoir à décider entre permettre aux compagnies canadiennes d'acheter des services bancaires à l'étranger, ou, au contraire, permettre aux banques étrangères de faire venir leurs experts au Canada et d'ouvrir des succursales qui offriront directement leurs services aux Canadiens. Ces différents choix sont examinés au chapitre 9, et on s'aperçoit qu'il est impossible d'établir un ordre de priorités clair, à moins que les qualités canadiennes soient "extrêmes". Un résultat général indique que l'importance des profits est proportionnelle à l'expansion de l'industrie des services. Ceci nous fournit une règle simple et pratique pour la formation des politiques. Puisque les profits sont proportionnels à l'expansion du secteur des services dans l'économie intérieure, les politiques devraient être formulées en fonction de la manière dont celles-ci affecteront l'industrie.

Des questions importantes, en rapport avec les investissements dans les industries de services, sont traitées au chapitre 10 : comment la productivité peut-elle être mesurée? Les changements techniques dans les services peuvent-ils constituer la base d'une croissance économique durable? Les moyens à notre disposition pour mesurer les changements techniques dans les services se sont avérés évasifs, en partie parce que les nouvelles technologies, dans ce domaine, sont souvent si différentes des anciennes que la comparaison est pratiquement impossible. Toutefois, il est clair qu'un grand nombre des progrès technologiques très importants qui ont été faits au fil des ans se sont produits dans le domaine des industries de services et qu'ils ont facilité le commerce et les communications. De fait, tout échange commercial requiert des services de transport, et par conséquent les profits commerciaux sont en fait des profits de services, et ceci englobe *tous* les échanges commerciaux, et non pas uniquement le commerce international. Ces constatations indiquent que les progrès technologiques accomplis dans les industries de services, et en particulier dans le domaine des transports et de la communication, peuvent fournir d'énormes bénéfices à la société; la politique sociale devrait donc encourager la recherche dans ces domaines d'importance capitale.

6. Conclusion

En conclusion, il semble important de reconnaître que la recherche dont il est question ici n'en est encore qu'à ses débuts, et qu'elle devrait être considérée comme un point de départ pour ce qui ne manquera pas de devenir, dans le futur, un domaine de recherche significatif. Les résultats théoriques que nous avons présentés doivent être considérés comme étant préliminaires, et sans nul doute de nombreux sujets importants ont été omis. Le fait que nous n'ayons pas pu savoir avec exactitude quels sont les services les plus importants pour le commerce international a rendu notre tâche difficile et nous ignorons si nous avons porté assez d'attention aux questions capitales. C'est pourquoi notre propos a gardé un caractère général, et la recherche future montrera sans doute que certaines des questions que nous avons examinées sont moins importantes que d'autres. Toutefois, nous espérons que la recherche présentée dans cette étude s'avérera de quelque utilité aux futurs chercheurs qui se pencheront sur les problèmes de commerce international des services.

Chapter I

Introduction

1.1 Introduction

In the last few years economists have begun to pay more attention to the role that services play in the economy, and there is now a substantial literature describing the rise of the service sector in the industrialized nations. The service sector now accounts for some 60% of the GNP of most countries, and the importance of the sector along with the real or perceived problems associated with productivity growth are now widely discussed. The role of services has not escaped the attention of trade treaty negotiators, and services have become an important item on the upcoming GATT round of trade talks. An important feature of the free trade negotiations between Canada and the United States was liberalization of restrictions in the service area, and it seems clear that in the future service trade will form an important component of bilateral and multilateral trade talks. The policy questions have lead international trade theorists to begin investigations of to what extent trade in services differs from trade in goods, and there is now a small and growing theoretical literature that addresses these issues.

While studies on the theoretical issues associated with trade in services have begun to appear, the research is widely dispersed among books, economic journals, and volumes of conference proceedings. The present study tries to bring together the various theoretical arguments under a unifying structure. It is hoped that this study will provide a building block that will facilitate further theoretical research in this

1

important area. The study focuses primarily on the series of research papers commissioned by the Institute for Research on Public Policy and financed by the Department of Regional Industrial Expansion, although some earlier theoretical works are reviewed in Chapter 2 and referred to throughout.

The principal issue when analyzing the consequences of trade in services is whether, in the context of traditional international trade theory, trade in services differs from trade in goods. In the final analysis it is found that, while there are fundamental similarities, there are, nevertheless, important differences. This study tries to identify both the similarities and the differences by bringing to bear on the issues of trade in services the analytical techniques and the theoretical models that would be found in a discussion of international trade in goods. The various techniques used in the chapters below are all familiar from traditional international trade theory, and the principal purpose of this analysis is to illustrate how the traditional conclusions must be modified when trade in services is considered. Of course the issue is not trade in services versus trade in goods, for it is difficult to imagine a world in which only trade in services occurs. Rather the issue is how appending trade in services to models in which trade in goods exists would be expected to change the theoretical conclusions and the policy implications.

As is true for any theoretical discussion of international trade, the final goal of this analysis is to provide a framework that will be useful for the analysis of real world problems and the formulation of economic policy. The primary motivation of the research is the question of whether the explicit introduction of services in trade models will fundamentally affect policy analysis. A variety of questions arise. For example, does the recognition that trade in services takes place require a reformulation of the effects of tariffs and other commercial policies? Can issues associated with trade in services be separated from issues concerning trade in goods or the questions associated with foreign investment? Will trade in services substitute for trade in goods, or will trade in goods and services be complements? Does the development of services facilitate or encourage the formation of multinationals, and if so, how would this be expected to affect trade patterns and the gains from international trade? All such questions have important policy implications, and these are examples of the issues that will be addressed in the chapters below.

1.2 Research Plan

We begin, in Chapter 2, with a review of some of the relevant literature. The emphasis in succeeding chapters is theoretical, and there does not exist a great deal of theoretical literature in the service trade area. There is some closely-related literature, however, and several authors have taken up the conceptual issue of the distinction between services and goods. A brief review of some of the most important contributions on these topics will be provided. In Chapter 3 we turn to the conceptual issue of what distinguishes services from goods. The basic argument is that services relate to the dimensionality of economic analysis, and that it is the struggle to overcome the constraints associated with time and space that produces the activities that have come to be known as services. It is also argued that there are a variety of different kinds of services having quite different characteristics, and that such a distinction is important, particularly when the issue of tradability is considered.

In Chapter 4 we consider the basic issue of the sources of comparative advantage in services. It is argued here and shown in subsequent chapters that the traditional sources of a comparative advantage described in the international trade literature will also exist for services. It is also argued, however, that the sources of comparative advantage in services may differ from those in traditional models because they tend to be footloose or ephemeral. The uncertainty surrounding this characteristic of many service industries is shown to have important policy implications; a theme which reoccurs in subsequent chapters.

Chapter 5 considers the transportation sector, and analyzes a variety of questions in terms of the Ricardian trade model. A simple example of transportation services is used to illustrate how technological change in a service industry can augment the gains from international exchange. Chapter 6 introduces trade in producer services and uses the Hechscher-Ohlin model to analyze the case where countries trade services for goods rather than goods for goods. This trade pattern is shown to require a rather fundamental reinterpretation of some of the traditional trade results, and in particular will require a reevaluation of the effects of commercial policy. Chapter 7 continues the discussion of factor services, but analyzes them in terms of a model with increasing returns to scale. It is argued that returns to scale are often associated with the formation of human capital, and this is shown to have important policy implications.

Chapter 8 investigates a number of questions concerning investment in service industries using the specific factor model, and considers the issue of whether a country would gain more from trade in service inputs or from trade in service commodities. These questions are related to the issue of whether it would be more appropriate to allow domestic consumers to buy service commodities from foreigners or to allow foreigners to establish plants in the domestic economy to produce these services. Chapter 9 investigates the role of services in the multinational enterprise and analyzes the issue of whether the existence of multinationals will be beneficial to both the host and home countries. The issue of licensing and franchising is also considered. Chapter 10 analyzes some of the issues concerned with productivity of services and argues that whether productivity improvement should be expected will very much depend on the kind of service being considered. We conclude the analysis in Chapter 11 with a summary of the policy conclusions derived from the analysis.

Chapter 2

Some Related Literature[1]

2.1 Introduction

For classical economists such as Adam Smith the distinction between goods and services was regarded as a matter of great importance. Over the years this distinction has diminished, and for the purpose of economic modelling, goods and services have been seen as equivalent. Indeed, at present, economists frequently refer to goods and services as if they were the same. When economists began to consider the importance of the services sector in modern western economies this treatment of the two concepts as theoretically equivalent came under increasing scrutiny. In addition, the fact that trade in services is to be considered in the next round of GATT talks has prompted economists to ask whether such trade can be adequately explained by existing models or whether there may be new insights to be gained by considering services as distinct from goods in such models.

2.2 Conceptual Issues

One of the principal difficulties in modelling services is the lack of a precise definition of services that clearly distinguishes them from goods. T.P. Hill (1977) was one of the first modern writers to focus on

5

this question. Hill rejects the notion that the distinction between goods and services should be dismissed or that services are, as Marshall suggested, simply immaterial goods. He also suggests that, while the output of goods is distinct, and therefore easily measurable, the output of services is not. Hill claims that "there is little understanding about the nature of the physical units in which most services should be quantified and consequently their prices are also vague and ill defined" (Hill, 1977, p. 315). He suggests that without such an understanding about quantities and prices "economic theory becomes irrelevant" (Hill, 1977, p. 315).

Hill, in order to distinguish goods from services, proposes a definition of each. A good, he states, "may be defined as a physical object which is appropriable and, therefore, transferable between economic units" (Hill, 1977, p. 317). In contrast, a service is defined as "a change in the condition of a person, or a good belonging to some economic unit, which is brought about as a result of the activity of some other economic unit, with the prior agreement of the former person or economic unit" (Hill, 1977, p. 318). He suggests that goods and services have distinct characteristics and that they "belong to quite different logical categories" (Hill, 1977, p. 318). Services must be applied directly to the good or person requiring the service, he argues, so that the consumption of a service must take place simultaneously with its production. One consequence of the simultaneity of production and consumption is that services, unlike goods, cannot be stored. Another consequence of this simultaneity is that services cannot be transferred from one economic unit to another. Thus Hill claims, "models of pure exchange economies of a Walrasian type...are quite inapplicable and irrelevant" (Hill, 1977, p. 319).

It should be noted that Hill's definition can be applied not only to services that are the output of a production process but also to services that are labour inputs and, with some minor modification, to public goods and externalities.

Hill constructs an elaborate classification system for services. He notes that any service activity may be applied to either goods or persons, that they may be temporary or permanent, that they may be reversible or irreversible, and that they may result in physical or mental changes. He analyzes each classification in turn and suggests that perhaps the appropriate distinction is not that between goods and services but between services to persons and services to goods. This suggestion arises from the observation that the problem of measurement is a feature particular to services to persons. He notes that while the servicing of a boiler is easily measurable, it is often impossible to measure the output of individuals such as teachers, professors, doctors, actors or musicians. This is because, when considering services to a person, it is difficult to attribute the degree of change due to the input of the servicer, and furthermore the change affected can vary according to the individual serviced.

Zweifel (1986) suggests a definition that is very similar to Hill's. Zweifel, however, suggests that an additional restriction, namely the preservation of the identity of the product being serviced, is necessary for the definition of a service. While this restriction is noted by Hill he does not consider it as central to the definition of a service. The motivation for Zweifel's additional restriction is that in a service process the good cannot "lose its identity in the way that material inputs do in the course of production . . . (and) the consumer of the service must be able to recognize and claim his good at any point in the process" (Hill, 1977, p. 320).

An alternative classification to the one proposed by Hill is suggested by Sampson and Snape (1985). They seek to classify services by the form of the transaction involved. For some services, such as tourism or surgical services, either the receiver or the producer of the service must move. This corresponds to the assertion of Hill that services must be consumed where they are produced. However, Sampson and Snape do not see the movement of agents as central to the definition of a service since they point out that other services can be carried out at 'arm's length' by means of post, telephone or computer links. Services such as banking, insurance, or technical advice can be provided in one country for consumers in another. The restrictiveness of Hill's definition has also been noted by Sapir (1985) and Hindley and Smith (1984).

Baumol (1985, p. 302-303) suggests three broad headings under which services should be listed and analyzed. They are: Stagnant Personal Services (for example, haircuts), Progressive Personal Services (for example, electronic communications), and Asymptotically Stagnant Impersonal Services (which is an amalgam of the first two). Asymptotically Stagnant Impersonal Services include such activities as computation, which involves computer software development (which is an example of Stagnant Personal Services) and computer hardware (which is an example of Progressive Personal Services).

The problem of devising a precise definition of services has also been discussed in the literature. Kravis (1983) claims that the proposed definitions often fail to make clear-cut distinctions between goods and services and that it is possible to find an activity that is commonly agreed to be a service that does not fit any definition proposed. This may explain the fact that some writers abandon the search for a definition and resort simply to listing the activities that are commonly known as services. In one of the earliest recent papers on services, Fuchs (1968) presents a taxonomy of services which has been employed by other writers such as Leveson (1985) and, with one minor alteration, by Summers (1985). Other examples of this method are to be found in Sapir (1985) and Benz (1985). A more indirect definition of services is presented by Shelp (1981) who defines a service as being any production activity that is not included in manufacturing, mining or agriculture.

From the multitude of definitions, classifications and tax-onomies, it seems that we are far from an agreement on a precise definition of a service. Inman (1985, p. 4) suggests that "like beauty, the definition of a service activity is often in the eye of the beholder." It is not at all clear that an unambiguous and widely accepted definition is possible, even though it is commonly believed that services are different from goods in some fundamental way.

2.3 Empirical Issues

As indicated in the introduction, economists are becoming increasingly aware of the relative importance of services in modern western economies. Indeed much of the early work on services concentrated on an empirical description and analysis of the services sector. This research is so extensive that a complete survey would be impossible in this chapter, and thus our objective here will be to summarize the principal issues raised in this literature.[2] The relative importance of the service sector is well documented in Benz (1985). He notes that in 1982, the services sector accounted for 69% of GNP in the United States economy, 74% of jobs, 86% of job growth and 37% of export related employment. In Canada, services are almost equally important, accounting for approximately 62% of current GNP.[3] However, despite the significance of these figures there is still a belief that they understate the case and that many services are currently subsumed under other headings. Rugman (1986) suggests that payment for the export of managerial services in multinational enterprises are hidden in repatriated-profits, while Inman (1985, p. 2) suggests that it is only with economic growth and specialization that many firms contract out services which enables them to be counted as a separate market activity. Benz suggests that with the increased focus on services there will be an improved accounting of service activities, and that it is possible that the share of the services sector in the United States economy may be even higher than present figures indicate. He further suggests that one of the reasons for the reluctance of the European nations to discuss trade in services at the forthcoming GATT talks may be the lack of an accurate European data base.

Another pervasive theme in the empirical literature is the effect of changes in technology on employment in the various sectors of the economy. It is commonly perceived that as labour is replaced in the manufacturing sector by computers and robots the services sector will expand to absorb the excess supply of labour. This hypothesis is examined by Inman (1985) who uses a version of Baumol's (1967) two-sector growth model, to analyze the possibility that the expansion of the service sector is a result of technical change.

An important issue in the empirical literature is the measurement of productivity, and the evidence of Baumol (1967), Fuchs (1968), and Kuznets (1972) suggests that productivity growth in the services sector has been slow. This has been seen as an explanation for the fall in overall productivity growth in the U.S. economy.[4] This hypothesis does not command universal support. Nordhaus (1972), Thurow (1979), and Wolff (1981) reject what Inman has called the Baumol-Fuchs hypothesis and suggest that the services sector has traditionally been more productive than other sectors and thus as labour moves into the services sector productivity must rise on average. Baumol (1985) disputes this argument and suggests that the services sector which is "presumably more labour intensive than most economic activities...cannot be characterized by a relatively high value of...absolute labour productivity" (Baumol, 1985, p. 316). He concludes that services will always lag behind other sectors of the economy in productivity development. In recent papers, Summers (1985) and Saxonhouse (1985) support Baumol's view

2.4 Comparative Advantage in Services

There is very little evidence in the conceptual discussions to suggest that the distinction between goods and services necessarily has any theoretical implications. Indeed it can be argued that Hill's work, with the exception of his remark about the inappropriateness of Walrasian exchange models, pays little attention to the theoretical implications of his distinction between goods and services. Further, Hill does not suggest any reasons why theorems generally associated with trade in a Walrasian exchange model would fail in an alternative framework where services are specified formally.

In contrast to Hill, Hindley and Smith (1984) can see no reason for concern at the neglect of the distinction between goods and services. They argue that goods are not a homogeneous commodity but rather that different goods have quite distinct characteristics. Nevertheless despite these differences in characteristics we would expect the theory of comparative advantage to apply. Hindley and Smith suggest that the same argument should apply to services, and that there is therefore no theoretical reason why goods and services should be distinguished *per se*.

Hindley and Smith, however, do allow that service industries have certain features, such as the prevalence of government regulation or the requirement that factors move, that may affect the observation of comparative advantage. They note that licensing and regulation is a feature of many service industries and some economic rationale has to be advanced to explain this. A common argument is that licensing and regulation is needed either to protect buyers who are unable to assess the service received or to prevent 'destructive competition'. Hindley and Smith dismiss the destructive competition argument on the grounds that regulation is simply an attempt to collect economic rent, much as are tariffs or quotas. This view is supported by Benz (1985) and Ewing (1985) who suggest that many services are not traded because of barriers erected by governments to serve the interests of domestic producers, to the detriment of consumers. Inman (1985) suggests that in the presence of asymmetric information problems, where buyers may have difficulty in assessing the value or quality of a service, government regulation may have a role to play. In any case, Hindley and Smith do not see any particular problem with the application of the principle of comparative advantage to these services. They point out that one would not expect any distinction between the need to regulate domestic suppliers of services and the need to regulate foreign suppliers and thus that the principle should continue to be applicable.

Like Hill, Hindley and Smith also note that many services cannot be physically traded and thus producers may have to relocate rather than export their goods internationally. They point out that an assessment of eighteen services industries suggests that foreign direct investment and labour migration can act as a substitute for trade in goods. They claim that while positive trade theory may be unable to predict whether a comparative advantage will manifest itself as a trade flow, an investment flow or a labour flow, the principle itself should not be violated. Thus a country with a higher pre-trade price for a service will gain either by importing services or by allowing immigration of labour or by receiving foreign direct investment. The topic of factor migration will be dealt with more extensively in Section 2.5.

Deardorff (1985) also considers the application of the principle of comparative advantage in the context of trade in services. Deardorff argues that there are at least three characteristics that may potentially lead to a violation of the principle. The first is that some services are only demanded as a consequence of trade in goods and thus have no autarky price. The second characteristic is the one discussed above by Hindley and Smith, namely that many services involve factors relocating when a country moves from autarky to free trade. The third characteristic is the fact that some factor services, such as management or technical expertise, can be supplied from a foreign country. The second of these, factor movements, is shown by Deardorff not to involve any conflict with the principle of comparative advantage. The general area is discussed in more detail in Section 2.5 and will not be considered further here.

Deardorff shows that when services are demanded only as a consequence of trade in goods the principle of comparative advantage can also be shown to hold. To demonstrate this he assumes that there are N countries and M goods, and that there are T services that are only employed if there is trade in goods. These services are used to carry a country's exports to a single market-clearing port and they can be provided by any of the N countries. Let X^i be a vector of a country's output of goods, C^i a vector of its consumption of goods, S^i a vector of its production services and U^i a vector of the trade services used in the course of trade. Further, let p^i and q^i be vectors representing the prices of goods and services respectively, where the superscript i refers to the case where a country is either in autarky (a) or is engaged in free trade (f). Deardorff then specifies both the autarky and competitive equilibria and demonstrates, by means of a revealed preference argument, that the following inequality holds.

$$p^a X^f - p^a C^f + q^a S^f - q^a U^f \leq 0$$

This inequality establishes that, on average, the goods and services a country exports must be worth less to it in autarky than the goods and services it imports. Thus, the principle of comparative advantage holds. It should be noted that this average relationship does not rule out the possibility that some goods and services may be traded in a pattern that violates the principle of comparative advantage, but this is also true in a model with many goods and no services.

We now turn to his third case, trade in factor services. It was noted above that while some services have to be produced in the same location as the consumer, some factor inputs (such as management or technical expertise) can be supplied from abroad. In order to capture this notion Deardorff constructs a model along Heckscher-Ohlin lines where there are two countries, two factors, one good and one service. The service is not tradeable and the factors of production are labour and management.

Suppose there are two countries, A and B, where A has a relative abundance of labour. If services are labour intensive then, in autarky, country A will have a comparative advantage in services. However, since the source of the comparative advantage lies in the relatively cheap source of labour in A, managers in B have an incentive to relocate in A to combine with labour and supply services in country A in exchange for goods. Deardorff suggests that this result violates the principle of comparative advantage since the "labour-scarce country B exports labour-intensive services in spite of the fact that these services cost more in B than in country A in autarky" (Deardorff, 1985, p. 65).

There is, however, some confusion possible here, for trade in services is defined as the production of services in A by managers located in country B, rather than as the export of factor (management) services. Deardorff himself notes that the principle can be rehabilitated if it is reinterpreted to apply to the supply of management services. In this case country B has the comparative advantage since the relative salary of management in B is lower in autarky. Indeed, it should be noted that there is no apparent reason to call the non-traded sector a service at all. The same result would hold if the non-traded sector produced a good rather than a service.

However, Deardorff claims that such a reinterpretation will lead to problems if the comparative advantage in country A is based upon a technological advantage in the production of services. Deardorff assumes a neutral technological improvement in the production of services in A and further assumes that managers can take this new technology with them when they work in B. It is not exactly clear what this means, however. Does the fact that a manager in A works in B mean that the service industry in B is now as efficient as in A? If so is this true only for firms using foreign managers or for *all* firms? If the latter then we no longer have a technological advantage in A. Alternatively, if this is not the case, how can the two different technologies for producing services exist side by side in B? If the technology is factor augmenting, then we really have different factors in the two countries, and no longer any difficulty with defining comparative advantage (a point made by Jones (1985)).

Deardorff also worries about the fact that country A may "export" management services even though the returns to K are higher in A in autarky. This point seems to confuse the issue of what is being traded. While it is true that the returns to management is higher in A relative to the returns to labour, this is not the relevant comparison. The exchange is of management services for a commodity, and when these prices are compared, management is relatively inexpensive in A. This point is taken up in some detail in Chapter 6.

2.5 Services and Factor Movements

A recurring theme in much of the work reviewed so far is the fact that many services require direct contact between the producer and the consumer. Thus, medical operations and haircuts require that either the producer or the consumer migrate if the service is to be provided by a non-resident producer. The possibility of factor migration acting as a substitute or as a complement to trade has already received considerable attention in the traditional theoretical literature. Mundell (1957a) showed that in the Heckscher-Ohlin model factor mobility could act as a substitute for trade in goods, since countries can eliminate their differences in endowments by means of factor migration. In a model with increasing returns to scale, Melvin (1969) has shown that in addition to gains for trade there will be gains to factor movements, and thus trade and factor flows are complimentary. A similar result is derived by Krugman (1979) who shows that factors may all migrate to one country because of the gains arising from increasing returns to scale. There are other circumstances when factor movement in the presence of scale economies or imperfect competition may be complementary to trade in goods. Markusen (1983) develops a model where both countries have identical factor endowments but where one country is technically superior in the production of one good, and he shows that factor mobility is complimentary to trade in goods. In such a model, factor migration permits a country to become relatively better endowed with the factor employed intensively in its export industry, and the volume of trade consequently increases.

There is also an extensive literature on optimal factor migration policies when a country can discriminate between returns to domestic and foreign factors. Ramaswami (1968) showed that if one factor is immobile, then the country should allow the mobile factor to move until the rents to the home country are maximized. The economic rationale is simply that any country with monopoly or monopsony power will choose the appropriate amount of factor migration such that its rents are maximized. If a country can choose to either import the scarce resource or export the abundant factor, then the former policy is optimal from the perspective of the domestic economy since this permits factors to be used in the same ratio throughout its economy. If the factors are exported then there is an efficiency loss in the home country, since its mobile factor is being used more intensively in one country than another. If, however, discrimination is not possible then Calvo and Wellisz (1983) have shown that it is preferable to export the abundant factor. Kuhn and Wooton (1987), in an extension of a paper by Jones, Coelho, and Easton (1986), include a third fixed factor, land. Under these circumstances a richer set of policy outcomes is possible, including the exportation of both capital and labour if the home country can discriminate.

2.6 The Characteristics Approach

The implications for trade theory when services require the mobility of factors was discussed above. The observation of Hindley and Smith (1984), Benz (1985) and Ewing (1985) that governments tend to impose restrictions on the movement of factors that are more restrictive than comparable restrictions on goods was also noted. These more severe restrictions may be due to the difficulty of collecting rents by discriminating between payments to foreign and domestic labour, or it may be due to sociological factors, such as preservation of culture or national identity. Whatever the reason for these restrictions, services are often seen as a distinct group of economic activities that lie outside the scope of international trade. Indeed, the extensive literature on trade in the presence of non-traded goods often refers to services as examples of non-traded goods (see Aukrust (1977) or Dornbusch (1980)).

But as we have also seen above, many services can be traded even when they involve personal contact between producer and consumer. Thus, engineering or management consulting can be conducted by post, telephone or computer, while repairs and alterations to goods can be conducted by transferring the product. The question of precisely how tradeable services are is addressed by Zweifel (1986). In order to analyze the tradeability of services, he uses a version of the demand model developed by Lancaster (1966), in which the characteristics of a good, rather than the good itself, form the arguments of an agent's utility function. Both Inman (1985) and Kierzkowski (1987) have suggested that this may be an appropriate model for analyzing trade in services since many services have several characteristics that can yield consumer utility.

Lancaster (1980) and Helpman (1981) show that the demand for characteristics leads to a demand for variety. In the presence of increasing returns to scale, a larger international market allows for a greater variety of goods to be produced, and hence agents are better off. Kierzkowski (1987) presents a simplified version of these models in which there are two industries, one producing a homogeneous good and the other producing differentiated products. Each 'model' (or type) of the differentiated product, which is produced under an increasing-returns-to-scale technology, can be represented as embodying a set of characteristics distributed among a unit circle. Consumers each have a preferred set of characteristics and hence have a preference for a specific model of the differentiated good. These agents are assumed to be distributed uniformly around the unit circle. Since the differentiated good is assumed to be produced under increasing returns to scale it may be more efficient to produce a limited range of the differentiated good rather than a specific good for each agent. The costs of production are assumed to be identical for all models, and, because of increasing returns, will depend upon the extent of the market. These costs, along with the tastes of consumers, will determine how many goods are produced, and producers will locate equidistant from one another and supply agents in their neighbourhood. If international trade is possible the market for a good is larger, and thus more goods are supplied at a lower cost and all agents are better off.

The variant of this model envisaged by Zweifel is one in which agents can combine goods linearly in order to obtain a bundle that more closely represents their desired bundle of characteristics.[5] Services, however, because of their nature, cannot be combined in this fashion. If a good possessed by a consumer requires some alteration or repair then the set of possible outcomes is restricted by the fact that the identity of the good must be preserved in the service process. It was noted above that Zweifel attaches considerable importance to identity preservation as one of the features of a service (a restriction also noted by Hill). He defines services as "activity inputs provided by a separate economic unit, to a production process resulting in identity-preserving change of characteristics of a person or a good in his personal property" (Zweifel, 1986, p. 10). It is the identity-preservation restriction that differentiates this definition from Hill's. Like Hill, he suggests that in the repair or transportation of a good, the identity of the good cannot be transformed out of all recognition, and hence the range of permissible changes are limited to some region of the original characteristics.

The difficulty about the provision of services in these circumstances, according to Zweifel, is that they are almost never consumed in linear combinations. This may be due to the fact that it is difficult to apportion the degree of repair or alteration effected by an individual servicer, the fact that property rights remain with the individual who is being serviced or whose good is being serviced or the fact that servicers cannot simultaneously work on a project and that the efforts of one servicer may impinge on the output of another.

The example presented by Zweifel is that of a watch repair servicer, where each servicer offers a fixed bundle of accuracy and elegance restoration. However, it is difficult to believe that watch repairs are so specialized that a servicer could not offer whatever bundle a particular consumer requires. The services of a medical, legal, or dental specialist would be other examples. Obviously the conflicting expert assessment of two cancer specialists on the need for an operation cannot be linearly combined.

Zweifel suggests that the inability to combine services linearly implies that services are more likely to be traded than goods. Since services cannot be combined to yield the desired characteristics, the need for variety is greater and thus international trade is of more importance. Zweifel also suggests that, due to the uncertainty associated with the quality of output of some servicers, one would expect to see government restrictions on the tradeability of personal services. This is precisely the point raised earlier by Hindley and Smith. They maintained, however, that the need for protection of consumers should be no different if foreigners rather than domestic producers supply the service and thus this should not have any special implications for the theory of comparative advantage.

2.7 Transport Services

There is a considerable body of literature on transportation services; not a surprising fact given their importance in world trade. Kierzkowski (1986) points out that existing figures for the value of transportation services put them at approximately 7.5% of the value of world merchandise trade. There are considerable problems with these data, however. Balance of Payments aggregation for IMF countries show that there is systematic under-reporting of transportation service costs. This may be due in part to the fact that neither the Eastern Block's large commercial fleet, nor the fleets associated with countries who operate so-called flags of convenience are included. Kierzkowski argues that the value of transportation services may be as much as 13% of the value of world merchandise trade.

There has been some theoretical treatment of transport costs. Samuelson (1954) and Mundell (1957b) modelled transportation by assuming that a fixed percentage of output is used up when a good is transported from one location to another. It is typically assumed that the "disappearance" is proportional to distance, and this model is sometimes referred to as the 'iceberg' model of transportation costs. This approach implies that the production side of the economy is unaffected, since no resources are absorbed in the production of transportation services. Domestic prices will be affected, however, and this will alter equilibrium output and consumption. The major drawbacks of the Mundell-Samuelson model is that transport costs are not determined endogenously, and that the model does not suggest which country will supply transport services. Herberg (1970) attempted to relax the fixed cost assumption, but he makes the additional restrictive assumption that each country must carry its own imports.

The principal result of modelling transport in this fashion is that high transport costs may act as a barrier to trade, just as do tariffs. This distortion will also mean that the factor-price-equalization theorem will not be satisfied even if all the usual necessary conditions are present. On the other hand, the presence of transportation costs does not necessarily imply that the price of imports must rise. Iceberg transportation costs have the same effect on offer curves as a tariff, that is, the curve is shifted proportionally downwards towards the importing axis. As a consequence, if the foreign country's offer curve is inelastic, then an effect similar to the Metzler paradox can occur leading to a lower price for imports.

Falvey (1976) and Cassing (1978) incorporated a transport-service sector into the traditional Heckscher-Ohlin model. By treating transportation as just another production sector, Falvey is able to allow market conditions to determine which country will supply services. As with any Heckscher-Ohlin model, the result will depend crucially upon the relative factor intensities of the three sectors and the factor endowment of the countries. If transportation services are more capital intensive than both of the goods then the capital-rich country will produce transportation. If transportation is more capital intensive than only one of the goods, then we cannot predict *a priori* which will supply the transport services. Cassing points out that for the purpose of the Metzler paradox it is important to differentiate between the case where tariffs are imposed on f.o.b. (point of sale) prices and tariffs imposed on c.i.f. (delivery) prices.

Casas (1983), in a comprehensive survey of transport services, suggests that resources from both countries will be used in international transportation since ports and airports involve the use of domestic resources even if the foreign country supplies the services. The contribution of each country will depend once again upon technology, endowments and market conditions. Sapir and Lutz (1981) extended this approach and tested the predictions of the Heckscher-Ohlin model with regard to trade in freight, insurance and passenger services. They assume that services are capital intensive and found that the model did have considerable predictive power.

Kierzkowski (1986) suggests that since many services such as shipping and telecommunications are characterized by oligopolistic market structures, it would be more appropriate to use a version of the intra-industry trade model employed by Brander and Krugman (1983) and Brander and Spencer (1984). Kierzkowski develops a duopoly model of international services by assuming that there are two countries each with a well specified import demand function and each with a shipping company that acts as a Cournot duopolist. Each shipping company chooses the quantity of goods it will carry in each direction and perfect competition is assumed to obtain in the market for goods. The import demand function for country i is defined as

$$M^i = Y_i \varepsilon(i) \, (eP^i + et_{i,j})$$

where M^i is the quantity of imports, Y_i is the real income of country i, $\varepsilon(i)$ is the import elasticity of country i, P^i is the price of imports in country i, $t_{i,j}$ is the price of transportation to country i from country j, and e is the exchange rate in units of country i. All variables are held constant, except for the quantity of imports and the transportation rates which are endogenous. By solving the above equation for freight rates and by setting the total supply of services equal to some fixed fraction of total imports, it is possible to derive the profit function and hence the reaction function of both shipping companies.

This model resembles the Samuelson-Mundell model in some regards, except that prices rather than transport cost are exogenous. The pattern of trade here is not affected by changes in the exogenous variables, but both the volume of trade and the relative share of the transportation market obtained by the two countries' shipping companies will be. The principal results of the Kierzkowski model are that 'ceteris paribus', an increase in country i's costs will reduce the market share of its shipping company, raise the prices of transportation in both countries and reduce the overall level of services. If both countries' costs were to rise, due to an oil price shock for example, then the total level of services would fall, but the relative market share of each country would remain constant.

2.8 Educational Services

Another area of the trade theory literature that relates to trade and services is that on the formation of human capital. Findlay and Kierzkowski (1983) developed a model where there are two goods, x and y, and two factor inputs, skilled and unskilled labour. Unlike the traditional Heckscher-Ohlin model, the endowment of these two factors is not determined exogenously, but rather the quantity of skilled labour is an endogenous variable. They assume that there is a stationary population, in which N agents are born (with a life span of T periods), and N agents die in each period. Individuals have a choice of entering the labour force immediately or of combining their labour input (for n periods) with a fixed educational factor in order to become skilled workers. In a competitive stationary equilibrium the number of skilled workers in an economy will depend upon the quantity of the fixed educational factor and the agents' rate of time preference. Thus in a world with free trade in goods, the country with the higher discount rate or the higher stock of educational capital can be expected to export the skilled-labour-intensive good and import the unskilled-labour-intensive good.

As Kierzkowski (1987) points out, there is no reason to believe that returns to each type of factor will be equalized in this model. Rather the wealth of each nation will depend crucially upon the endowment of the fixed educational factor. If there were some way of guaranteeing equal access to this factor for all the population in the world, then the discounted income of all agents would be equal. Thus welfare could be increased if foreign labourers could avail themselves of the fixed educational factor, thereby equalizing the return to the educational factor in the two countries. Once again, free trade in services requires that the receivers of the service (students) or the providers of the service (professors) migrate. Alternatively, education can be exported via books or, as in the case of Britain's Open University, by television.

2.9 Conclusions

Although economists have always distinguished between goods and services, in the recent history of economic analysis this distinction has become more performa than real, and there has been very little discussion on whether and why one should distinguish between goods and services. Hill (1977) provided the first significant contribution to the recent discussion of this issue and has provided some very thoughtful insights into the conceptual issue of what distinguishes services from goods. Recent years have seen a flurry of activity in the services area, and the contributions of a variety of authors have been summarized above. But while there is a growing literature on this topic, it nevertheless seems fair to say that we have not yet reached a concensus on exactly why services exist or what their importance is in a modern industrialized economy. We take up this conceptual issue in Chapter 3, where we argue that services can be seen as the mechanism through which economic units overcome the constraints associated with the dimensions of time and space.

One aspect of services that has received a good deal of attention is its empirical importance in modern industrialized nations. As was suggested above, the service industries are now the most important sector of most economies, both in terms of employment and in terms of their contribution to GNP. In Canada, for example, some 62% of GNP is attributable to service industries, and this may well be an understatement, for many service activities performed internally by firms are not reported separately as belonging to the service industries. This growth in the service sector has led many economists to be concerned about whether the predominance of services in national output has contributed to the decline in productivity growth. This concern seems largely unfounded. As will be shown in Chapter 4, an increase in service activity, even if services do not enter consumers' utility functions directly, and even if the output of consumer goods falls, can still result in an increase in utility for consumers. At the same time it is recognized that the issue of measuring productivity in service industries is a difficult one, since measures of inputs and outputs are often difficult to disentangle. In Chapter 10 it will be argued that the appropriate measure of productivity growth in services should be related to the question of whether the service has resulted in a reduction in the gap between consumer and producer prices.

While the conceptual and empirical issues relating to services have received some attention, there have been almost no contributions to the theoretical question of the importance of services in trade. Of course there is a good deal of related literature, for many service sectors are important for international trade, and many of these have been discussed by theorists. For example, transportation is an important service sector, and there is a literature on transportation, both for domestic economies and for international trade. In many situations services are associated with factor movements, and there is certainly no shortage of literature in this area. Education and human capital is a very important component of many service sectors and these issues have also been extensively discussed by economists. But while all these issues have been discussed, there has been no attempt to formally incorporate these services in a traditional general equilibrium, international trade model. Thus, while there has been some discussion of the importance of transportation for international trade, there has been almost no discussion of the general issue of whether the formal introduction of services into the standard international trade models would require a fundamental reformulation of basic trade theory. The single exception to this is the excellent paper by Deardorff (1985).

While some progress has been made in defining services and analyzing their consequences, much remains to be done. Of particular importance is the question of the effects that the explicit recognition of the importance of service trade will have for international trade theory. Trade in services is now being discussed in connection with trade liberalization, and it is obviously important if progress is to be made in this area that negotiators have an understanding of the precise role that services play. It is to this issue that the remaining chapters in this volume are addressed, and it is hoped that the discussion here will contribute to the ongoing and very important debate on the role and importance of services for a trading economy.

Notes

1. This chapter closely follows Ryan (1988). For another survey of services and international trade see Kierzkowski (1984).

2. For an introduction to the empirical work in this area see Inman (1985), Part I, or Gershuny and Mills (1983), Ch. 4.

3. See Table H.5, Bank of Canada Review (1987), National Income Accounts, GNP at factor cost by industry.

4. The work of Baumol (1967) and Fuchs (1968) are discussed by Inman (1985, pp. 2-4), and Kuznets (1972) contributions are cited by Gershuny and Mills (1983, p. 45).

5. Combining the differentiated product approach and the characteristics approach has also been suggested by Kierzkwoski (1987).

Chapter 3

The Conceptual Issues

3.1 Introduction

The main purpose of this chapter is to describe circumstances in which services exist and to provide a classification of these services.* Our purpose is not primarily to define services nor to distinguish them from goods, although the analysis may well prove useful in addressing such issues. Our concern is *why* services exist rather than *what* services are. In particular it is argued that the commodities usually called services are produced in response to the desire of economic units to overcome the constraints of time and space. The difficulty economists have in coming to grips with the role that services play in economic analysis may be due, at least in part, to the fact that time and space have not received the attention they deserve in traditional theoretical discussions. The goal of the chapter is to provide an analysis of services that will be helpful in understanding some of the questions that have arisen concerning the role of services in the economy, and that will be useful in analyzing such issues as productivity in the service sector and the importance of services for international trade.

We begin in Section 3.2 with a brief description of the economic model that will serve as a standard of comparison for later analysis. Section 3.3 considers the coincidence question and intermediation

---

* The analysis here follows Melvin (1987a).

services are discussed in Section 3.4. In Section 3.5 a formal model of trade in services is formulated, and the question of relaxing the dimensionality constraint is taken up in Section 3.6. The conclusions and policy implications are summarized in the final section.

3.2 The Standard Model

Consider the market for some commodity Y. On the supply side a production function is assumed that employs factors of production, usually under conditions of homogeneity of the first degree, to produce an output. This can be characterized as:

(3.1) $Y = F(K,L)$.

For simplicity only two factor inputs, capital and labour, have been assumed. On the demand side consumer preferences are represented by a utility function such as:

(3.2) $U = U(Y,X)$

where again we have assumed two commodities. The production function in (3.1) can be used to obtain a supply relationship under the assumption of profit maximization by the industry. From equation (3.2) a demand curve for Y can be derived from the assumption of utility maximization. These demand and supply relationships are assumed to be independent, and this independence makes it unnecessary for demanders and suppliers to have any direct inter-action with one another.

A simple general equilibrium model could be constructed by adding to equations (3.1) and (3.2) a production function for commodity X and by imposing constraints on the availability of capital and labour. The simplest such model assumes that all consumers have identical and homothetic preferences, but no difficulty is encountered in defining an equilibrium even if all consumers have different tastes. Such two-sector general equilibrium models are the cornerstone of international trade theory.

In the simple model just described no explicit account is taken of either space or time, and implicitly all economic activity is assumed to occur instantly and at one location. There is seldom any discussion of even the elementary questions of the process through which consumers obtain X and Y from producers, or how firms arrange for the delivery of the appropriate quantities of the factors of production they require. Even international trade theory which deals explicitly with different countries implicitly assumes countries to be points where all economic activity takes place, and abstracts almost entirely from both intranational and international transportation costs.[1] Nor is there much discussion, in such simple models, of how arrangements can be made to consume commodities in one period that are produced in another. Such models are completely without dimension; there is no space and no time. A principal argument of this chapter is that it is the explicit recognition of time and space that necessitates the introduction of services, and furthermore that the explicit introduction of services requires consideration of the process of intermediation.

Of course, there are circumstances in which a simple model without services would provide a perfectly acceptable characterization of economic activity. For primitive tribes that are isolated from the rest of the world notions of space are not very important. Neither is time an important factor in economic activity in such societies, for if hunting and gathering are used to provide food, neither the present nor the past has much influence on day-to-day activity. Furthermore, even for much more complex societies, the simple dimensionless model provides an extremely useful starting point for the analysis of economic activity. It is, however, just the starting point, for it does not address questions associated with the interaction of activities over space nor with the interrelationships which exist through time. Basic economic analysis which employs the simple models of production and consumption has not carefully integrated the aspects of time and space. Of course Arrow-Debru models have commodities indexed with respect to both time and space, so that physically identical items become different commodities if their time or space indices differ. There is not, however, an explicit consideration of the role that introducing these dimensionality constraints plays in the economic analysis.

This is not to suggest that time and space have been ignored in economic analysis. Spatial and regional research have a long history in economic theory, but the space aspect has never become central to the basic model. The treatment of time in economics has an equally long and much richer history, and includes economic dynamics, growth theory, consumption theory, investment theory and risk and uncertainty. More recently an extensive literature on intertemporal economic activity has developed. Again, however, it would seem fair to suggest that such analysis is seen more as the introduction of new theoretical topics rather than as an integral part of the basic economic model. It will be argued that it is the introduction of an explicit recognition of space and time into the basic economic model which produces the activities referred to as services.

Perhaps a major reason for the failure of economists to fully incorporate dimensionality into economic models is their concentration on the scarcity problem as *the* raison d'être of economic analysis. Of course scarcity *is* central to the maximization problem for both producers and consumers. Furthermore time and space are required inputs for both production and consumption, and thus both can be scarce. Certainly not having enough time or space could be a serious production constraint. But while time and space can be scarce there can also be too much. Dimensionality can also impose constraints if producers and consumers are too far apart either in time or in space. Thus as well as the scarcity problem we can have a superfluity problem, and it is the attempt to deal with this later difficulty that requires the existence of services. Thus while economic goods are a consequence of the scarcity of factors of production, some economic services (but, as we will see, not all) are a consequence of the superfluity of time and space. Time and space are inputs for which there is no free disposal, and overcoming these dimensionality constraints will require the use of resources to produce services. Such services do not directly increase utility but rather serve to facilitate market clearing.

The constraints associated with the superfluity of time and space are associated not so much with the separate activities of production or consumption as with the process by which producers and consumers are brought together, or in other words with distribution. Of course the problem of distribution can be overcome by the very simple procedure of having consumption and production occur at the same place and at the same time. Indeed for some activities market clearing *requires* this double coincidence of time and place, and such economic events form one group of activities that has become known as services. Haircuts and medical services are in this class. For most commodities, however, such a coincidence of time and space is not required, and when demanders and suppliers are separated either by time or space, the services of an intermediator are essential. Of course in general this intermediation could be performed by either the producer or the consumer, and what is essential is that third party intermediation is possible. Transportation and storage are examples of such activities, and these form a second class of services. There are other activities where, although direct personal contact between producers and consumers may be preferred, close substitutes can be provided through intermediation. Examples include live theatre and sporting events, and these form a third class of services. These three classes of services are considered in greater detail in the next two sections.

3.3 The Coincidence Question

A central feature of the simple model described at the beginning of Section 3.2 is the independence of demand and supply activities. Producers of apples or cookies neither know nor care when these outputs will be purchased nor who will consume them. Similarly the consumer of a bag of cookies is typically not interested in whether they were produced in Toronto or New York, and is concerned with when they were produced only insofar as it affects the quality of the product.

This happy independence of time and space is not true for all activity however. The markets for such things as haircuts, prostitution, and medical services such as appendectomies operate quite differently. Here production and consumption are not independent, but in fact are the same activity. For such commodities the joint production and consumption activity requires that there be a coincidence of both time and space. We no longer have the traditional separation between production and consumption, and thus rather than equations (3.1) and (3.2) we have the single equation (3.3).

$$(3.3) \qquad U = U(F(K,L),X).$$

Here utility is obtained from the consumption of commodity X and from the simultaneous production and consumption of commodity Y. For commodity Y there is an activity which is seen by the consumer as consumption and by the producer as production, but they are one and the same activity.

An important feature of such services as appendectomies and prostitution is the inseparability of the production and consumption activities, both in space and time. We will define these as contact services to indicate that intermediation to relax the constraints of time and space is not possible, and that actual physical contact between the economic agents is often present.[2] Any attempt to relax either of the dimensionality constraints results in nonprovision of the service. Such services also typically do not have close substitutes.[3] The formulation shown in equation (3.3) does not distinguish between the activity of purchasing or obtaining a service and the provision of utility from the consumption or use of this service. Hill (1977, p. 322) emphasizes the importance of such a distinction and argues that ". . . there is a tendency to confuse the services themselves with the benefits the consumer expects to derive from them, and great care is needed to keep them distinct from each other." There is certainly no question that, at least for some services, such a distinction can be made. One has a tooth pulled or has a surgical operation not because the service itself provides utility but rather because of the expectation that utility will be higher in the future than it would have been otherwise. This, of course, is not a distinction unique to services (as Hill also notes) for one purchases a coat to keep warm, and it is not the purchase of an apple but rather its eventual consumption that we have in mind when we write down utility functions such as (3.2).

For some services, however, such a distinction is anything but clear. For live theatre and live athletic events (and the purchase of prostitution services) it is difficult to argue that a distinction can be made between provision of the service and the increase in utility. Indeed for some services the *anticipation* of the event may be the major source of the increase in utility.

The important issue, however, is not whether one can distinguish between the provision of a service and the utility it provides, but rather whether such a distinction is required. It would not be difficult to formulate the problem so that the provision or purchase of a service and utility generated from it are distinct, but at least for our purposes there would seem to be no advantage in such further complication of the problem. Thus we will follow the tradition employed in standard economic analysis of subsuming the acquisition of a service and the provision of utility in the same equation.

We have defined contact services as services which *require* a double coincidence of time and space and for which no close substitutes exist. There are some services that are often provided at the same time and place but for which close substitutes are available. These would include live theatre, concerts and sporting events. Close substitutes are available via T.V. and high fidelity recordings that can relax either or both of the space and time constraints. We will define these as *substitution services* to suggest that while it is attractive to be a participant at the event, a significant proportion of the utility of the activity can be obtained through the substitution of another form of entertainment, or the transmission of the event itself through space or time (or both). There are many examples of such services. Person-to-person communication has a time constraint, but the telephone frees such communicators from the space constraint. This is a type of spatial intermediation. This illustrates the point that technological advance in the service area can be seen as providing intermediation that frees economic actors from the dimensional constraints. In primitive societies all communications require coincidence of both time and space. The development of long-distance transmissions of sound removed the space constraint for communication, and television removed the space constraint for visual performance. The more recent development of VCRs has substantially reduced the time constraint for visual performances.

3.4 Intermediation

There is a large class of services that is quite distinct from the contact and substitution services discussed above. For the standard production model described in Section 3.2 where the demand and supply activities are independent, services are often required to facilitate market clearing. Thus an apple must be transported from the producer to the consumer, and savings must be transported through time to allow consumption in the future. These are arm's length activities (or at least can be) in that for spatial activities producers and consumers need not know each other, and of course all intertemporal activities avoid direct contact between the two economic actors as long as the time periods are not contiguous. We will refer to all such activities as *intermediation services* to suggest that the service could (but need not) be provided at arm's length by a third party.

Intermediation services is clearly the largest of our three classifications, at least as far as value of output is concerned. Transportation facilities intermediate commodities over space. Insurance intermediates risk over time. Accounting and record keeping intermediate information over time and space. Advisers and consultants intermediate knowledge and information over time and space. The government service sector intermediates transfer payments, information, and to a limited extent, commodities between the government and the citizens. All such activities have expanded tremendously in the last several decades, and as a result the service sector accounts for a large fraction of the national income of all developed countries.

The intermediation and substitution services introduce further complications to the simple production and consumption structure outlined in Section 3.2. The provision of these services, for example, almost always involves the use of a durable good. These could be consumer durables such as refrigerators and T.V.s or producer durables such as trucks or airplanes.[4] With such services we must introduce a production activity that does not directly increase utility, for the durable good is not desired for its own sake. One does not purchase a refrigerator or a television set because of the utility derived directly from these appliances, but rather because one gets utility from cold beer and football games. Note that such durables are directly related to the constraints imposed by time and space. Appliances such as refrigerators exist because of the existence of the time dimension. Obviously without time there would be no demand for storage of any kind. Durables such as radios, telephones, and T.V.s are associated with the dimension of space and provide the substitution service of communication. Durables such as trucks, trains, and planes are also associated with space, but are used for intermediation, for here transportation is the essential service.

As was emphasized earlier it is important to distinguish carefully between time and space as constraints on the distribution of commodities and time and space as necessary inputs to the production and consumption processes. Our concern in this chapter is not scarcity but rather the problems associated with the superfluity of time and space. Intermediation and substitution services arise when there is too much space and/or time separating producers and consumers.

Of course the scarcity constraints of time and space are relevant to service industries just as they are for other producers. The time required for travel can be an important economic consideration, but this is not the aspect of time with which we are here concerned. The time constraint that generates the need for a service activity is the problem of moving things through time. If one has a basket of apples today the problem is how one can insure that they can be consumed next month, or how, in the face of uncertainty, one can guarantee that one's income or assets are sufficient for next year's needs. One has well defined starting points and end points in mind with "time travel" just as one has with transportation through space, and the concern is not with the speed at which some activity can be undertaken. Increasing the speed at which some activity can be accomplished may increase the efficiency of the operation and therefore reduce cost, and this may be an important consideration for service industries such as transportation. Such increases in speed may improve the efficiency of the transportation sector, that is, may improve efficiency in the *space* dimension, but this is not the aspect of time which is our principal concern here.

3.5 A Formal Model

Having described three distinct types of services, or situations in which services arise, we now formulate a general model that can be used to analyze any of the three cases. The basic problem is to convert or transform the output of the production process, defined as X_p, into a commodity that can provide utility for the consumer, defined as X_c. In general terms a service transformation function can be written as

$$(3.4) \qquad X_c = S(X_p, ...) ,$$

where the other inputs to this transformation process will be various kinds of capital, labour and intermediate inputs.

We first consider transformations associated with the need to overcome the constraint of space. A more specific form of (3.4) could be

$$(3.5) \qquad X_c = G(X_p, K_g, L_g) + D(X_p, K_d, L_d) \, Q(d)$$

where K, L and d are capital, labour and distance. Associated with this transformation we have the cost function

$$(3.6) \qquad C_d = X_p P_p + K_g r + L_g w + K_d r + L_d w .$$

The problem is to minimize C_d subject to the transformation function (3.5).

The first term $G(X_p, K_g, L_g)$ in (3.5) describes the technology for producing a unit of X_c from a unit of X_p, where X_p and X_c are in contiguous locations. A contiguous location could be "a kilometer distant", but the definition of contiguous may well depend on the nature of X. The important point is that X_c and X_p are not at the same location. The nature of G will depend on the nature of the commodity X. For goods such as apples and chairs, where no physical transformation of the commodity is required, $K_g = L_g = 0$ and we have $G = X_p$. If X is an appendectomy or a haircut, then no method of transformation is known and a G does not exist. For substitute services such as a live production or a baseball game, the X_p can be transformed into X_c through the use of the capital and labour inputs associated with television transmission. The function $G(X_p, K_g, L_g)$ is meant to capture the *physical transformation* of a commodity required to produce a unit of X_c from a unit of X_p where X_c and X_p are at different locations. For some commodities it is presently not possible, for others it is trivially easy, and for some it can be accomplished only through a complex production process.

The second term of (3.5) relates to the actual process of transformation or transmission—in the present example the transportation component. The function $Q(d)$ explicitly introduces the distance variable d. It is assumed that $Q(0) = 0$ and that $Q'(d) > 0$, where primes indicate partial derivatives. Thus if X_c and X_p are in fact at the same location, the second term of (3.5) becomes zero. The function $D(X_p, K_d, L_d)$ is the transportation function, and incorporates the assumptions that transportation will depend on the quantity of X_p to be transported and that inputs of K and L will be required.

The three types of services described earlier can be seen as special cases of (3.5). Note first that for *any* situation where X_c and X_p are in the same location we have $X_c \equiv X_p$. This follows from the assumptions that $Q(d) = 0$ and that G is defined for contiguous locations. Contact services can be defined as the group of commodities for which G is not known to exist. Haircuts are such a commodity, as was instantaneous long distance communication before the invention of the telegraph. In such cases consumption is possible only when $d = 0$. Thus for an individual to consume such a service he or she must travel to the producer, or alternatively persuade the producer to travel to the site where consumption takes place.

Substitution services exist when a close enough substitute for the "real thing" exists. Here a physical transformation is often required so that G will typically be an important part of the transformation process. The function D, which incorporates the actual distance travelled, may well be less important for substitution services than the function G, as it is for television and telephone conversations. Certainly marginal costs of D are often small. For substitution services the consumer usually has the choice of consuming either X_c or X_p. One can always go to the Stanley Cup playoffs rather than watch them on T.V., and one can insist on face to face meetings when verbal communication is required. The choice by the consumer will depend on the relative costs of X_c and X_p, the budget constraint, and the extent to which the consumer views X_c as a substitute for X_p.

For intermediation services the emphasis is on D, the travel component, and often no physical transformation of the commodity is required. Of course after transportation commodities are often not exactly the same as they would have been if consumption had taken place at the production location (fresh fruit or vegetables for example).

The above discussion has been in terms of the spatial constraint of distance, but a similar formulation applies when the dimension to be overcome is time. In place of (3.5) we could have

(3.7) $X_c = H(X_p, K_h, L_h) + T(X_p, K_t, L_t) \; Q(t)$

where the interpretation of the terms in (3.7) is the same as for (3.5). There will also be a cost function corresponding to (3.6). If consumption and production take place in the same time period (within the next hour or the next day, perhaps) then no physical transformation is required so that $K_h = L_h = 0$ and $t = 0$ implying that $X_c \equiv X_p$. For contact services such as appendectomies there is no known technology for transferring output from one period to another, so that only if $t = 0$ can the output be consumed. For substitution services such as recorded concerts the component H is generally the more important component of cost with the actual cost of storage a minor element of total cost. For intermediation services where storage is the important feature, such as with potatoes or savings, then the function T is the most important cost component in the transformation.

If both space and time are constraints, then the total cost of transformation will become the sum of the costs associated with equations (3.5) and (3.7). In some cases G and H may be the same process (for frozen fish, for example) but they certainly need not be. Generally the time and space transformations of D and T will be independent.[5]

It will never be clear where to draw the line between costs associated with intertemporal or interspatial services or between substitution services and intermediation services. Are frozen fish or canned beans substitutes for the original products or are they the same commodities in a different location in time or space? Does one freeze fish or can beans in order to store them or in order to transport them? Such distinctions are of no great importance, however, for both are included in the service production function (3.5) or (3.7). The more the commodity is transformed the relatively more important will the G or H part of (3.5) and (3.7) become, but whether or not one views X_c as the same as or different than X_p or whether the "differences" are due to the space or time constraints is largely irrelevant for our analysis.

3.6 Relaxing the Dimensionality Constraint

We have argued that the existence of services is intimately associated with the dimensionality of economic analysis. The constraints imposed by the dimensions of space and time are distance and uncertainty. While distance is most important for space, transportation through time may also require the provision of a service. Storage and refrigeration are two examples of services required for "time travel". Uncertainty is the more important constraint where time is concerned, but there may also be uncertainty associated with distance. While life insurance, fire insurance, and crop insurance are associated with uncertainty through time, cargo insurance is primarily concerned with the uncertainty of transportation through space.

The history of the development of intermediation services can be seen as a continuous attempt by economic agents to overcome these dimensionality constraints, and typically these have taken the form of replacing a contact service with a substitution or intermediation service. In a primitive society even the basic activity of communication requires a double coincidence of time and place. The invention of the written word was perhaps the first major development in the process of relaxing these constraints, for it allowed communication over both time and space. The development of radio and the telephone further relaxed the space constraint in the communication area.

The space constraint associated with the consumption of goods was relaxed by the invention of the wheel and the many transportation facilities which developed thereafter. The development of first the railway and then aircraft were significant milestones in man's struggle to overcome the constraints of space.[6] The invention of banking was also an important step in the development of the service sector. Banking deals with the space dimension by providing intermediation between loaners and borrowers, but may also have been the first major attempt to deal with the problem of uncertainty. Banks, by facilitating borrowing and lending, allow intermediation through time as well as through space.[7] Other important developments in the time dimension were insurance, accounting, and record keeping in general.[8]

The development of the computer and data processing along with the advances in electronic communication are the most recent advance in the struggle against dimension. These recent developments are services that substitute for other services such as record keeping, bookkeeping, data storage, and secretarial services, most of which have traditionally been contact services. Historically, secretaries and research assistants were constrained by time and space, but recent developments have begun to relax both of these restrictions. It would now be possible for the secretarial staff of a firm to be located in another city or even in another country. One can confidently predict that the large office complexes associated with industries such as insurance will gradually become decentralized. Such developments will produce significant improvements in efficiency by reducing travel and by freeing individuals from the constraints of working from 9 to 5. It is noteworthy that some of the gains from such developments will show up as increases in utility for consumers and will be difficult or impossible to measure.[9] It seems probable that the communications revolution presently under way will overshadow even the railroad and the airplane in terms of its effect on the welfare of individuals.

3.7 Conclusions and Policy Implications

It has been argued that services play a distinct role in economic activity and in that sense are fundamentally different than goods. Services are inherently related to the dimensionality of economic analysis and are created either by our inability to intermediate or by our attempts to overcome the constraints of distance and uncertainty associated with space and time. An important property of many services is the required coincidence of time and space in the production and consumption activities. For substitution and intermediation services, on the other hand, a service is provided when the time and space constraints are relaxed. A formal model of services was constructed to illustrate the various types of services, and this model will prove useful in analyzing the question of productivity in the service sector to be considered in Chapter 10.

Many of the issues considered here will be discussed in more detail in subsequent chapters. While this chapter has served merely as an introduction to the question of what services are and what role they play in the economy, some tentative policy implications can already be suggested. For example, if we accept the notion that services are intimately associated with the dimensions of time and space, and given the substantial importance of distance in the Canadian economy, it seems clear that an efficient service sector will be important to the economy. This will be particularly true for services such as transportation, communication and banking and finance.

It is argued in Chapter 4 that comparative advantage in service industries sometimes develops because of the need to overcome dimensionality and other economic constraints. Because of the physical nature of the country, Canadians have always been concerned with distance, and some of the Canadian service industries have developed comparative advantages by international standards. The branch-banking system developed in Canada was an efficient way of overcoming the distance constraints, and the expertise acquired in the domestic economy led to the expansion of Canadian banks throughout the world. In recent years Canada has been at the forefront of certain types of long distance communication developments, and it seems probable that this will be a source of comparative advantage in the future. Even in the transportation sector several industries have become major exporters. Snowmobiles were developed in Canada, certain types of aircraft used for short-distance transportation have become an important export item, and Canada has obtained contracts to install intra-urban transportation systems. All of these examples suggest that support for services associated with distance could be a productive social policy.

Finally, there is a somewhat different lesson that can be inferred from the discussion of this chapter. Overcoming the constraints of distance is costly for consumers, and anything that will reduce transportation costs will increase welfare. The history of Canada can be characterized as an attempt to overcome the long distances associated with the fact that the population is stretched along the Canadian-U.S. border, and although to some extent Canadians have been successful the cost has been high. An obvious alternative to transporting goods within the country is to trade with the nearer U.S. markets. In other words, one effective way of reducing transportation costs is to trade with producers that are closer. The theme of the importance of transportation costs for a trading regional economy has been taken up in detail by Melvin (1985b).

Notes

1. For a discussion of the consequences of introducing interregional transportation into an international trade model see Melvin (1985a, 1985b).

2. Crimes such as muggings, shootings, and rape are the undesirable counterparts of utility-producing contact services, just as "bads" are the undesirable counterparts of goods. Perhaps they could be called contact disservices.

3. Note that it is the *services* that do not have close substitutes and not necessarily the providers of the services. Haircuts have no close substitutes, but if a qualified barber is not available one's spouse might do an acceptable job. Provision becomes much more problematic with services such as appendectomies.

4. On the production side producer durables are capital, and there is certainly no shortage of literature in this area. We are differentiating here between capital which provides a service, such as transportation, and capital which is a required input to the production process. This distinction is admittedly somewhat forced.

5.   Note that the fact that time and space costs are independent does not imply that the speed of transportation does not affect transport cost. As noted earlier, speed of travel is an aspect of the efficiency of transportation and not a dimensionality constraint. The additive separability of d and t rather implies that if you store apples for six months and also move them from Ontario to Saskatchewan, the locational change does not affect the storage costs. Although there may be some interaction the differences are likely to be small.

6.   One could go further and argue that the development of language was the first attempt to overcome dimensionality, for language provides some relaxation of the space constraint.

7.   Of course storage of any sort allows goods to be moved through time.

8.   The provision of advice is also a service, and this is undoubtedly a primitive activity.

9.   Through the use of computer terminals, some employees can work at home at their convenience. While their incomes may be the same, the relaxation of the constraints on their time may substantially increase their utility.

Chapter 4

Trade and Comparative Advantage: An Introduction

4.1 Introduction

Before we begin our systematic analysis of trade in services in Chapter 5, it will be useful to provide some preliminary remarks on the form that trade in services takes and the nature of the restrictions that can be placed on trade in services. These topics will be considered in the following two sections. In Section 4.4 we introduce the notion of comparative advantage and briefly summarize the traditional determinants of trade patterns. The next section argues that comparative advantage in services may differ from that found for most traded commodities, and Section 4.6 discusses Canadian exports in relation to the service industries. The final section presents a summary of the policy implications.

4.2 International Trade in Services

In Chapter 3 we considered the role that services play in trades among producers and consumers. International trade in services is just the recognition that some of these transactions are made across international borders. The question of interest here is whether such transactions differ substantially from the traditional trade in goods, and whether the methods of restricting such trade and the consequences of such restriction differ from those found in the traditional international trade literature.

Before discussing international trade in services it will be useful to define international trade in goods. By international trade one typically means that some commodity produced in one country is consumed in another. The traditional economic good described in Chapter 3 presents no problems with such a definition. Because of the independence of the demand and supply activities, apples and cookies can easily be produced in one country and consumed in another.

Difficulties with our simple definition of trade arise, however, as soon as trade in contact services is considered. For services requiring coincidence in time and space one clearly cannot have production in one country and consumption in the other since the production and consumption activities are one and the same. The export of haircuts must involve the consumer crossing the border to obtain haircuts or the barber crossing the border to provide this service.[1] But while commodity trade of the usual kind does not take place in this situation, the economic consequences of such activities are the same as for trade in commodities. It seems appropriate, therefore, to regard such transactions as international trade in services. All that is required is that we amend the definition of international trade to include transactions which take place between residents of different countries regardless of where production and consumption actually take place.

When intermediation services are considered the issue of international trade becomes more complex. Does one regard international telephone calls or radio broadcasts as trade, and if so, what is being traded? Certainly in some circumstances information which is valuable—perhaps even crucial—to productive activities is provided. This is part of the "export of technology" issue, and as such has received a good deal of attention. The principal question here is not so much how the information is transmitted, for mail or personal visits could presumably produce the same result, but rather how one determines the value of this particular service. For arm's-length transactions this is presumably not an issue, since firms will make a payment for this service. With intrafirm transactions, however, there need not be any direct payment, and indeed the firms themselves may not be able to place a value on each specific activity of this type. Arm's-length transactions in services for which payments are made show up in the trade statistics while intrafirm activities for which no such payments are required do not, and the problem here is similar to the under-invoicing issue. The problems are exacerbated by the fact that it may be difficult to place an accurate value on these services.

A more important issue than the inability to keep track of international transactions in services is the possibility that such service flows may provide cost advantages to some firms. If some producers receive valuable services at very low cost while others must pay market prices, the former receives a significant advantage in the marketplace. If a multinational enterprise makes a service available to a foreign subsidiary at zero cost or at less than market price, then this may give the subsidiary a significant advantage over local firms. And often such producer services are produced with high fixed cost and very low marginal cost so that once the service has been provided to the domestic firm it may be possible to supply the foreign subsidiary at very low marginal cost. Services provided at less than market price are analogous in their economic effects to subsidies.

Similar problems may arise in the more traditional service industries such as transportation and insurance. If a trucking firm contracts to transport commodities for a third party in a foreign country a service will be provided which will be paid for and recorded in international trade statistics in the usual way. Similarly insurance provided by a firm in one country to producers or consumers in another will result in a payment which will be recorded as a balance of payments transaction. Difficulties may arise, however, with multinational corporations for which arm's-length transactions cannot be assumed. If a company with a fleet of trucks provides all the international transportation from the home country, then the foreign subsidiary should be charged for this service. If it is not then we have a distortion exactly analogous to that associated with the free transmission of information or technology. Insurance provided in one country for activities which take place in another provides similar possibilities for under-billing.

While trade in services produces some complications the difficulties seem to be overemphasized by some researchers. One of the sources of confusion in the literature on trade in services is the failure to distinguish between trade in services and services provided to domestics by a foreign subsidiary. In banking, for example, there is a tendency to count all foreign activities of a domestic bank as trade in services. But if a bank sets up a branch in a foreign country and then provides banking services to the residents of that country this does not represent trade in services. This situation is not essentially different from that of an automobile firm setting up a plant in a foreign country and selling cars to local consumers. These automobiles are not regarded as the exports of the home country. Of course foreign branches of banks or other firms may indeed produce trade in services if they intermediate between residents of different countries, but this is not what the statistics typically capture.

The same kind of difficulty occurs for franchise operations, where the entire activities of such firms are often counted as exports. For franchise operations it is difficult to see why exports of services would arise at all, other than for personnel training and common advertising and promotion campaigns. Overall, the importance of international service trade seems exaggerated. The suggestion that there could be as much as $120 billion exports of services from the U.S. (Stalson 1985, p. 9) is difficult to accept, and such figures almost certainly include services which are not traded at all.

Some of these problems can be illustrated by considering the production activity shown in equation (4.1)

(4.1) $Y = F(X_2, X_2)$,

where Y is some output, either a good or service, and where X_1 and X_2 are imports, one of which may be a service. Suppose that production takes place in Canada and that X_1 is supplied by the United States. The question is what is being exported by the U.S.? If Y represents automobiles, X_2 represents Canadian labour and X_1 U.S. capital, then we have a situation where there is foreign investment by the U.S. in Canada but no trade. Suppose, however, that X_1 represents foreign know-how or management services. In this case we could quite legitimately regard X_1 as an export of services from the United States. To take quite a different example suppose that Y represents haircuts, that X_1 represents barbers who commute from the United States, and that X_2 represents some rented facilities for providing haircuts. Most economists would not object to Y being regarded as U.S. exports of haircuts, even though the production of this service actually takes place in Canada. As an even more extreme example suppose X_1 are Japanese cars, X_2 are Canadian dealerships that provide the service of selling these automobiles and that Y are Japanese cars sold in Canada. Again we would have no difficulty in persuading ourselves that Y is the imported commodity even though some value has been added by the service industry in Canada.

The point is that while the formal production and trade structure in all these examples is the same, they lead to quite a different interpretation of what is being imported, depending on what the production process actually does. One way of avoiding this confusion is to concentrate on international payments and to define an import to have taken place if an international payment is made for X_1, whether X_1 is capital, a service, or an intermediate commodity. Thus in our example X_1 is always the import and Y is domestic production. In the haircut example, the import is barbers' services, not haircuts. This is not a trivial distinction and indeed is crucial if certain apparent paradoxes and theoretical inconsistencies are to be avoided.

4.3 Restrictions on Trade in Services

The U.S. trade negotiators have argued that restrictions on trade in services should be a part of the upcoming trade liberalization talks. Various proposals to ensure that at least no new restrictions are created have been suggested (see Stalson, 1985). But when one examines the ways in which international flows of service can be controlled it is not clear that the issue is one of trade restrictions. Certainly traditional tariffs and quotas will generally be ineffective in restricting service trade, for such restrictions require the identification of the traded items at the border.[2] Contact and substitution services typically do not cross the border but are produced on site, and even if all such activities could be monitored there is still the difficulty, referred to above, of valuation. For intermediation services evaluation at the border may be almost as difficult even when they can be identified.

One of the principal concerns in the service literature relates to right of establishment in foreign countries, but while this may be an important problem it does not seem to be a trade issue. The typical argument is that, for a country to provide a service in a foreign country, a presence is required. Thus if Canada is to provide banking services in the U.S. it would be efficient to set up branches in that country. The fact that many states do not allow branch banking means, it is suggested, that there is a restriction on service trade. The issue here, however, does not seem fundamentally different than what would be involved if a U.S. company wished to supply concrete to the Edmonton construction industry. To do so efficiently the company would want to set up a plant in Edmonton, and if the building industry were restricted to local firms this would prevent foreign participation in this market. It does not seem useful, however, to think of this as a restriction on international trade. Note that the only fundamental difference between this cement example and the banking or insurance industry is the kind of output that the various companies produce. There may well be an important issue in terms of international investment in the right of establishment debate, but no trade issues per se are involved.

But even if the present volume of international service trade is overstated, it is clear that trade in services is important and will increase in significance in the future. We previously referred to the fact that the communications revolution has broken down both the time and space barriers in this industry. In the future it seems probable that services such as typing, data processing, and basic research activities will become important components of the international trade markets. One would expect this trade would be governed by the usual rules of comparative advantage and therefore subject to the traditional analysis. And as in the traditional analysis such trade can be seen essentially as a substitute for factor mobility. But whether trade negotiators in high-wage countries such as Canada and the United States should insist that there be no restrictions on such trade is anything but clear. Many of these service industries are particularly labour intensive, and in the past the jobs of such workers have been protected by the restrictions imposed by dimensionality. Thus in the past one could obtain secretarial service from a foreign worker only through immigration, or in the short run through guest worker provisions. Opening up the entire service sector to foreign competition would not be unlike opening the borders to foreign labour, and while this would undoubtedly increase world utility in the long run it is not clear that the short-run benefits to the United States or Canada would be large. Certainly domestic labour would be seriously disadvantaged. Of course in the short run language differences will provide an effective constraint for many foreign countries, but even these are likely to be reduced over time.

4.4 Traditional Comparative Advantage

A principal concern of this study is the role that services can play in the trading pattern of an economy. Any investigation of the causes and consequences of international trade must begin with a discussion of why trade takes place, or in other words with the determinants of trade. The theme of this section is that the determinants of service trade will sometimes differ from the determinants of trade traditionally discussed in the international trade literature, and that these differences will be important for policy issues when services are considered.

Trade among nations, just as is true with any other kind of trade, such as trade among regions or among individuals, ultimately depends on price differences. A nation will find it profitable to export a particular commodity if there is some production advantage available to that country, and conversely a country will import a commodity if that particular good or service can be produced more efficiently elsewhere. Thus the search for determinants of trade is just a search for reasons why prices will differ between countries. Several determinants of trade have been extensively discussed in the international trade literature. Still the most popular explanation of trade is endowment differences, or the Heckscher-Ohlin model, which attributes trade to differences in capital-labour ratios between regions or countries. It is this endowment model that is central to most modern international trade theory, and that has provided most of the standard trade propositions. An analysis of services in a Heckscher-Ohlin model is considered in Chapter 6.

An alternative determinant of trade is differences in production functions, and an early version of this explanation is the Ricardian model. This model assumes a single factor of production, and while this significantly simplifies the analysis, one does not obtain the relationships between factor prices and commodity prices that is such an important feature of the Heckscher-Ohlin model. Nevertheless the simple Ricardian model has often proved useful in illustrating basic concepts such as gains from trade or the effects of technical change. Indeed we will use the Ricardian model to illustrate the effects of technical progress in transportation in Chapter 5.

Other explanations of trade that have recently become popular are increasing returns to scale and imperfect competition. Early contributions include Herberg and Kemp (1969) and Melvin (1969) and more recent contributions include Markusen and Melvin (1981) and Ethier (1979) and (1982). Here there are a wide variety of models, depending on such things as the nature of the returns to scale assumed, whether increasing returns exist in all industries or only in some, and whether the returns to scale are consistent with perfect competition or whether some form of imperfect competition must be assumed. Although these models are richer in terms of the choice of technology that can be assumed, they do not provide the clear and unambiguous conclusions and policy prescriptions that can be derived from the Heckscher-Ohlin approach. Several models dealing with increasing returns to scale and imperfect competition will be considered in Chapters 8 and 9.

A variety of other possible explanations of trade have also been considered in the literature. As was noted earlier, anything that results in price differences can cause trade, and thus distortion such as taxes can be a determinant of trade. An earlier analysis of this problem is contained in Melvin (1970) and more recently Deardorff (1987) has considered some related issues. A popular model that has become an alternative to the Heckscher-Ohlin approach was developed by Jones (1971) and Samuelson (1971), and has come to be known as the specific factor model. The specific factors could be capital in place, in which case the model could be seen as a short-run version of the Heckscher-Ohlin model, or alternatively the specific factors could be resources, in which case the model would provide an explanation of trade patterns based on natural resources. This model presents quite different implications for the relationships between commodity prices and factor prices and between changes in endowments and changes in the outputs of produced commodities. The implications of specific factor models for trade in services are considered in Chapter 7.

It is clear from the above that there is no shortage of explanations of why trade takes place, and it is well known that the implications of trade caused by these various factors can be quite different. The issue at hand is whether trade in service commodities can be seen as arising primarily from one of the determinants listed above, or whether service trade can be caused by any or all of the above determinants. A third possibility is that service trade depends on yet a different set of factors that have not been seen as primary determinants of trade in goods. Certainly there is no difficulty in relating certain types of service trade to the determinants of trade listed above. Indeed the theoretical studies of trade in services sponsored by the IRPP on which this study is based do just that. Melvin (1989) has analyzed trade in services within the context of the traditional Heckscher-Ohlin model, where trade in services and goods can be related to the endowments of capital and labour. Markusen (1989a and 1989b) has analyzed the effects of producer services in the presence of increasing returns to scale and imperfect competition. Burgess (1989) and Jones and Ruane (1989) have used the specific factor model to investigate various questions concerning trade in services, while Ryan (1987) has examined the implications of service trade in a Ricardian model. Thus, at least to some extent, trade in services can be seen to be determined by the same factors that determine trade in goods.

4.5 Ephemeral Comparative Advantage in Services

While the basic determinants of trade apply to services just as they do to goods, there is one fundamental difference that seems to reappear in most of these discussions. In Melvin (1989) for example, the factor capital can be interpreted to be the services of managers, and it is this factor service that is assumed to be mobile between countries. A similar approach to the consideration of services in the context of the Heckscher-Ohlin model was employed by Deardorff (1985). In Markusen (1989a and 1989b) there were returns to scale assumed at the level of factor input and these returns to scale were associated with the acquisition of skills or education. The returns to scale were generated by the fact that acquiring skills such as engineering expertise requires a relatively large initial fixed cost, but the provision of the subsequent service can be provided at very low marginal cost. These models, then, while very much in the tradition of the international trade literature that has developed in recent years, differ somewhat in the definitions of the factors of production. Capital, rather than being physical machines, is human capital provided by education, training, and research and development. The comparative advantage generated by these factors therefore depends crucially on the ability of the economy to provide facilities for education, training, and research and development. Thus, compared to the long-lasting and stable comparative advantage provided by such factors as resource abundance and plentiful labour, comparative advantage in the service industries may be fleeting and ephemeral.

The ephemerality of service comparative advantage arises from at least two sources. First, the skills and knowledge associated with human capital are, by definition, embodied in individuals, and these individuals are free to move from place to place. This footloose feature of comparative advantage in services will be important for countries, but may be even more important for regions within a country, due to the differences in labour mobility. The regional comparative advantage associated with skilled engineers, accountants or lawyers depends on the ability of the region or the country to be able to retain these individuals within their jurisdictions. Second, the comparative advantage associated with these human capital skills can generally be acquired by others through education and training. Thus the advantage endowed by superior technological know-how or modern engineering techniques may quickly disappear as other regions or other countries acquire the same level of skill and training.

The ephemeral nature of comparative advantage in service industries presents nations and regions with difficulties somewhat different than those associated with the traditional sources of comparative advantage. Uncertainties surrounding how long a particular advantage can be expected to persist will make it difficult to plan for the provision of infrastuctures such as transportation. The importance of human capital in the comparative advantage in services spotlights the importance of education and training, and this raises further questions in terms of public policy. For example Markusen (1988) has shown that the general provision of education and skill training to the population at large will generally be inefficient, since the region or economy has no guarantee that the individuals trained will remain within that jurisdiction. Engineers trained in Newfoundland, for example, may very well seek employment in Toronto, resulting in a loss to Newfoundland, both of the skilled worker and of the resource cost of providing the education. A more efficient method of providing subsidies to training and education would be to give the subsidies to the producer rather than to the individual worker, but this is often not feasible. Certainly one could not delay the provision of basic education until individuals are employed, nor does it seem reasonable to suppose that professional training could be provided at the level of the firm producing the service. Furthermore, even if one provided in-house training and education there would be nothing to prevent the individuals, once having acquired the human capital, from moving elsewhere. In general it will be difficult to ensure that producers are able to keep control of the skill, education, and research and development potential embodied in workers that is acquired through subsidized learning.

As more and more production and trade is associated with service industries, the difficulties associated with the ephemerality of comparative advantage in the production of services will become a more and more important policy issue. This will be true both for regions and for countries, and if a country is to be successful in the provision of service outputs then the mechanisms through which human capital is acquired will deserve more serious consideration. It is also clear that policies that are appropriate for regions would not necessarily be appropriate for countries, because of the differences between interregional and international mobility of labour. A high degree of interregional labour mobility, which in the limit means that the location of training is unimportant in determining where a factor will be used in the production process, suggests that higher education and skill training should be financed by federal rather than provincial governments. On the international side, since countries have much more control over immigration and emigration than do regions, concerns about a net loss of educated and skilled workers may not be as great. A country such as Canada can almost certainly attract as many skilled workers through immigration as it loses through emigration. It will still, however, be efficient to target educational subsidies to ensure that the system does not produce skilled individuals who cannot, because of the structure of production in the economy, obtain employment. Training individuals in the horticulture associated with growing oranges and bananas (and probably grapes) is clearly not an activity in which a country such as Canada should engage.

4.6 Service Industries and Canadian Exports

While Canada has traditionally been seen as an exporter of raw materials and products that rely on natural resources as inputs, a good deal of the activity in international markets, both through trade and foreign investment, can be seen to depend on service industries in Canada. These sources of comparative advantage very often can be seen to depend on particular constraints that Canadians have been required to overcome; constraints that very often depend on the physical nature of the country. There are at least two ways in which Canadian service industries influence exports and investment. First there are the direct exports of service products such as engineering skills and banking services, and second there are exports of products that have developed because of the existence of particular service industries in Canada. These two factors are not independent and indeed the former is often a consequence of the latter.

Because the Canadian population lives in a narrow band along the United States border, communication and transportation have always posed difficult problems for Canadians. Communication and transportation have always been important priorities, and this has given rise to the development of expertise in several areas. At present Canada is a leader in the field of long-distance telecommunications, and several companies have developed world-wide reputations for producing communication equipment such as telephones and other communication equipment. In the transportation area Canadians have developed aircraft that are useful both for moving passengers and freight under conditions of severe weather and limited runways, and these aircraft have found markets in the rest of the world. Canada also exports diesel locomotives and is at the forefront of the technology for intra-urban transportation systems.

It could be argued that the Canadian branch-banking system was an efficient method of overcoming the constraints of distance and difficulties associated with a sparsely populated country. The development of an efficient banking system has resulted in Canada becoming a substantial exporter of banking services, and Canadian banks are now found in many foreign countries.

Other services exported by Canadians include engineering and consulting, and in particular, expertise has developed in areas relating to the construction of major hydro-electric projects such as the James Bay hydro-electric facility. Thus the development of such projects, which depend for their existence on the unique Canadian geography, have resulted in spinoffs leading to the export of engineering services. In recent years Canadians have also been active in land development in foreign countries. Mario Polese has suggested that one of the reasons for this international comparative advantage was the expertise gained through the development of real estate projects in Toronto and Montreal. The ability to put together parcels of land, provide servicing and financing and organize construction were skills that could be transferred to foreign markets, particularly in the United States.

The service exports described above all share two characteristics. First, they all depend, to at least some extent, on the development of an industry or product in Canada that, in turn, was often related to the difficulties associated with overcoming the constraints of distance. Second, the comparative advantages in these industries is clearly ephemeral and could easily vanish if the circumstances that led to the development of these industries were to disappear. Canadian exports of grain, wood and wood products, and metals, depend for their existence on resourse endowments, a source of comparative advantage that has a certain permanency. A continued comparative advantage in service industries, however, is much less certain and may be much more sensitive to domestic economic policy.

4.7 Summary and Policy Conclusions

The purpose of this chapter has been to provide an introduction to the discussion of trade in services. An initial requirement in any such discussion is to have a clear understanding of what trade in services means, and some way of distinguishing among trade in services, foreign investment, and factor flows. With services, because of the close relationships with factor flows and investments, such a distinction is often difficult. This raises the related and equally as difficult issue of measuring the international flows of services. Restrictions on service trade also presents different problems than restrictions on trade in goods, for the traditional commercial policy tools of tariffs and quotas will often not be effective. Such issues will be taken up in more detail in Chapter 6.

Comparative advantage in services may develop from any of the traditional determinants of trade discussed in the international trade literature, but many service exports are faced with a difficulty not encountered for goods. Comparative advantage is often based on human capital, and thus is often footloose and ephemeral, due either to the fact that the individuals who possess the special knowledge are mobile, or from the fact that the required knowledge and information can be acquired in other countries. The ephemeral nature of comparative advantage in services raises some unique policy issues. Human capital is often the reason for the success of service industries, and this highlights the role of education and research and development in maintaining such industries. The ephemeral nature of comparative advantage in services can be illustrated by specific reference to some Canadian service industries.

The provision and maintenance of an efficient transportation and communications network is not only important for the efficient production of Canadian exports, but it also often leads to spillovers which allow for the export of certain distance-related services. Again we find that public policy is often crucial for the provision of such transportation and communication networks. We will have more to say on these issues in subsequent chapters.

Notes

1.   As is argued below, if barbers move it is more appropriate to regard this as a flow of factor services.

2.   In Chapter 6 it will be shown that for trade in factor services, commercial policy can take the form of restrictions on the repatriation of foreign earnings.

Chapter 5

Transportation: An Analysis Using the Ricardian Model

5.1 Introduction

This is the first of five chapters that examine the phenomenon of service trade with specific reference to traditional models from international trade theory. In the present chapter we concentrate on transportation and use, as the starting point, the Ricardian model. We begin by examining a model of a simple closed economy that produces two commodities, and where transportation of these commodities between production locations is required if individuals are to consume both goods. Services are shown to arise endogenously, and the allocation of labour among the three industries is found to depend on the technology used in the production of goods and services and on consumers' preferences. Changes in technology, both in services and in the production of commodities, are assumed, and the welfare consequences of such changes derived. A simple trading world is then examined where it is assumed that service technologies differ between countries. The consequences of having differences in the production function for commodities is also examined, and the distribution of gains from trade between the two countries is considered.

We then move to the consideration of a more traditional transportation model which concentrates on regional and international transportation costs (as opposed to considering the transportation costs associated with *all* trades) and consider the consequences of technological change. Because of the importance of interregional trade in the Canadian economy, the regional

47

implications of transportation costs are emphasized in this section. Extensions of this model to the case where there are more than two factors is then considered briefly, and the chapter concludes with a summary and some policy conclusions.

The focus of this chapter is on transportation, and while this service sector has always been important for international trade, there has been surprisingly little discussion of transportation in the trade literature. As was noted in Chapter 2, early contributions include those of Samuelson (1954) and Mundell (1957a), and in these papers the so-called "iceberg model" of transportation cost was employed. It was assumed that, in transit, some of the commodity disappeared, so that the amount reaching the consuming country was smaller than the amount that left the producing nation. This assumption was a proxy for the notion that transportation cost used real resources, and for some purposes it was quite appropriate. On the other hand, it is clear that transportation does not necessarily use factors of production in the same proportions as is required for the production of the commodities that are being moved, and thus the iceberg model is not an appropriate assumption if one wants to focus on the commodity-price and factor-price effects of explicitly introducing a transportation sector. Furthermore, the iceberg model does not permit transportation to be a traded commodity, since by definition transportation is uniquely associated with the trade of a commodity. One could certainly not analyze, for example, the possibility of one country providing transportation services for another in exchange for goods.

Subsequent work on transportation, particularly that of Falvey (1976) and Cassing (1978) specifically included transportation as a resource-using productive activity. As was noted in Chapter 2, with this approach the capital-labour ratio in the transportation sector is crucial in determining which country will be the major provider of transportation services. Other contributors to this literature include Casas (1983) who surveyed and extended the produced transportation cost literature, and Melvin (1985b) who analyzed the effects of transportation costs in a regional trade model.

The traditional discussions of transportation costs in the international trade literature have made another important simplifying assumption, for most contributors have assumed that transportation is required only for international transactions. Even Melvin (1985b), who explicitly introduces transportation costs between regions within a country, abstracts from transportation costs that may be required within a region. While transportation costs are obviously required for international trade, transportation is no less important for the exchange that takes place entirely among domestic citizens. Furthermore, transportation across international borders is most appropriately thought of as an extension of the transportation activity that exists within an economy. Certainly the discussion of technological change and of comparative advantage in transportation should be analyzed in terms of a transportation sector that is required for commerce in general and not specifically targeted to international transactions. Of course in many circumstances international transportation does differ from domestic transportation and such differences must be taken into account. Nevertheless it would seem that the appropriate approach is to begin with a discussion of why transportation would arise in a closed economy and then extend the model to one in which international trade takes place. This is the approach that is taken in Section 5.3.

5.2 The Model

Throughout most of the discussion we will employ the simple Ricardian model which assumes that labour, L, is the single factor of production. Our analysis follows Ryan (1987) and assumes that two consumer goods, X and Y, are produced using labour. Individuals can choose to produce either X or Y, but cannot produce both.[1] Furthermore, the production locations for X and Y are separated, so that consumption of both commodities by any consumer will require trade, which in turn requires transportation. It is assumed that there is a transportation sector, S, which can facilitate the required exchange, and for simplicity we will assume that a worker who chooses to work in the transportation sector must produce transportation exclusively and cannot produce either X or Y. This is a stronger assumption than required, for we could allow producers to produce X and S or Y and S (but not both X and Y).[2]

Although labour is the only identified factor of production, it is clear that, just as in the traditional Ricardian model, other factors of production are lurking in the background. These could be resources, capital, or Ricardo's "climate", and our assumption is essentially that these other factors do not impose constraints on the production process. We could thus imagine two production activities, each of which requires some resource which is geographically specific. Producers have the option of locating at either resource and producing the commodity associated with it, or of engaging in the transportation activity.

The analysis presented here and in the following section is a simplification of results due to Ryan (1987). We will use simple geometric techniques to illustrate the principal results, and we will make no attempt to prove all of the propositions. It is assumed that all individuals have identical preferences defined over the two commodities, X and Y. Preferences are assumed to be homothetic so that community indifference curves can be constructed. Thus the basic model consists of the three production functions, (5.1), (5.2), (5.3), and the utility function (5.4) shown below. The model is completed by noting that the total amount of labour, L, must be divided up among the three industries as indicated in equation (5.5).

(5.1) $X = F_X(L_X)$

(5.2) $Y = F_Y(L_Y)$

(5.3) $S = F_S(L_S)$

(5.4) $U = U(X,Y)$

(5.5) $L = L_X + L_Y + L_S$

   We further simplify the model by assuming that the production functions for X and Y are identical in the sense that a unit of X and Y require the same input of labour. We also assume that the utility function is symmetric, which means that interchanging the units of X and Y in the utility function does not affect the utility level. Thus ten units of X and two units of Y give exactly the same utility as two units of X and ten units of Y.
   In this analysis the form of the utility function is obviously important in determining the final equilibrium. Two extreme cases are of interest. If the utility function is Leontief, with the elasticity of substitution in consumption equal to zero, then exchange between the two groups of producers is essential for positive utility, and some amount of trade must take place. As another extreme, suppose there is infinite substitution in consumption, which implies that the indifference curves are linear. In this case the two commodities are indistinguishable as far as consumers are concerned, and thus there is no reason for trade even if transportation costs were zero. Thus the form of the utility function will determine how much trade takes place, which in turn will determine the need for the transportation service. Other things being equal, the need to provide transportation will reduce the labour available for producing consumer goods X and Y, and thus the utility function will also affect the overall level of utility enjoyed by consumers.
   We begin by analyzing, in Figure 5.1, a situation where there are three individuals, where each has chosen one of the three productive activities. The process works as follows. The Y producer produces fifteen units of Y and the X producer fifteen units of X giving them initial endowments of Y_0 and X_0 in Figure 5.1. The servicer travels to the Y producer where he offers to trade five units of X in exchange for ten units of Y. The servicer takes these ten units of Y, consumes five,

and transports the other five to the X producer. The X producer exchanges ten units of X for five units of Y, the servicer consumes five units of X and transports the other five units of X back to the Y producer. All three individuals have consumed five units of X and five units of Y, and because preferences are identical with no substitution in consumption, this situation is an equilibrium. We note that in this model prices faced by all three individuals will differ, and that an equilibrium is described by a situation in which utility levels reached by all three agents are the same. Should utility levels be unequal, some individuals will move into the occupation providing the higher utility, and this will continue until an equilibrium is reached.

Now suppose there is a substantial improvement in the service technology such that a labourer in the transportation sector can transport twelve units of Y in one direction and twelve units of X in the other. It is clear now that each servicer can provide transportation for at least two pairs of producers of X and Y of the kind shown in Figure 5.1. Indeed, it can be seen from Figure 5.1 that such an allocation will result in a new equilibrium. Suppose a servicer visits the Y producer and offers to exchange nine Y for six X. On receiving the nine Y the servicer can consume three, transport the remaining six Y to the producer of commodity X, and exchange them for nine units of X. The servicer can consume three X and transport the remaining six units of X back to the Y producer, thus completing the trade. This gives position C_2 in Figure 5.1. We note that the two producers each consume six units of Y and six units of X, so that their total consumption adds to point B, where $20C_2 = 0B$. The servicer has received three units of X and three units of Y, which is vector BE, one half the length of vector C_2B. The servicer, because of the technological improvement, has also been able to provide transportation between two other producers and has thus received another three units of X and three units of Y, giving total consumption of six units of each. Thus we again have an equilibrium where all individuals have consumed six units of X and six units of Y.

How will the total output for the economy have changed with this technological improvement? To continue our specific example suppose the economy has 300 workers, and that in the initial situation 100 were allocated to each of the three productive activities. Total output of the economy would be 1500 X and 1500 Y, with 100 workers being required to provide the necessary transportation service. Now consider the technological improvement that allowed each servicer to carry twelve units of X and Y. Only half as many services are required, which means that 50 workers can be reallocated to other activities. Of course they cannot all be allocated to the production of X and Y for if they were there would be no one to carry out the required

Figure 5.1

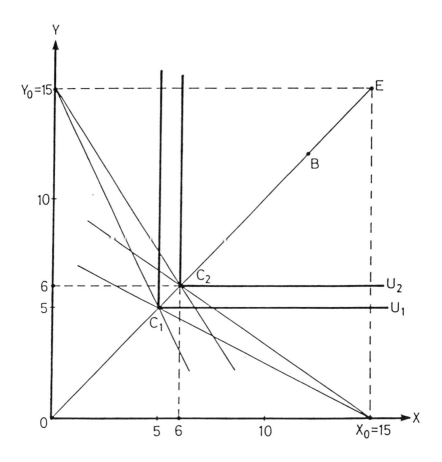

trades between these new producers. It is easily seen that of the 50 workers, 20 will be allocated to Y production, 20 to X production, with the remaining 10 carrying out the additional transportation that will be required. Note that we now have a total of 120 workers in each consumer-good industry, giving rise to a total output of 1800 units of X and Y. We still have 300 workers in total and thus each consumes six units of X and six units of Y.

This simple example illustrates several interesting points. First we note that the technological improvement has resulted in an increase in consumption from five to six units of both commodities for all individuals, and thus utility for everyone has increased. The total production of X (or Y) has increased from 1500 to 1800 units, while trade has increased from 500 to 720 units. Thus while production and consumption have increased by 20 percent, trade has increased by 24 percent, and all these changes are a result of a 140 percent improvement in the transportation technology.

The case of Leontief preferences is very special and of limited interest because it does not allow for any substitution in consumption. A more interesting example is shown in Figure 5.2 where preferences for all consumers have been assumed to be Cobb-Douglas. It is again assumed that Y producers and X producers produce Y_0 and X_0 respectively, and we consider an initial situation with prices P_y and P_x resulting in consumption at C_y and C_x for Y and X producers respectively. Because utility functions are Cobb-Douglas, each producer will consume exactly half of his own output. The transportation technology is assumed to be such that a servicer can carry Y_x of Y and X_y of X. The story is then as follows. The servicer goes to a Y producer and promises to provide X_y in exchange for Y_y. On receipt of Y_y he consumes $Y_x Y_y$ and transports Y_x to the X producer, and exchanges it for X_x. He then consumes $X_y X_x$ and takes X_y to the Y producer, completing the exchange. The sum of the consumption vectors for the Y and X producers gives C_1, which leaves $C_1 E$ of output available for the servicer with $C_1 E$ equal to OC_0 (and also equal to the two quantities $Y_x Y_y$ and $X_y X_x$). The servicer thus receives the consumption bundle C_0, so that the utility of all three individuals is identical and we have an equilibrium.

Now suppose we have an improvement in the technology of transportation that allows a servicer to carry $2Y'_x$ of Y and an equivalent amount of X. The technological improvement will result in a reduction in the price of imports for both producers, and because utility functions are Cobb-Douglas this will result in an increase in the consumption of import goods but no change in the consumption of their own output. Thus we would obtain consumption points for producers Y and X of C'_y and C'_x respectively, giving rise to an aggregate

Figure 5.2

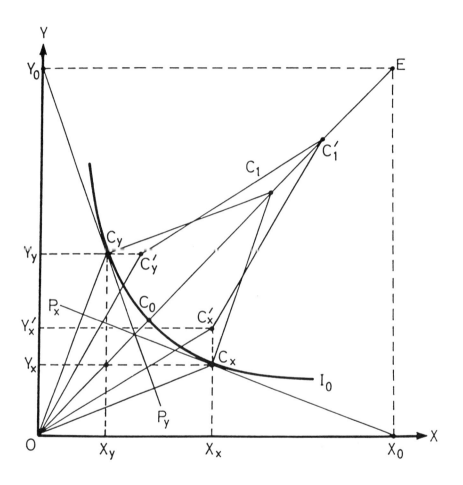

consumption point for these two producers of C'_1. Thus the amount of X and Y available for the servicer is C'_1E, and doubling this amount would put the servicer on the indifference curve that passes through C'_y and C'_x.

We find that in the Cobb-Douglas case the results are very similar to those found in Figure 5.1. An improvement in the service technology will result in an increase in the level of utility enjoyed both by producers and servicers. Fewer services are required for each pair of producers, and thus labour will be transferred from the service sector to the production sector, resulting in a larger aggregate output of both commodities. Trade by each producer will increase, but this increased trade volume can easily be handled by the improvement in the efficiency in the transportation sector. Thus we have our first major result:

PROPOSITION 5.1: In a Ricardian world, services will arise endogenously if producers of the consumption good are in different locations. For symmetric Leontief or Cobb-Douglas preferences, an improvement in the service technology will increase output of both consumer goods, will increase trade, and will increase the utility of all consumers.

Figure 5.3 shows a situation where the elasticity of substitution in consumption is greater than one, and in this case the results can be quite different from those found for Leontief or Cobb-Douglas utility functions. With prices P_y and P_x facing Y producers and X producers respectively we find the two consumption points are C_y and C_x. Total consumption for the two producers is C_1, found by completing the parallelogram $OC_yC_1C_x$. The vector C_1E is the amount of output available to the service sector, and since OC_0 equal $4C_1E$, each servicer must be able to provide servicing for four pairs of producers if the situation shown in Figure 5.3 is to be in equilibrium. We note that with an elasticity of substitution in consumption greater than 1, producers are inclined to consume a large amount of their own output unless the cost of transportation is relatively low. Thus in this world transportation must be more efficient than in the Cobb-Douglas or Leontief cases shown in Figures 5.1 and 5.2, for otherwise no trade would take place.

We now suppose a 50% improvement in technology in the service sector, which gives rise to a reduction in the price of imports for both producers, and gives the new consumption points C'_y and C'_x. The sum of the two consumption vectors produces point $\hat{C}_1$, and we note that this implies a smaller total consumption of X and Y for the two producers than point C_1, the consumption point before the technological change. At the same time the welfare level for both producers has increased, since C'_y and C'_x are on a higher indifference curve than are C_y and C_x.

Another difference seen when Figure 5.3 is compared to earlier diagrams is that the technological change has resulted in a very substantial increase in the amount of trade between these two producers. In Figure 5.3 trade has increased from $Y_s Y_y$ to $Y'_s Y'_y$, an increase of approximately 300%.[3] Obviously the 50% technological improvement in the transportation sector will not permit the existing transportation industry to complete all the trades required by this proposed equilibrium. In the initial situation each servicer could supply transportation for four pairs of producers, but now, because of the increase in demand for transportation, a servicer will be able to provide transportation for only two pairs of producers. Could this still result in an equilibrium? The answer is yes, for because the aggregate consumption point is now less than it was previously, there is more X and Y available to pay the service sector. Since the distance $C'_1 E$ is more than twice $C_1 E$, servicers receive enough X and Y to allow them to be on the same indifference curve as the two producers. Of course this is not the end of the story, for we now do not have enough servicers to provide the transportation required for all the exchanges associated with this new equilibrium. Indeed we will need twice as many labourers allocated to the service sector, and of course we can have more servicers only if we have less producers of X and Y. Thus in the final equilibrium we will have less production of both X and Y, more trade, more factors allocated to the service sector, but nevertheless all individuals will have higher utility levels than before the technological change took place. We thus have the following proposition:

PROPOSITION 5.2: If the elasticity of substitution in consumption is greater than one, an improvement in technology in the service sector will increase the utility of all consumers, will result in more trade, but may result in a smaller aggregate output of both consumer goods.

The results of Proposition 5.2 are of interest because they illustrate the fact that a relatively fast-growing service sector is not necessarily associated with a slowdown in the growth of real national income as measured by utility. Indeed, a rise in service activity combined with a fall in the production of all consumer goods may still leave consumers better off. As Ryan (1987) has noted, some authors have expressed concern about the growth of the service sector, and have argued that the fall in real consumer products has been harmful to society.

Figure 5.3

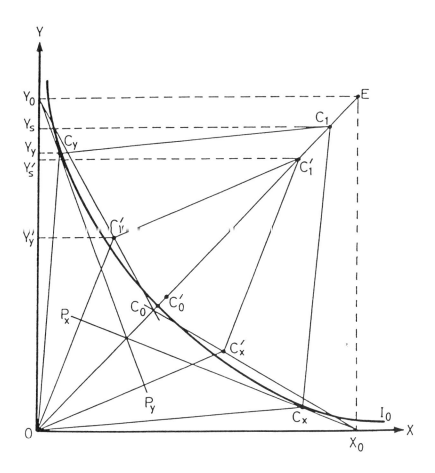

Ryan (1987) has shown that, when one plots the quantity of labour allocated to services against the technology in the service sector, L_S initially rises, attains a maximum, and then asymptotically approaches zero. This result can be confirmed by the example of Figure 5.3. Note, first, that if transportation was very inefficient, then because of the high elasticity of substitution in consumption, producers would choose to consume only their own output and there would be no trade at all, and thus no service sector. In this case C_1 would correspond to point E, which means that all output produced is allocated to the two producers. As technology improves there will be some point at which producers will be willing to exchange some of their output for the output of the other sector, and we will have an equilibrium such as the initial situation of Figure 5.3 with aggregate consumption for the two producers at C_1. As technology continues to improve, so that services are able to carry more and more output, at some point the aggregate consumption point will again start to move back towards E, and of course in the limit, as transportation costs approach zero, the number of labourers in the service sector will also approach zero and the aggregate consumption point for the producers will approach point E.

In the three cases discussed so far we have assumed a very symmetrical world. Not only have we assumed symmetry between the two producers and in the utility function we have also assumed symmetrical improvements in the transportation technology. We now want to consider relaxing these assumptions, and we begin by assuming that technological change takes place only in the X industry. It is important to recall that we have assumed that a single servicer carries X in one direction and Y in the other. Thus an improvement in servicing for X producers would mean that more X could be carried than previously. But if there is no improvement in the transportation for Y, there can be no additional trades, for while a servicer would be prepared to carry more X to trade with a Y producer, he could not bring back any more Y to pay for it. Thus technological improvement in transportation in only one good will simply result in excess capacity in one direction, but will not otherwise change our equilibrium. Thus we have the following:

PROPOSITION 5.3: When servicers transport both com-modities, technological improvement in transportation for one sector will produce excess capacity in the transportation sector but will not change output or utility for any of the consumers in the economy.

Of course, if at some subsequent stage there is an improvement in the technology in the transportation of X, then a real increase both in output and in utility would be observed. Thus whether or not technological improvement in the service industry for a single product will result in an improvement in welfare and an increase in output will depend on whether or not there is excess capacity in the service sector for the other industry.

Another important symmetry in the model is the assumption that a labour unit can produce exactly the same number of units of X and Y. We now assume technological improvement in the production of X but no change in the production of Y. In Figure 5.2 this would move X_0 further out along the X axis. With no change in the service technology servicers cannot transport any more X, even though the output of X has increased. This is not the end of the story, however, for with a larger output of X, even if the same amount of X is transported to the Y producers, there is nevertheless more X to be consumed. Thus either X producers or servicers (or both) will be able to consume more X and will therefore be on a higher indifference curve. Of course if X producers are on a higher indifference curve than are Y producers, then we no longer have an equilibrium and further adjustments will be required. The price of X paid by Y producers must fall and a new equilibrium will be reached with more trade and a higher level of utility for all consumers.

Figure 5.4 illustrates the case where there has been technological improvement in the X industry. The technological change results in a maximum output shift of from X_0 to X'_0, and the new equilibrium shows consumption at C'_y and C'_x for the Y and X producers. We thus have our next result:

PROPOSITION 5.4: **A technological improvement in the production of either good will increase the utility for all consumers in the economy.**

The assumed change in the technology in the X industry has destroyed the symmetry of the problem. Thus the consumption bundles for the two producers are no longer symmetric, and we no longer have $P_x = 1/P_y$. And because the consumption bundles are not symmetric there must be excess capacity in the service sector. Recall that the services can transport equal quantities of the two commodities, but now the producers consume different amounts of the transported good, so that full utilization of the transportation facility is not possible.

If instead of assuming an increase in the technology for producing X we had relaxed the assumption of symmetry in the utility function we would have observed similar adjustments. Prices in the two industries would no longer be symmetric, but all consumers would nevertheless be on the same indifference curve in equilibrium. It is

Figure 5.4

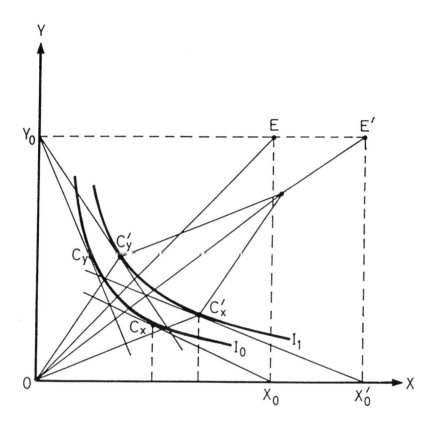

impossible to compare welfare in this case, however, for a change in the utility function means that utility comparisons cannot be made.

5.3   International Trade with Endogenous Transportation

To this point we have considered transportation within a closed economy, and we now want to analyze the consequences of two such economies engaged in international trade. Of course if the two economies are identical, because of our assumption of constant returns to scale in all productive activities, no trade would take place. Thus some difference between the two economies must be assumed. Two differences will be considered. We will first suppose that the service technology is more efficient in country H, and we will next consider the case where the production of the two goods differs and where the service technology is identical. We first suppose two economies with identical production functions for X and Y and identical endowments of factors of production. We assume that these countries are unable to trade due to tariffs or to some natural transportation barrier. The service technology in country H is assumed to be more efficient, and thus in the initial situation pairs of producers in the two countries could be as represented by the two equilibrium situations in Figure 5.2.

If free trade is now permitted, producers in country F will all want to obtain the other consumption good from servicers in country H, since the technological advantage in country H provides a more favourable exchange rate for both producers. Servicers in F will be eliminated from the market and will switch to producing commodities X or Y. In the final equilibrium all transportation will be provided by servicers in country H as long as the population of H is large enough to provide transportation for both countries. If we designate the populations in countries H and F as N_h and N_f respectively, and if the amount of labour required to provide transportation in both countries is L^w_s, then the condition $L^w_s < N_h$ guarantees that all servicing can be carried out by the home country.

In this model we note that the integration of the two economies has resulted in the consumers of both economies enjoying the higher consumption points associated with C'_y and C'_x in Figure 5.2. Thus trade has allowed the consumers in country F to take advantage of an improved technology not previously available. We also note that as long as the condition $L^w_s < N_h$ holds, so that all trading can be carried out by the efficient home country servicers, while the residents of country H have been made better off, there has been no change in the welfare of individuals in country H. We thus have the following result:

PROPOSITION 5.5: If two countries are identical except that H has a more efficient transportation system, and if $L^w{}_s < N_h$, then country H will provide all the servicing for consumers in country F, country F will gain from trade but country H will not.

In the situation of Proposition 5.5 the opening up of trade has allowed residents of country H to take advantage of an improvement in the technology of transportation, and all consumers in the world now enjoy the same utility level. A somewhat different result will occur if country H is small enough, relative to country F, that we obtain the inequality $L^w{}_s > N_h$. In this situation residents of H cannot provide transportation for all exchanges in the world and now some transportation must be carried out by the inefficient servicers in country F. In this situation the price of servicing must be determined by the inefficient servicers in F, or otherwise they would not provide any service output. Thus in the final equilibrium the world price of services would be the price that prevailed in country F in autarky, and this will result in gains to all consumers in country H (all of whom are now engaged in transportation) since their more efficient transportation system provides them with a higher utility level than is possible in country F. Thus if country H is small the distribution of the gains from trade are the opposite of those in Proposition 5.5. Consumers in H benefit, consumers in F are unaffected, and in the final equilibrium all consumers in country H are better off than any consumer in country F. We thus have the following proposition:

PROPOSITION 5.6: If country H is small relative to country F and if country H has the efficient transportation sector, then trade may result in a welfare improvement for all residents of H but no change in welfare for consumers in F.

These two propositions illustrate, in terms of a model with endogenous transportation, a well-known proposition in Ricardian trade theory, namely that the gains from trade very much depend on the size of the two countries. It can also be shown that an intermediate case exists where gains from trade can be enjoyed by both countries.[4]

There is another observation that can be made from the trade patterns associated with both Propositions 5.5 and 5.6. In both cases country H provides transportation services and in exchange receives outputs of X and Y. Indeed the trade pattern shows a flow of X and Y from F to H but no commodity flows in the other direction. Country H has a merchandise trade deficit because it is receiving commodities in exchange for its export of services. We thus have the following proposition:

PROPOSITION 5.7: **If the efficiencies of service sectors differ among countries a merchandise trade deficit by the efficient country is to be expected.**

Although Proposition 5.7 is a simple consequence of our model, it may nevertheless be relevant to a good deal of the current trade policy debate. In particular the United States has been concerned with the deficit in the merchandise trade account, while at the same time arguing that there should be unrestricted trade in service sectors. It seems quite possible that the merchandise trade deficit is simply a reflection of the efficiency of U.S. service sectors. As we shall see in subsequent chapters this is a feature which arises in several of the trade models, and is thus quite a general result.

We now turn to the consideration of the case where the two countries have different production functions for the two commodities but the same service technology. We initially assume that country H is more efficient in the production of commodity X and that country F is more efficient in the production of Y. Note that in making these assumptions we must necessarily relax the assumption that production within an economy is symmetric. Thus we have the situation shown in Figure 5.4 where the production of a unit of one commodity requires less labour than the production of a unit of the other. To simplify the analysis we assume that the efficiency differences of the two industries are symmetric between the two countries. Thus, for example, we might assume that industry X in country H uses 10% less labour than the production of Y, while industry Y in country F uses 10% less labour than is required to produce X. We further normalize by assuming that industry Y in country H and industry X in country F have identical technologies in the sense that both produce the same number of units of output for the same factor inputs. This is not a restrictive assumption because it can always be accomplished by an appropriate normalization. Finally we assume that the two countries have identical endowments of labour.

When trade is allowed in this model we observe the standard Ricardian result, namely that country H will specialize in and export commodity X, while country F will specialize in and export commodity Y. Thus we observe the standard gains from trade found in any Ricardian model. Both countries specialize completely and consume bundles of X and Y that were unavailable before trade was allowed.

But there is an additional source of gains from trade in this model that does not occur in the traditional Ricardian analysis. Because countries were asymmetric in production in the initial autarky situation, and given our maintained assumption that the service technology can carry equal amounts of X and Y, it is clear that the service industries in both countries had excess capacity in autarky.

When trade is permitted servicers from both countries carry commodities from the efficient X industry in country H to the efficient Y producers in country F, and given our assumption of symmetrical and identical utility functions between countries, desired trade volumes will again balance. Thus the introduction of international trade has again re-established symmetry on the production side of the model, since only the two efficient industries will be used to produce the world's output. Trade therefore allows the excess transportation capacity that existed in autarky to be used, and this is equivalent to an improvement in technology. Indeed, exactly the same world output would have been produced had we assumed that in the absence of trade, the two inefficient industries (one in each country) became as efficient as their foreign competitors.

The increase in production symmetry generated by the introduction of international trade can now, from the point of view of the world, be analyzed in the same way that an improvement in technology was analyzed in Section 5.2. If utility functions are Cobb-Douglas or Leontief, then the technological change will allow labour in the service sector to transfer to the production of commodities X and Y, and output of both consumer goods will rise. If the elasticity of substitution in consumption is greater than one, then more workers may be required in the service sector and total world output of consumer goods will fall. But in either case, as was shown in Propositions 5.1 and 5.2, the utility of all consumers will rise. We thus have the following result:

PROPOSITION 5.8: If two countries differ symmetrically in terms of the efficiency of their goods-producing sectors, and have the same service technologies, then international trade will result in specialization and the usual Ricardian gains from trade will be observed. In addition, however, trade will permit an effective technological improvement in the service industries, and will result in additional gains for all consumers in both countries.

The symmetry assumptions that have been used here are quite severe, and in general there would be no reason to believe that the technological superiority is perfectly symmetrical between the two countries. This strong assumption is not required for the results, however. Even if we relaxed the strong asymmetry assumptions, trade will produce both of the gains described in Proposition 5.8, as long as, in the initial autarky situation, there was excess capacity in the service sectors in both countries. If we do not have complete symmetry, then after trade there will still be excess capacity in one direction, but there will be gains associated with the elimination of an equal amount of excess capacity in both directions. The efficiency gain will be limited by the amount of excess capacity in one of the two sectors, and the total gains, while less than in the perfect symmetrical case, will nevertheless be positive.

5.4 Transportation and Trade: The Traditional Model

We have considered a model with endogenous transportation, where transportation is assumed to be required for *all* trades, both domestic and foreign. While this approach is more general than what is usually assumed, it does have the disadvantage of being quite complex and difficult to generalize. In this section we consider a simpler model where transportation is required only for transactions between trading areas, such as countries or regions. This model may be appropriate for small countries where internal distances are insignificant relative to international distances, but it will also be relevant for countries such as Canada, where a significant amount of trade takes place between regions. Indeed, transportation among regions may well be more important than transportation between Canadian and U.S. centres, and to focus attention on regional trade we will identify the two trading areas as E and W to represent eastern and western Canada. Thus we are assuming that transportation between regions (or countries) uses resources, but we ignore the resource costs of trades *within* a region.

We begin by assuming that there are two regions, E and W, and initially simplify the analysis by assuming a single factor of production, labour. As before suppose that there are three commodities, each produced under conditions of constant returns to scale. As well as the two consumption goods, X and Y, we assume a produced transportation service T.[5] We initially assume that T is not tradable, and that each region (or country) produces the amount of transportation required for its own trade in X and Y. We could suppose that each region provides the transportation for its own export (or import) or alternatively that all goods traded are transported to some intermediate location, and that each region provides the transportation to and from this transshipment point.

In Figure 5.5 the production possibility curves for the tradable commodities Y and X are T_EG_E for region E and T_WG_W for region W. We show only the outputs of the tradable goods, which means that the production of the transportation service is being suppressed. One can think of the production possibility curve of region E of Figure 5.5 as a two-dimensional representation of the three-dimensional production surface, where T_EG_E shows a slice through that surface at the

Figure 5.5

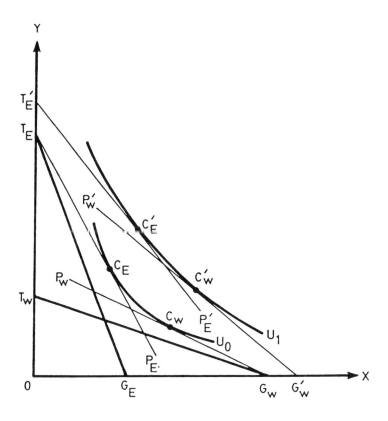

production point for T. Thus T_EG_E represents the available quantities of X and Y under the assumption that the amount of labour necessary to produce the required amount of commodity T needed for the transportation of the traded commodity has already been allocated to industry T. The initial equilibrium prices are assumed to be P_E and P_W for regions E and W respectively. These give rise to consumption at point C_E and C_W, where in order to simplify the diagram we have assumed both consumption points to be on the same community indifference curve.[6] The difference between the slopes of these price lines represents the transportation cost, and the fact that P_E is significantly steeper than P_W indicates that there are significant transportation costs between these two regions.

We now assume that a significant technological improvement occurs in the transportation sector. This will reduce transportation costs between the two regions and consequently will reduce the difference between the equilibrium prices faced by consumers in E and W. But the technological change in the transportation sector will have additional consequences. First, it will reduce, for both regions, the average cost of transporting a unit of either commodity. This conserves labour in the transportation sector and results in a larger quantity of labour being available for the production of commodities X and Y. At the same time, however, the reduction in transportation costs will generally increase the volume of trade, which in turn will require an increase in the labour needed to produce the additional transportation service. Thus we have two offsetting effects. The per unit labour cost of transportation will fall but more transportation will be required. Figure 5.5 illustrates the case where the savings in labour associated with the technological change outweigh the labour cost of the larger volume of trade, resulting in higher outputs for both commodity Y and commodity X. Thus the production point for region E shifts to T'_E and the production point for region W shifts to G_W. Consumption will now be C'_E and C'_W for regions E and W respectively. In the example shown there are two sources of welfare gains for consumers in both regions. First, because of the reduction in the transportation costs, the terms of trade become more favourable for both regions, and second, the output of both consumption goods is increased due to the savings associated with the technological improvement in the transportation sector.

Figure 5.6 illustrates the case where the savings associated with the lower per unit cost of transportation are more than offset by the larger volume of trade required in the new equilibrium. Here the total possible output of commodity Y in region E is reduced from TE to TE' while the total possible output of commodity X in region W is reduced from GW to G'W. Note, however, that even though the total output of both consumer goods has fallen, utility for the consumers of both regions has increased. The improvement in the terms of trade associated with the lower transportation cost leads to consumption at C'_E and C'_W for regions E and W respectively, on a higher indifference curve than C_E and C_W. It can easily be shown that this is a general result, and improvements in transportation technology can never make both regions worse off.[7] The basic argument is that the decision to trade implicitly takes into account the cost of transportation, and only when the real cost of obtaining the import is reduced will any technological change be undertaken. Thus we have a result similar to the one found in Section 5.2 for the closed economy:

PROPOSITION 5.9: An improvement in transportation technology may either increase or decrease the output of consumer goods for the trading regions, but in either case it will increase utility for consumers.

The situation of Figure 5.6 is of interest because it illustrates a case where technological change in the service sector reduces the aggregate output of both tradable commodities, but nevertheless increases the utility of all consumers.[8] A similar situation for a closed economy was described, but not illustrated, in Section 5.2. In this model, one way of measuring the technological change associated with the transportation sector from Figures 5.5 or 5.6 is to compare the prices for the two goods in the two regions both before and after the technological improvement. Technological improvement will always reduce the price differential for traded goods between regions. We will have more to say on the measurement of technological change in Chapter 10.

5.5 Transportation with Two Factors

A model with a single factor of production is useful for illustrating the production effects of technological change in the transportation sector, but does not provide us with information on how relative factor rewards might be affected. In Figure 5.7 we have illustrated the case corresponding to Figure 5.6 for region E for a Heckscher-Ohlin model with two factors of production, capital and labour. We assume that commodity Y is capital intensive relative to commodity X, and that region E is relatively well endowed with K. The initial situation has production at Q_E and consumption at C_E, and it is then assumed that a technological change takes place in the transportation sector. As before this will reduce the cost of imports for region E resulting in price line P'_E, and in the situation shown we have assumed that the increase in the volume of trade requires a larger bundle of factors than was

Figure 5.6

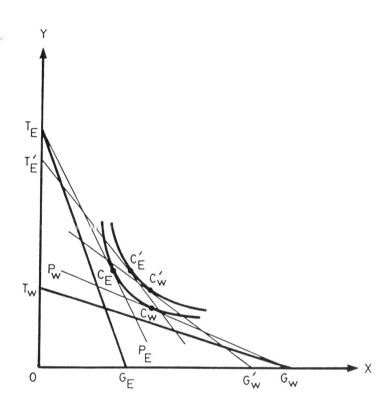

Figure 5.7

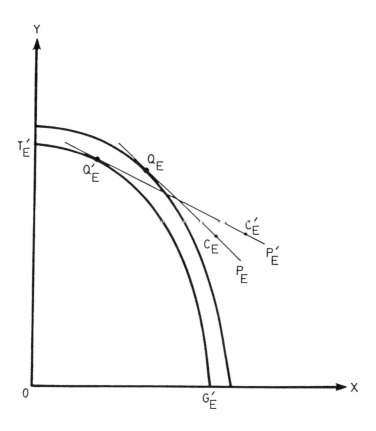

needed to produce T before the technological change. Again we find that improvement in the technology of the transportation sector has resulted in a smaller output of both the tradable goods X and Y, but has nevertheless resulted in a higher utility level for consumers in this region.

We also note that the increase in the price of Y has resulted in a larger Y/X ratio of production for region E. Because Y has been assumed to be the capital-intensive good, we know from the Stolper-Samuelson theorem that this relative change in outputs must be associated with a relative decrease in the wage rate, or in other words w/r must have been reduced. Of more importance is the fact that the real return to labour will have fallen, measured in terms of either commodity X or commodity Y, while the real return to capital will have increased. Thus for region E, technological improvement in the transportation sector, while improving the average welfare of all citizens in the community, nevertheless makes labour worse off.

But while labour in region E is disadvantaged, both relatively and absolutely, by the technological improvement in the transportation sector, just the opposite has happened in region W. There the relative price of X has increased and this will result in a real and relative increase in the return to labour but a real and relative fall in the return to capital. Again it will be true that the overall welfare for the citizens of region W will have improved so that on average individuals will be better off. Of course these same effects on factor rewards will hold even if the factor-saving effects of the technological change outweigh the larger volume of trade, resulting in an outward shift of the production possibility curve in a manner similar to that shown in Figure 5.5. We thus have the following proposition:

PROPOSITION 5.10: A technological improvement in transportation will lower the real return of the factor used intensively in the import industry.

One important implication of Proposition 5.10 is that improvements in transportation technology will reduce interregional factor price disparities. Note also that the same change in real factor rewards would occur if, through trade, we allowed more efficient foreign services to provide our domestic transportation. This is similar to a result found in Section 5.3.

5.6 Summary and Policy Conclusions

This chapter has focused on transportation, one of the most important service sectors, and has analyzed several comparative static changes in terms of a simple Ricardian model. We began by constructing a model in which a service sector arises endogenously from the desire of consumers to purchase commodities that they do not themselves produce. An equilibrium is defined as a situation in which the utility of all consumers is identical regardless of whether the individual is engaged in the production of X, the production of Y, or the production of the service commodity. It was shown that technological improvement in the service sector will increase utility for all consumers, even though it may result in the reduction of the output of consumer goods. These results have at least two important policy implications. First, they illustrate that the concern expressed by some economists, that the growth of the service sector, by inhibiting output of consumer goods and slowing down overall productivity increases, will reduce welfare for the economy, is unfounded. We have seen that growth in service sectors will increase welfare just as will growth in any other sector. Second, the fact that technological improvement in the service sector can have a substantial positive effect on utility emphasizes the importance of encouraging and maintaining efficiency in the transportation sector. This is of particular importance for a country such as Canada where distance is such an important obstacle in market activities. Public policy should certainly encourage efficiency in transportation, which suggests the importance of deregulation of transportation industries such as trucking.

When international trade is considered as an extension of domestic trade it was shown that domestic welfare can be improved by making use of a more efficient service technology that exists in a foreign country. For a small country it was shown that the use of foreign transportation, if more efficient, could release domestic labour to produce consumer goods that would be traded for the imported services. Domestics would be better off even if the local service sector disappeared. Restrictions on international trade in services would eliminate this potential welfare gain, which emphasizes the importance of free trade in the service industries. This type of gain was shown to be more likely for small economies.

When countries differ in the technology for producing goods but have identical service technologies, then as well as the traditional gains associated with Ricardian trade models there will be additional gains associated with the increase in the efficiency of the service sector. These gains can only be achieved if trade in goods is allowed, and the system will be most efficient if servicers are allowed to provide transportation in both economies.

In a more traditional model where transportation is assumed only to be necessary for international trade, similar results were found. When this model was extended to a model with two factors it was found that, while trade will result in welfare gains, it will nevertheless result in a reduction in the return to the factor used intensively in the import industry. This is not a new result, of course, but is a simple application of the well-known Stolper-Samuelson theorem.

Transportation is an important service sector for an economy but is particularly important for a country such as Canada where producers and consumers must overcome vast distances. The treatment of transportation as a sector which arises endogenously from the need for domestic trade, emphasizes the importance of an efficient transportation system. Substantial gains for the economy will accrue to improvements in transportation, even if as a result less output of consumer goods is available. Furthermore, efficiency developed in the transportation sector may provide an economy such as Canada with a comparative advantage that will result in further gains in international markets. Several such examples were identified in Chapter 3.

Notes

1.   To ensure that each labour unit will produce only one commodity, Ryan assumes that there is increasing returns to scale for the individual. For a full discussion of this assumption see Ryan (1987).

2.   On this point see Ryan (1987).

3.   Note that of the total output Y_0, Y_y is consumed by Y producers, $Y_S Y_0$ is the amount the servicer receives, and thus $Y_y Y_S$ is the amount consumed by X producers, and thus the amount transported.

4.   For a discussion of this case see Ryan (1987).

5.   We define transportation as T to distinguish it from the more general form of transportation, S, used in previous sections.

6.   Note that while the assumption of equal utility levels was required in earlier discussions, since factors could move costlessly between occupations, that assumption is not being made here. Utility levels will generally differ between countries or regions in this model.

7.   In some circumstances it is possible for a technological improvement to reduce the welfare in one of the regions. This depends on adverse terms of trade changes (or no change at all for one region) and is a kind of immiserizing growth. On this point see Ryan (1987).

8.   For a more complete discussion of this and other related cases see Ryan (1987).

Chapter 6

Factor Services: A Heckscher-Ohlin Approach

6.1 Introduction

Factor services are often important inputs to a wide variety of production activities. Furthermore such services, examples of which are managerial skills and engineering expertise, can be traded, and comprise a very important component of service trade. In this chapter, which is an extension of Melvin (1989), we analyze the effect that factor services have when incorporated into the standard Heckscher-Ohlin model. It is shown that, contrary to the views of Hindley and Smith (1984) as outlined in Chapter 2, the introduction of services does provide difficulties and does result in an analysis that differs substantially from the traditional model. It is also shown that in some circumstances the law of comparative advantage, at least as usually defined, need not apply to service trade. It is found that commercial policy and domestic tax policy may have quite different effects in a world in which services are traded than they do in a standard Heckscher-Ohlin model.

The analysis presented here makes all of the assumptions common to the Heckscher-Ohlin trade model, including constant returns to scale. It is clear, however, that for some factor services such an assumption is inappropriate. Many skills and other forms of human capital that give rise to factor services are developed through expensive education and training, but thereafter can be provided at low marginal cost. Thus in some circumstances it would be more appropriate to assume that factor services are themselves produced

75

under conditions of increasing returns. This additional complication is considered in subsequent chapters.

6.2 Commodity Trade and Factor Flows

The model we will employ in our analysis is the standard two-factor, two-good model from international trade theory. In particular we assume that two commodities, X and Y are produced with two factors, K and L. Both production functions are homogeneous of the first degree and factors K and L are in fixed supply and are fully employed. Thus the production side of the model is described by equations (6.1) through (6.4).

(6.1) $X = F_X(K_X, L_X)$

(6.2) $Y = F_y(K_y, L_y)$

(6.3) $L = L_X + L_y$

(6.4) $K = K_X + K_y$

The foreign country is defined completely analogously, the only difference being that we assume that the home country is relatively well endowed with K. It is assumed that commodity Y is relatively K-intensive and for simplicity it is assumed that tastes are identical and homothetic in the two countries.

Our model differs from the traditional one in that we assume that one of the two commodities cannot be traded. The non-traded good may be a service, but this is not at all central to the major results. One of the factors, K in our analysis, provides a service which can be exported to the foreign country. We have in mind a factor which provides a service to producers in the foreign country, perhaps by visiting the foreign firm but again this is not essential. If the factor does visit the foreign country it is assumed to return once the service has been provided, and all consumption by the owner of this factor takes place in the country of domicile. It is not a factor flow as usually defined since it does not remain in the foreign country. The factor service could be engineering consulting, management services, or the services of truck drivers.

While the factor service flow does not represent an actual factor movement, since the factor returns to the home country, the production effect of this temporary reallocation of the factor is clearly similar to what would occur in a factor-flow model. Our model thus combines the characteristics of a trade model where commodities are exchanged and an investment or factor-flow model where factors move.

Trade is therefore an exchange of a commodity for the services of a factor. Because this model combines elements of trade and factor mobility the remainder of this section will provide a brief description of how these two types of exchange are related in terms of the traditional diagrammatic exposition.

Figure 6.1 shows the world factor box diagram, with E the division of the total world's capital and labour between the two countries.[1] Thus K_h and L_h represent country H's endowment of capital and labour as measured from O_x. Figure 6.2 shows the production possibility curve diagram for our two countries with $T'_hT'_h$ and $T'_fT'_f$ the production possibility curves for countries H and F respectively. A free trade equilibrium in Figure 6.2 is represented with consumption for countries H and F at C_h and C_f respectively. Consumption at C_h for country H is achieved by exporting Q_hB of Y in exchange for BC_h of X, with a similar trade triangle for country F.

Although these commodity trades are typically not represented in the factor box diagram of Figure 6.1 they easily can be. We first note that because of the assumptions of the model, and in particular the assumption of identical and homothetic preferences, the factors K and L embodied in the consumption vectors for the two countries must lie along the diagonal O_xO_y. Furthermore, because the value of production must equal the value of consumption for each country, so must the value of the factors embodied in production equal the value of factors embodied in consumption.[2] Thus a line through E with the slope of the equilibrium wage-rental ratio will give the consumption of embodied factors for the two countries at point C on line O_xO_y.[3] In Figure 6.1, k_y and k_x represent the capital-labour ratios for industries Y and X associated with equilibrium production at Q_h and Q_f in Figure 6.2. The factors of production embodied in the commodity trade bundles can be found by drawing line EL parallel to k_y and LC parallel to k_x, where L is the intersection of these two lines. Thus EL gives the vector of factors required to produce Q_hB from Figure 6.2 and LC shows the factors required to produce BC_h. Thus the factor flows embodied in the commodity trade triangles shown in Figure 6.2 are given by the factor-flow triangle ELC in Figure 6.1.

It was first shown by Mundell (1957a) that in the standard Heckscher-Ohlin model with factor price equalization, factor flows are a perfect substitute for commodity flows. Thus rather than the exchange of commodities shown in Figure 6.2, exactly the same final equilibrium position could be reached if an amount of capital ES moved from country H to country F and if an amount of labour SC moved from country F to country H. With these factor transfers both countries would produce and consume at point C and no commodity

Figure 6.1

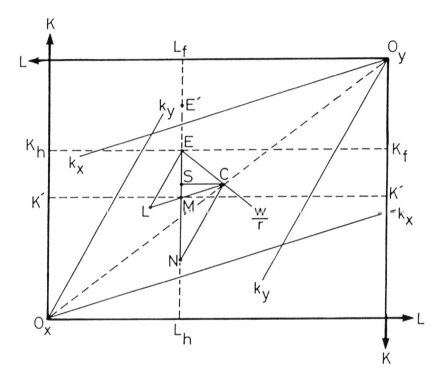

Figure 6.2

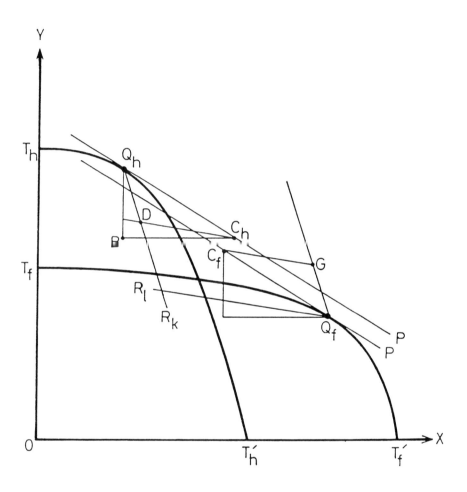

trade would be required.[4] A figure such as 6.2 would show the two countries identical except for scale.

These factor flows can also be represented in Figure 6.2. As capital leaves country H we move along the Rybczynski line R_k in Figure 6.2 from Q_h to D for country H and from Q_f to G for country F. With R_1 the Rybczynski line for labour transfers, the movement of labour from country F to country H is represented by the movements from D to C_h and from G to C_f for countries H and F respectively. The new transformation curves (not shown) would be tangent to the price lines P at C_f and C_h.

Figures 6.1 and 6.2 demonstrate the fact that the case of pure commodity flows and the case of pure factor flows can be represented either in factor space or in commodity space. Both, of course, give exactly the same final equilibrium for the two countries, given our assumption that factor prices are equalized by trade.

6.3 An Analysis of Trade in Services

The model for trade in services is exactly the same as described in Section 6.2, except that rather than either pure commodity flows or pure factor flows we have a combination of the two. Initially we assume that while commodity X is tradable, commodity Y is not. Y may be a consumer service but this is not essential to the argument. Factor L is assumed to be immobile between countries but the factor input K can be provided by factor owners in one country to producers in the other. The provision of this service may or may not involve the factor actually visiting the foreign country. For example K could represent managerial services that could be provided without any physical factor movements at all in the manner analyzed by Deardorff (1985). In any case no permanent movement of the factor K takes place. Thus in this first example we are assuming that the mobile commodity, X, uses the immobile factor, L, intensively.

We first ask whether the trade of a factor service for a commodity could produce exactly the same equilibrium as shown in Figures 6.1 and 6.2. That this indeed is possible can be seem by examining Figure 6.1 and Figure 6.3, where in 6.3 the figure has been simplified to show only the home country. From Figure 6.1 the transfer of an amount of capital EM from country H to F in exchange for an amount of X which has embodied factors equal to MC will result in the final equilibrium point C, the same as for trade or factor mobility. In this case although country H retains ownership of its full endowment of capital, the amount K_h K' is temporarily assigned for use in the foreign country. The foreign country pays for the factor service with the amount of commodity X using embodied factors MC. In Figure 6.3 the transfer of capital results in a movement along the Rybczynski line from Q to V, where V represents the domestic production point for country H. The new domestic production possibility curves associated with the use of K' and L_h will be tangent to price line P at V. Consumption point C is achieved by obtaining an amount of X equal to VC from the foreign country. Note that the equilibrium price ratio for country H at V will be equal to P, for world efficiency conditions have not been disturbed.

We thus conclude that in this particular example efficient equilibrium for the world can be achieved through the trade of a factor service for a commodity. The tradable commodity X is exported by the country with the relatively low price of X in autarky, so that trade conforms to the principal of comparative advantage. Furthermore we note that country H, the country well endowed with capital services, is exporting K and importing X, the commodity which uses labour most intensively. The pattern of trade is therefore consistent with the Heckscher-Ohlin theorem. We therefore have the following:

PROPOSITION 6.1: In a model with service trade, if the tradable commodity is intensive in the immobile factor, then an efficient world equilibrium can be achieved, trade will follow the principle of comparative advantage and the trade pattern will be consistent with the Heckscher-Ohlin prediction.

Figure 6.1 also allows a comparison of the efficiency of the three forms of exchange in terms of the embodied factors. Commodity trade involves an exchange of embodied factors EL for embodied factors LC, and this trade triangle is uniformly larger than ESC associated with a pure factor exchange. The trade of factor services (EM) for commodities (MC) lies intermediate between the other two in terms of the quantity of embodied factors which must be transported. Of course such comparisons will provide information on the relative efficiency of these exchanges only if the cost of transporting commodities is equal to the cost of transporting the embodied factors.

We now change the specification of the model by assuming that commodity Y is tradable but that commodity X is not. Now the tradable commodity uses the mobile factor service intensively. In this situation the home country, which is relatively well endowed with K and therefore has a relatively low price of capital services in autarky, also has the relatively low price of commodity Y, the tradable good. Can profitable exchange of capital services for commodity Y nevertheless take place? While at first glance it may seem that such an exchange is not possible, an examination of Figure 6.1 shows that trade of capital services for commodity Y can still take place and may well result in worldwide efficiency. If an amount of capital EN moves from the home to the foreign country and if this is exchanged for an

Figure 6.3

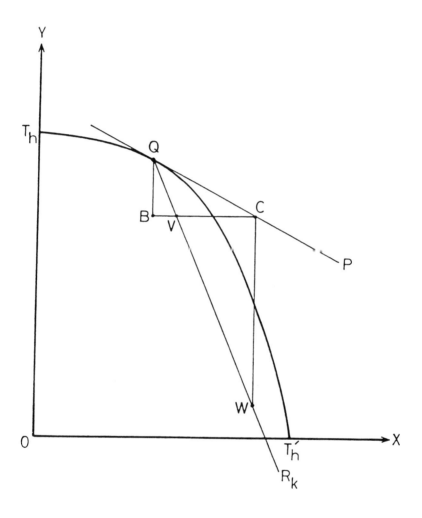

amount of Y with embodied factors NC, then the efficient consumption point C can be reached by both countries. In Figure 6.3 the transfer of capital services moves economy H down the Rybczynski line to W and consumption point C is achieved by importing CW of commodity Y.

This is an interesting result for we have the country that is well endowed with capital services importing the commodity that uses capital services intensively. Thus trade does not seem to conform to the Heckscher-Ohlin prediction when *only commodity trade* is considered, although all the required assumptions for the theorem are fulfilled. Furthermore country H is importing the commodity that was relatively cheap in autarky so that trade does not conform to the principal of comparative advantage as defined by relative *commodity* prices. We therefore have the following:

PROPOSITION 6.2: If the tradable commodity uses the mobile factor service intensively, then efficient world output is possible, but the imported commodity is the one that was relatively cheap in autarky, and commodity trade patterns will not be as predicted by the Heckscher-Ohlin theorem.

The reason for this seemingly paradoxical result is that the outflow of capital services from H leaves the country relatively poorly endowed with K from a *production* point of view. The temporary factor flow has been sufficient to change the relative productive endowments of the two countries. The Heckscher-Ohlin theorem can be "rescued" by noting that in this model capital services are being exchanged for commodity Y and that capital services are, by definition, more K-intensive than any commodity. Nevertheless in empirical work aimed at testing trade theories it is common to compare commodity trade bundles, and I have found no examples where flows of capital services are included in calculations used to test the Heckscher-Ohlin theorem. Of course in the present model such tests could not be undertaken since only one commodity is exchanged internationally. Modest changes in the assumptions could create a much more normal looking world, however. With more than two commodities it is easy to imagine that the country well endowed with capital could export capital services and some quantity of a third good in exchange for imports of the capital-intensive commodity Y. An examination of the factor content of commodity trade could easily produce results that do not conform to the Heckscher-Ohlin prediction. Examples can also be constructed if the assumption that only one commodity is tradable is relaxed. This model is examined in Chapter 10. We can conclude, then, that trade in services can provide yet another explanation of the Leontief Paradox, namely that a capital intensive country may import the capital intensive good.

We noted in Proposition 6.2 that a country could be observed to import the commodity that had the lower relativity price in autarky. On the face of it this seems to contradict the law of comparative advantage. This result is understandable, however, when we note that since we are not trading commodity X for commodity Y, it is not the commodity terms of trade that are relevant for the issue of comparative advantage. The tradables in this case are commodity Y and factor service K, and in autarky the price of Y is more expensive in H *relative to the price of factor K*. Thus, properly interpreted, the law of comparative advantage holds in this case as well.

It is also noteworthy that while the exchange of capital services for Y results in efficient world output in the simple frictionless world we are considering here, achieving this equilibrium requires a substantial movement of both factor services and commodities. Certainly this is the least efficient trade pattern so far considered from a transportation point of view. Furthermore it may not be possible for equilibrium to be achieved by this trading pattern. If, in Figure 6.1, we make country H smaller we could easily produce a situation where country H does not have enough capital to satisfy the requirements of the foreign country. In this case point N would have to lie below the L axis in Figure 6.1—an impossible situation. Note also that if N lies between the line k_X and the L axis, while enough capital is available in H to satisfy country F's requirements, world production will not be efficient, since H must specialize in commodity X with factor prices different from those implied by efficient world production. There are certainly many situations where either commodity trade or pure factor exchanges would lead to an efficient equilibrium while an exchange of capital services for commodity Y would not.

Alternatively we can see that there are many situations where trade in factor services for commodities will result in efficient world output where efficiency production cannot be achieved with trade in goods only. If X is the tradable commodity then trade in commodities for services will result in efficient world output for *any* allocation of capital between the two countries.[5] Note also that the initial allocation of L is unimportant in this case. This can be shown as follows. Choose any initial allocation of capital and labour for the two countries within the world factor box. Then through this endowment point draw the wage-rental ratio which would exist if world production were efficient. The intersection of this wage-rental ratio and the diagonal of the factor box gives the efficient equilibrium consumption point potentially available for both countries. Then a temporary flow of capital services in exchange for a flow of commodity X producing a trade triangle similar to EMC can *always* be constructed to yield consumption at the efficient world consumption point.[6] Thus we have the following:

PROPOSITION 6.3: If the tradable commodity uses the immobile factor intensively, then trade of commodities for factor services will <u>always</u> result in efficient world output regardless of the initial endowment of factors.

For the case where the non-tradable commodity uses the immobile factor intensively, then as we have already seen, efficient world output is not guaranteed. Changes in the dimensions of Figure 6.1 could produce a situation where country H does not have enough capital to supply the requirements of country F. Alternatively, endowment points outside the factor price equalization parallelogram could result in efficient world production. Thus if the endowment point were E' and if w/r were equal to the slope of E'C, then world efficiency can still be achieved by trading commodity Y for factor services, while world efficiency cannot be achieved by trade in commodities only. In this case, however, general results where world efficiency is guaranteed are not apparent.[7]

We have noted that in this model commodity trade is unbalanced, and thus we have:

PROPOSITION 6.4: When trading commodities for factor services, the country exporting services will be observed to have a merchandise trade deficit.

Although this is an obvious result given the assumptions of the model, it nevertheless provides important insights into some of the trade policy debates currently in progress in Canada and the United States. The United States has stressed the importance of including trade in services in GATT tariff negotiations, and the general concensus is that the United States has a comparative advantage in many service industries. At the same time there has been a great deal of concern among U.S. politicians with the U.S. merchandise trade deficit, and there have been suggestions that an import surcharge should be levied against countries running a merchandise surplus with the U.S. The U.S. merchandise deficit, however, may simply be a reflection of a trade surplus on the service account. Correction of the merchandise imbalance, in this case, can only be accomplished by reducing service exports. Certainly in the context of Canadian-U.S. trade, the observation of a rising U.S. merchandise trade deficit combined with a falling Canadian dollar suggests that there has been an increasing surplus in service exports to Canada by the U.S.

6.4 Commercial Policy and Service Trade

We now examine the consequences of commercial policy in the model of trade in services and we will begin with an investigation of the effect of tariffs for the case where X is the tradable good. We initially consider the small open economy with the terms of trade given exogenously. As noted earlier, it is important to remember that this is not the standard commodity trade model where we are exchanging X for Y. Instead we are trading a factor service for a commodity, and thus the terms of trade is not the commodity price ratio but rather the ratio of the price of K to the price of commodity X.

In the standard commodity trade model we can analyze the consequences of a tariff by supposing that a shipment of our exports is made to a foreign country and that these exports are paid for by the return shipment of a quantity of our import good. When a tariff is imposed the government simply collects some quantity of this imported commodity at the border, and this means that, from the domestic point of view, we are receiving less for our exports than we did prior to the tariff. Thus a tariff results in a reduction in the price of our export commodity. The same approach can be used in the present model. Domestic owners of K provide some of this factor service to foreigners and receive as payment some quantity of commodity X which they bring back to the domestic economy either for consumption or for exchange with other domestic consumers. When a tariff is imposed on X the amount of X that capital owners receive for the services rendered abroad is reduced, and thus domestic owners of K find it less profitable than before to provide this service to foreign producers. They thus reallocate some of their factor service back to the domestic economy, making K more abundant than previously, thereby reducing the price of Y, the commodity which uses K intensively, relative to the price of commodity X. The consequences of a tariff are therefore the usual ones. In the domestic economy P_X rises relative to P_y, r falls relative to both commodity prices, and w rises relative to both commodity prices. Thus we have the following:

PROPOSITION 6.5: If the imported commodity uses the immobile factor intensively, then in a service-trade model tariffs will have the traditional consequences.

Now consider the model where X is the non-traded commodity and Y is the tradable good. The international exchange rate is the ratio of the price of the traded factor service to the price of commodity Y. Domestic owners of factor service K who provide their services to firms abroad receive payment in units of commodity Y. When a tariff is imposed on Y some of this Y is confiscated by the government at the border and consequently domestic K owners find that the price they receive for their factor services abroad has been reduced. This reduction in their payments from abroad means that they allocate more of their factor services to the domestic economy, increasing the supply of K, and therefore reducing the relative commodity price of Y which uses K intensively. We therefore have an increase in P_x/P_y and associated with this a reduction in r and an increase in w.

This result may seem somewhat paradoxical for what we have shown is that a tariff on the imports of the commodity Y will reduce the price of Y relative to X in sharp contrast to the usual effects of a tariff. Thus a tariff on Y has precisely the same effect as a tariff on X, and we have the following:

PROPOSITION 6.6: If the imported commodity uses the mobile factor service intensively, then a tariff will reduce the price of the import relative to other commodity prices. Furthermore the tariff will result in a relative and real reduction in the return to the factor used extensively in the import-competing industry.

This seemingly paradoxical result is easily resolved when we recall that in the present model the terms of trade are not commodity price ratios but rather the ratio of a factor price to a commodity price. In this model there can be no presumption as to how a tariff will affect relative commodity prices.

These conclusions can be verified by referring to the popular algebraic formulation of the Heckscher-Ohlin model first introduced by Jones (1965). Defining dP_x/P_x as $\hat{P}_x$ with percentage changes similarly defined for all other variables, we can show that, for any price change, either

$$(6.5) \qquad \hat{w} > \hat{P}_x > \hat{P}_y > \hat{r}$$

or

$$(6.6) \qquad \hat{w} < \hat{P}_x < \hat{P}_y < \hat{r},$$

which is what Jones (1965) has called the magnification effect.

Now consider the imposition of a tariff on X. A tariff increases the price of X relative to the price of K and thus equation (6.5) must hold. We note that the tariff raises the price of X relative to the price of Y, and we have the standard tariff result as noted in Proposition 6.5.

For the case of a tariff on Y we have an increase in P_y relative to r and thus equation (6.5) is again relevant. Again we find that P_x rises relative to P_y, and thus a tariff on Y increases P_x relative to P_y and increases the output of X relative to the output of Y. Thus we have Proposition 6.6.

These results are significant, for the common presumption is that tariffs protect the import-competing industry by raising import prices relative to other commodity prices. However if service flows play an important part in the balance of payments, it is possible that tariffs will have the opposite effect on relative commodity prices than expected from traditional analysis.

The implications of tariffs for domestic factor payments are also important. We note from equation (6.5) that whether a tariff is applied to commodity X or commodity Y the returns to K will fall and the returns to w will rise. Thus in this model labour will benefit from a tariff regardless of which commodity is being imported. Conversely we can argue that trade liberalization will always make the owners of capital services better off regardless of which good is imported. We therefore have:

PROPOSITION 6.7: With internationally-mobile capital services and with commodity-service trade, a tariff on either commodity will increase the real and relative return to labour. More generally any tariff will increase the return to the immobile factor.

There has been a considerable amount of discussion in the literature on why labour has been observed to favour tariffs in spite of the fact that the standard trade model shows that tariff will harm labour if the import commodity is capital intensive. The present model provides a possible explanation, for as long as labour is relatively internationally immobile there is a presumption that tariffs will always increase real wages.

We now consider the case where country H is not small. At fixed terms of trade the tariff has reduced the trade triangle for H, and thus the domestic price of K will rise relative to the price of the import. This will increase welfare for domestic consumers, and may even increase welfare above the free trade level. There will, in general, be an optimum tariff. Note that a tariff on X or a tariff on Y will produce the same welfare result. In the cases considered below, the consequences of moving from the small country case to the two-country model will depend mainly on the terms-of-trade effects, and the conclusions derived can be reinforced or offset by terms-of-trade changes. These will not be discussed in detail, but terms-of-trade changes should be borne in mind and will affect overall welfare results.

Now consider a tax on the export of capital services. It comes as no surprise to find that the welfare consequences and the effects on factor prices are precisely the same as for a tariff on imports. This is just the well-known Lerner symmetry theorem. Indeed in the present model these two cases are more than symmetrical, they are precisely the same. We have an owner of capital services providing an input to the production process in a foreign country for which a payment is received in terms of commodity X. The government can hardly tax the export of this factor service before production in the foreign country takes place, since theretofore no income has been earned, and thus the tax must be collected in units of commodity X received as payment. This is precisely the same as collecting an import tax on commodity X. Thus we have:

PROPOSITION 6.8: When commodities are traded for factor services, a tax on exports is exactly equivalent to a tariff.

Of course even in a standard trade model too much is often made of the distinction between an import tariff and an export tax. If one considers both activities as being carried out by an import-export company then the choice the government gives the firm is whether they wish to pay the tax in units of Y or in units of X. This choice will be of no consequence either for the import-export company or for the government.

Export subsidies are a somewhat neglected aspect of commercial policy in the theoretical literature, but are quite important aspects of the commercial policy of most countries. Certainly the countervail cases brought by the U.S. government against foreign imports depend on providing evidence of subsidies to exports or to export-producing firms in foreign countries. Policy makers and domestic import-competing firms certainly feel that foreign subsidies are an important aspect of foreign trade policy. In the present model export subsidies would be payments to capital services working abroad, and could take the form of favourable tax treatment on foreign-earned income. In this case the inequality shown in (6.6) is relevant and we note that such subsidies will increase the domestic returns to capital services relative to all other prices and that such subsidies will increase P_y relative to P_x regardless of which of the two commodities is being imported. Furthermore such favourable treatment of factor services employed abroad will be harmful to labour in terms of both commodity X and commodity Y. Thus we have the following:

PROPOSITION 6.9: Favourable tax treatment of foreign-earned service income is equivalent to an export subsidy in a model of commodities-for-service trade. Such tax treatment will increase the relative price of the commodity that uses service inputs intensively and will reduce the real and relative returns to the immobile factor labour.

Of course such subsidies to K will result in a larger allocation of capital services to the foreign country and will result in an increase in the output of commodity Y relative to commodity X. Traditional international trade policy has generally not considered the treatment of foreign-earned income as a major determinant of trade flows, commodity prices and relative factor incomes. The present model makes it clear that special treatment for foreign-source income may well be as important for trade policy as such traditional commercial policy tools as tariffs and subsidies.

Also neglected in traditional commercial policy discussions is the role of import subsidies. In the present model just as one cannot distinguish between import tariffs and export taxes neither can one distinguish between export subsidies and import subsidies. In both the latter cases the factor providing the capital services abroad receives a larger income; for an export subsidy income is augmented when the service is exported, while for an import subsidy income is subsidized when payment for the export is repatriated. Thus we have:

PROPOSITION 6.10: When commodities are traded for factor services, import subsidies and export subsidies are exactly equivalent. An example of either is favourable tax treatment of foreign-earned service income.

This observation is important not because import subsidies are likely to become an important commercial policy tool, but only because it points out the fact that import subsidies and favourable treatment of foreign-earned income produce exactly the same economic consequences. While foreign-earned income is sometimes preferentially treated, it is difficult to imagine a government directly subsidizing imports.

To this point our attention has focused entirely on the country that has been assumed to import a commodity in exchange for the export of a factor service. For country H, while tariffs may not always have the expected result, tariffs can be imposed. For the foreign country, however, this is not the case, for no commodity is imported. Import taxes must take the form of a tax on the earnings of the imported service. In our model service income is paid in units of commodity X or Y, and thus import taxes are equivalent to a tax on exports. This is the result from Proposition 6.8. In general a tariff will be any differential tax on foreign service income, such as a withholding tax on repatriated foreign-service income. Thus we have the following:

PROPOSITION 6.11: When factor services are imported, a tariff takes the form of a tax on repatriated service income.

Proposition 6.11 has two important implications. First, any country that imposes a withholding tax or that otherwise taxes income earned by foreigners at a rate different than applies to domestic factors is imposing a tariff insofar as the taxed income is the payment for service imports. Free trade in services thus requires the elimination of such taxes. In practice, of course, it will be very difficult to distinguish between foreign-service income and other types of international monetary flows. A second implication is that countries that are large service importers would be expected to resort to taxes on foreign-source income if they become involved in tariff wars with service exporting countries.

For countries that import services in exchange for commodity exports, export subsidies can be imposed, but since these exports are the income of the owners of foreign services, export subsidies are equivalent to subsidies to foreign-earned income. Thus we have:

PROPOSITION 6.12: For service-importing countries, export subsidies are equivalent to subsidies to foreign-earned income.

6.5 Service Trade and Commodity Taxation

In the standard two-sector trade model it is well known that any tariff system can be duplicated by an appropriately chosen set of domestic taxes. It is of interest to see whether similar conclusions hold for the present model. We begin first by considering the consequences of domestic commodity taxation for the small open economy.

Assume that at the free trade equilibrium with X the mobile commodity and where H exports capital services, the government imposes a consumption tax on commodity X raising the relative commodity price ratio to P_t as shown in Figure 6.4. This wedge between producer and consumer prices will result in a shift in consumer purchases away from commodity X and with unchanged production will create an excess supply of commodity X. This will put downward pressure on the producer price of X which in turn will put upward pressure on r in the domestic economy. This will result in a withdrawal of K from foreign production and this will continue until a new equilibrium is reached. Such an equilibrium is shown in Figure 6.4 with consumption at C_t and imports of commodity X of $V_t C_t$. We note that the effect on consumer welfare of the consumption tax on X is exactly the same as it is in the traditional commodity trade model. In both cases consumption moves from C to C_t.

If we now relax the small country assumption we note that at world terms of trade P our trade triangle has been reduced from QVC to $QV_t C_t$. The standard offer curve diagram would show a resulting

Figure 6.4

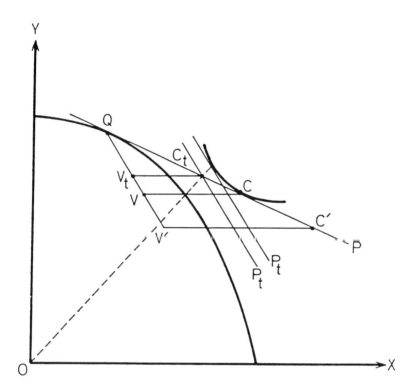

improvement in the world terms of trade which would improve domestic welfare. It is possible that the final equilibrium would be superior to consumption point C, and in general there will be an optimal tax just as there is an optimal tariff. Note also, however, that a high enough tax on X could make things worse than any tariff. This is most easily seen for the small country case where a high enough tax could move consumption to Q, a position which is clearly inferior to autarky.

A consumption tax imposed on commodity Y can be analyzed in a completely analogous fashion. In this case the relative price of Y to consumers is increased, and consumption will move to a point such as C' with imports of X equal to V'C'. Again it is possible in the small country case for the tax to result in a final consumption position inferior to autarky.

Relaxing the small country assumption for the case of a tax on the consumption of Y we note that the increase in the trade triangle to QV'C' will deteriorate the terms of trade and this will further reduce domestic welfare. The optimal consumption tax on Y is therefore zero. A high enough tax will completely eliminate trade and move the economy back to autarky. From the above we therefore have the following:

PROPOSITION 6.13: For a service exporting country, consumption taxes on either commodity have exactly the same effect as in a commodity trade model.

We now consider a production tax and first consider a tax collected from the producers of commodity X. This will reduce the relative price of X for producers which in turn will increase the domestic price of K. For the small-country case with fixed terms of trade between r and P_X the tax will introduce a fixed wedge between the foreign and domestic prices of K, and thus all K will return to the domestic economy and the autarky position will be re-established.

Now consider a production tax on Y. This will reduce the domestic price of Y for producers and will result in a fall in the return to K. This gap between the domestic and foreign prices of the mobile factor K will result in an outflow of K that will only cease when all K has been employed in the foreign economy. Clearly production taxes in this model have a very different effect than in the traditional commodity trade model.

Relaxing the small-country assumption does not change the conclusions regarding the effect of a production tax in any substantive way. While the world terms of trade between K and X will be affected the domestic production tax will nevertheless maintain the wedge between domestic factor prices and foreign factor prices and the conclusions derived above will still follow. This leads to the following result:

PROPOSITION 6.14:   For a service exporting country, a production tax on the commodity that uses the immobile factor intensively will eliminate all trade.   A production tax on the commodity intensive in the internationally mobile service will result in all this service being fully employed in the foreign country.

The analyses in this section have been carried out in terms of the model where commodity X is the mobile good. An examination of Figure 6.3, however, makes it clear that a similar analysis will hold for the case where commodity Y is the tradable good. We note only that a consumption tax on X could easily result in the use of the entire supply of the home country's K in the foreign country.

Another domestic tax that can have international repercussions in this model is a differential tax on factor incomes. Suppose, for example, that in the domestic economy the returns to capital are taxed more heavily than the returns to labour. Such a tax will initially lower r relative to w, but of course in doing so must also, from equation (6.5), reduce r relative to both P_y and P_x. From a production point of view this is completely analogous to the effect of a tariff on either X or Y, or alternatively to an export tax on the mobile K. Similarly a factor tax that reduces w relative to r will mirror the production effects of an import or export subsidy. Thus in this model domestic factor taxes are analogous, in terms of their effect on the production side, to commodity trade taxes or subsidies. Of course domestic factor taxes will not produce a distortion on the consumption side of the market, although the relative prices of X and Y in the domestic economy will change as shown by equation (6.5). Thus we have:

PROPOSITION 6.15:   When factor services are traded, differential domestic factor income taxes have the same production effects as tariffs and trade taxes.

We find, then, that there is a symmetry between import tariffs and domestic taxes. While the symmetry is quite different than in the traditional commodity trade model it is, perhaps, the expected one in terms of a model in which factor services are exchanged for a commodity. Specifically we have:

PROPOSITION 6.16:   In a model with trade in services, a domestic consumption tax combined with a tax on the factor income of the internationally mobile service is equivalent to a

tariff. An income tax on the immobile factor combined with a consumption tax is equivalent to a trade subsidy.

6.6 Summary and Policy Implications

There are those who claim that goods and services really do not differ, and that even if they did there would be no reason to expect that the usual results from trade theory would not hold. We have shown, however, that in a simple model of service trade the results derived are quite different from those of the traditional Heckscher-Ohlin model. While the export of a factor service in exchange for a commodity will, in situations where both goods continue to be produced in both countries, produce the same world equilibrium as either commodity flows or factor flows, the world may look quite different after trade has taken place. In particular if the mobile service is used intensively in the production of the mobile commodity, then efficient world production can be achieved only if the factor service employed in the other country is enough to produce a switch in effective relative endowments. In this case the country that is well endowed with the factor K will nevertheless import the K-intensive commodity.

One implication of the service trade model is that a service exporting country will be observed to have a merchandise trade deficit. Such deficits should not be seen as a problem but rather a reflection of a comparative advantage in the service sector.

Tariffs have unexpected results in terms of the traditional model, for regardless of whether X or Y is imported a tariff will result in an increase in P_X relative to P_Y. This occurs because the direct effect of the tariff is not on relative commodity prices but on the price of the imported commodity relative to the price of the internationally mobile factor service. A commodity tariff will also always be beneficial to the immobile domestic factor whether the tariff is on X or Y.

A reinterpretation of traditional results is also required for other trade taxes. A tax on the export of capital services is shown to produce identical results to a tariff. Thus in this model just as there is an optimal tariff so is there an optimal tax on the repatriation of foreign earnings. An export subsidy is found to be exactly equivalent to an import subsidy, and both will reduce welfare and deteriorate the terms of trade.

With trade in services, some domestic taxes have unexpected effects on the trade sector. It is shown that favourable income tax treatment of foreign-source service income is equivalent to an export subsidy. For countries importing services, a tariff is equivalent to a domestic tax on repatriated foreign-earned income.

While a tax collected from domestic consumers produces identical outcomes to those found in the commodity trade model, changing the relative price of commodities at the production level has quite different effects. A tax which raises the price of the commodity which uses the mobile factor intensively will increase the price of this factor relative to its price in the foreign country and this will result in the repatriation of the K previously employed abroad. The final equilibrium will be the autarky position. If the tax reduces the price of the commodity that uses the internationally-mobile factor intensively then all units of this factor will seek employment in the foreign economy. On the other hand, domestic factor taxes are shown to have exactly the same effect as tariffs and thus there is a symmetry between domestic taxes and trade taxes. In particular an import tariff can be duplicated by a commodity tax combined with a domestic factor income tax.

Notes

1. The analysis here employs the technique first used by Lancaster (1957).

2. We have assumed that trade equalizes commodity prices. Then, since the endowment point lies within the parallelogram formed by the equilibrium capital-labour ratios for the two industries, factor prices will be equalized in the two countries. Note that Figure 6.1 excludes the possibility of factor-intensity reversal since both countries have endowments in the same cone of diversification.

3. The assumption of identical tastes in the two countries is not important for the analysis and can easily be relaxed. With different tastes the ratio of factors embodied in consumption, which we will call the factor-consumption ray, will differ and will intersect at a consumption point C not on the diagonal. Otherwise the argument is the same.

4. The factor-flow triangle ESC is the one which will produce the same consumption point for both countries. If the final consumption point is not constrained to be C there are an infinity of factor-flow triangles that will produce equilibrium in the world economy with the same equilibrium world prices. Indeed any reallocation of factors that gives an endowment point on O_xO_y will produce this result. Note that if tastes differ between countries there will be a unique factor-flow triangle that will produce the same equilibrium world prices as exist with free trade.

    Figure 6.1 can conveniently be used to illustrate the central features of the transfer problem. With identical homothetic preferences in the two countries, any transfer of commodities (or factors) within the factor-intensity parallelogram will result in a consumption point on O_xO_y and will not change the terms of trade. Different tastes will result in consumption points not on the diagonal and thus a transfer that would move the effective endowment from E to L for example, would require a commodity price change to reestablish a consumption equilibrium on the joint intersection of the two factor-consumption rays and the wage-rental ratio. The commodity price change will depend uniquely on how preferences differ.

5. Although we are considering the case where country H is well endowed with capital, efficient world production is also assured when F is well endowed with K.

6. This is similar to the condition required for efficiency in the commodity trade model, namely that both countries' endowment rays lie in the same cone of diversification (that E is in the factor intensity parallelogram of Figure 1). For

trade of capital services for Y the "cone of diversification" is formed by the K axis and k_x *for whichever country is the exporter of capital services.* The exporter of capital services must be relatively well endowed with K (i.e., E is above O_xO_y) so that E is necessarily in this diversification cone.

7.   Special cases where world efficiency necessarily results from the exchange of Y for the services of K can be constructed. For example, if the intersection of k_y and k_x above the diagonal is to the right of the intersection below the diagonal, and if the allocation of L is between these two points, then trade of factor services for Y will result in world efficiency for any allocation of K between the two countries. A description of such cases is, however, taxonomic, not intuitively appealing, and does not produce general conclusions.

Chapter 7

Producer Services and Increasing Returns to Scale

7.1 Introduction

In Chapter 6 we examined some of the implications of producer services in a trade model using the standard Heckscher-Ohlin assumption of constant returns to scale. As was noted, while this is an interesting framework for considering many questions concerning trade in services, many producer services are more appropriately modelled with an increasing-returns-to-scale technology. In this chapter we continue our discussion of producer services and concentrate mainly on the case where there is increasing returns to scale in the production of producer services, and where these services in turn enter the production of the consumer goods for the economy. Before embarking on that discussion, however, we will begin with a more general discussion of returns to scale, and in particular will ask whether issues concerning returns to scale for services will differ from the traditional returns to scale for goods.

In Section 7.2 we begin our analysis by reviewing how returns to scale could be important for service industries, and we argue that there may be a kind of returns to scale that is intimately associated with the dimensionality of space; what we define as economies of dispersion. In Section 7.3 we introduce a model in which there are returns to scale in the production of service inputs to the goods production sector, and show that trade in services may have quite different effects than the traditional trade in goods. In Section 7.4 we turn to the question of the relative size of countries, and show that the implications of returns to scale in this model of producer services are quite different than traditional increasing-returns-to-scale models. Section 7.5 compares trade in services with trade in goods, and Section 7.6 presents some preliminary results on the effects of tariffs. In Section 7.7 we provide some concluding comments and review the policy implications.

7.2 Economies of Scale and Economies of Dispersion[1]

An issue that has received a good deal of attention in Canada in recent years, both in the theoretical literature and in more policy-related discussions, has been the question of whether returns to scale are an important determinant of trade for the Canadian economy. In the context of the present discussion three issues arise. First, would we expect to observe economies of scale of the traditional kind in the service industries? Second, are there economies of scale that arise because of the characteristics of service sectors and that are therefore different from the traditional sources of economies of scale? Third, if economies of scale are important for the service sector, how can they best be modelled, and what are the policy implications? We take up the first two of these questions in this section and address the third in the remainder of this chapter.

For what we might regard as the traditional contact services such as haircuts, medical treatment, retail activities, and restaurant services it would be difficult to argue that there are significant returns to scale at the production level. Certainly for such contact services, traditional *external* economies of scale would not be expected, for it is difficult to imagine economies of scale that depend on the level of industry output and that are not internal to firms. It is also generally supposed that most of the traditional contact service industries operate more or less competitively, which suggests that there are not significant *internal* economies of scale at the production level. There may, however, be some economies of scale associated with the provision of inputs for some of these industries. Thus chains of retail outlets may benefit from their ability to buy in large quantity at lower price.

Turning from the traditional contact services to the service areas that have experienced rapid technological change in recent years, such as communications and data processing and the related activities in banking, insurance, and international finance, it seems clear that economies of scale are present. Whether the economies are external or internal is not always clear, and there are probably examples of both. However, the fact that most of these industries are imperfectly competitive or monopolistic suggests that some of the benefits of the economies are captured by the firms, which suggests that the economies are internal.

But as well as the traditional internal and external economies, there would seem to be economies associated with what we have argued are the fundamental defining characteristics of services, namely their relationship to the dimensions of time and space. Consider, for example, two trucking firms that are identical in every respect, except that one operates entirely out of Toronto, while the other has equal-size branches in both Toronto and Montreal. While firm A, based in Toronto, will be well located to transport freight from Toronto to Montreal (and of course elsewhere), the fact that the other firm, firm B, has branches in both cities may well make it easier to arrange for profitable backhauls. As an extreme case we can imagine firm A hauling commodities only from Toronto to Montreal, while firm B is able to arrange to have its trucks full in both directions. There may be, in other words, economies associated with decentralization, or having one's operations dispersed throughout the economy. We will refer to such economies as economies of dispersion to distinguish them from the traditional external and internal economies of scale.

Economies of dispersion can be identified in a variety of different industries. It is generally recognized that the banking system can operate more efficiently if branch banking is allowed, for branches allow the bank to more closely match borrowers and lenders than will be possible if banking operations were restricted to the area served by a particular establishment. Such economies depend on there being differences in the saving, expenditure and investment patterns of firms and individuals among regions, and it is generally believed that such differences do exist in Canada.

Economies of dispersion can also be identified in many of the well-known franchise operations. Car rental companies can operate more efficiently if drop-offs in different cities are permitted. Fast food outlets such as McDonalds can benefit from operating in different locations for a variety of reasons. First, advertising, whether through television, radio, or newspapers, will typically reach a larger population than could be served by a single outlet. There are therefore clear economies associated with having a number of outlets which cover the advertising area. Furthermore, there are advantages in being recognized in different locations. Travellers are much more likely to frequent restaurants and hotels with which they are familiar, and which offer, with reasonable certainty, "no surprises". One could hypothesize that the large amount of mobility in North America, both temporary and permanent, has contributed to the rapid increase in franchise operations in fast-food chains, grocery stores, hotels and motels, and real estate brokers.

The economies of dispersion described above are clearly associated with the dimensions of time and space, and therefore, by our earlier arguments, are properties that are unique to service industries.

Note, for example, that were we to consider any of the activities described above in a model where all production and consumption was assumed to occur at the same time and place, there would be no need for the dispersion of activity that we have described.

We have argued that internal and external economies of scale could well be characteristics of service industries, and furthermore that a somewhat different type of scale economy, what we have called economies of dispersion, may often be an important feature of service industries. The next issue is whether such economies will have important trade implications. With regard to the traditional returns to scale, the evidence on the effects on individual countries is mixed. If increasing returns are assumed to be external to the firm then, as Markusen and Melvin (1981) have shown, there is a presumption that a small country or a small region will be at a disadvantage when trade is allowed. The Markusen-Melvin model assumes two countries that have the same overall capital-labour ratios but that differ in size. It is assumed that one industry is characterized by increasing returns to scale and that constant returns to scale exist in the other. When trade is allowed, and assuming that tastes are the same, the large country will generally be expected to have an advantage in the commodity that exhibits increasing returns to scale, since prices for that commodity will be lower in autarky. In this model it can be shown that a sufficient condition for gains from trade is that the output of the industry with increasing returns to scale increase, and such increases are more likely in the large economy. With internal economies, on the other hand, and where the economies are associated with factor inputs, Markusen (1987a) has shown that when there is trade in both commodities and factor services, there is a presumption that the small country or region will be the principal benefactor from such trade. This argument is examined in some detail in Section 7.3.

Thus again we find that the type of returns to scale assumed will be of importance in determining whether or not a country would be expected to gain from trade. While external economies have a long history in the international trade literature, it is not clear that they are particularly relevant to discussions of trade and services. On the other hand the Markusen analysis is specifically concerned with services that become inputs to the production processes, and certainly factor services are one of the important examples where services can be traded. There may, then, be a presumption that smaller countries will be the largest benefactors from service trade. It is important to note, however, that this does not imply that larger countries will lose. There will generally be gains from trade for all countries, and what we have argued is that a larger share of such gains may go to smaller countries. Of course all of this presumes that the small countries will be producers of the commodities that use these factor services. If countries do not produce such commodities then gains from trade in factor services cannot be expected.

Finally, with regard to economies of dispersion, these feature significantly in international trade discussions. The existence of multinationals and international franchising operations is often related to such economies, and these have become very important aspects of trade in recent years. Several aspects of trade relating to multinations and franchising will be considered in more detail in Chapter 8.

7.3 Returns to Scale in the Production of Producer Services

We are interested here, as we were in Chapter 6, with producer services, by which we mean such production inputs as accounting, legal counsel, insurance, architecture, engineering consulting, and management consulting. These are intermediate inputs to the production process, and are generally characterized by having large amounts of human capital embodied in them. The provision of services such as legal advice and engineering skills can be provided only by individuals or groups of individuals who have undertaken significant periods of specialized training. The acquisition of the human capital typically involves a fairly lengthy period during which little or no returns to the individual are forthcoming, and which are typically quite costly to acquire. Once these skills have been acquired, however, they can typically be provided to firms at low marginal cost. Indeed, in many circumstances the output of such service producers may have a marginal cost approaching zero and the inputs may take on public good characteristics. Thus a skilled engineer or architect can provide sophisticated plans to many firms in many different locations simply by sending detailed blueprints and other forms of instruction.

It is the production of this human capital, and its implication as a service input to the production process, that we focus on for the remainder of this chapter. We assume that a factor service requires a significant fixed cost before any of the input can be provided, and assume that inputs can be produced at low and constant marginal cost. Thus the service inputs are produced under conditions of increasing returns to scale.

The model itself assumes that there are two consumer goods, X and Y, both produced under conditions of constant returns to scale. Commodity Y uses labour and capital as inputs, while commodity X uses only factor services as inputs, and initially we assume that there are only two of these, S_1 and S_2. The factor services in turn are produced using only labour, and these production functions exhibit the type of returns to scale discussed above. The amount of capital in the economy is fixed and is used only in the production of Y, and the fixed supply of labour is allocated between the production of Y and the service inputs. On the demand side we assume that consumers obtain utility from X and Y, and that individual utility functions are homothetic and identical for all consumers in the economy. These two assumptions permit aggregation of individual utility functions into an aggregate function, which in turn is homothetic. The model is therefore described by equations (7.1) through (7.6).

(7.1) $Y = F_y(L_y, K_y)$

(7.2) $X = F_x(S, ..., S_i, ..., S_n)$

(7.3) $S_i = F_i(L_i)$ $i = 1, ..., n$

(7.4) $\bar{K} = K_y$

(7.5) $\bar{L} = L_y + \sum_{i=1}^{n} L_i$

(7.6) $U = U(X, Y)$

In general, any number of service inputs can be considered, and indeed the number of services provided in each country will be endogenous. This general form of the model has been examined by Markusen (1989a). In the analysis here we present a somewhat simpler version of his model and initially assume that only two services are produced. In Section 7.4 we will extend the analysis slightly to include three services, but will not provide further generalizations. The simplified and mainly geometric version of Markusen's model presented here has both advantages and disadvantages. Among the disadvantages is the fact that we are unable to provide the rigorous proofs developed by Markusen. On the other hand, our simple version has the advantage of allowing us to relax some of the symmetrical features of the model that are necessary for the rigorous demonstration of some of the general results.

We begin by focusing on the production of X, and initially assume that X is produced using two factor services. Each factor service is produced using labour, where it is assumed that some fixed labour cost is required before any output can be produced. Thus the cost function for S_1 is given by equation (7.7)

(7.7) $C_1 = wF_1 + wS_1$

where F_1 is the fixed cost, S_1 is the level of output of the service, and where w is the wage rate. There is a similar, but not necessarily identical, cost function for S_2. The input constraints to the production of X associated with the production of S_1 and S_2 are illustrated in Figure 7.1. We begin by assuming that some fixed amount of labour has been allocated to the production of S_1 and S_2, and that when all of this labour is allocated to the production of S_1 we obtain $\bar{S}_1$. Now suppose we wish to produce a unit of S_2. To do so we must undergo the full fixed cost of producing S_2, which is the distance $\bar{S}_1 F_2$. With fixed marginal cost for producing both S_1 and S_2, the various output combinations such that both services are produced lie along the straight line $F_2 F_1$. Should we decide to produce only S_2, we would no longer have to incur the fixed cost of producing S_1 which is the distance $F_1 \bar{S}_2$. Thus if only S_2 is to be produced we are able to produce the quantity $\bar{S}_2$. Thus the isocost line for inputs of services to the production of X consists of the line segments which make up the broken line $\bar{S}_1 F_2 F_1 \bar{S}_2$. The isoquant X_0 is the highest output level that can be produced subject to this cost constraint, and thus the equilibrium production point would be A. Thus for the particular allocation of labour to the production of S_1 and S_2 assumed in drawing Figure 7.1, X_0 represents the maximum amount of X that a closed economy could produce.

7.4 Trade in Factor Services

Now suppose we have two economies with identical production functions for S_1, S_2, and X, and for the moment assume that both economies allocate exactly the same amount of labour to the production of the service inputs. Thus in the initial autarky equilibrium both would be represented as in Figure 7.1, and both would produce X_0 at point A. Now suppose we allow trade between these two countries, and initially assume that trade is restricted to trade in S_1 and S_2. If country H specializes in S_1 and produces at $\bar{S}_1$ and if country F specializes in S_2 and produces at $\bar{S}_2$, then by trading S_1 for S_2 they can both achieve the higher output levels for commodity X associated with the points A_f and A_h for countries F and H respectively. Thus the possibility of international trade allows both countries to specialize and trade to obtain an input bundle which contains some of both services, and this allows a larger output of X than would be possible in autarky. We thus have the following result:

PROPOSITION 7.1: With increasing returns in the production of services, trade in services only can generate a larger output of the commodity using services as an input.

Figure 7.1

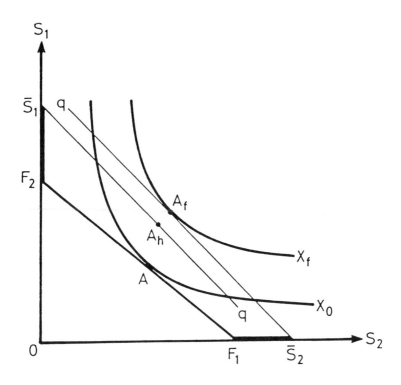

We note that while trade in services may allow an increase in the output of X in both countries, this is not a necessary consequence of service trade. In Figure 7.1, for example, suppose that the production technology requires relatively more S_2 so that points A_h and A_f are closer to the S_2 axis. This would result in a higher relative price of S_2 (a steeper q) if trade is to be balanced, and it is possible that A_h could be on a lower isoquant than A. In this case either there would be no trade, or the output of X in H would fall. This is a standard result in increasing returns models and is examined in Melvin (1969). Thus while substantial gains from trade are possible, positive gains cannot be guaranteed.

Many variants of the situation shown in Figure 7.1 are possible, and Figure 7.2 provides a special case that is of some interest. In constructing Figure 7.2 we have assumed a completely symmetrical world. The production functions for S_1 and S_2 have been assumed to be identical, which means that both the fixed cost and the marginal cost are identical for the two services. The production function for X has been assumed to be symmetrical with respect to the inputs, which implies that if the prices of S_1 and S_2 are the same then these two inputs would be used in the same proportions. Finally, we have assumed that the elasticity of substitution in production for X is relatively low, and that the isoquants intersect the two axes. Note that because of the symmetry, an isoquant such as X_0 will go through both $\bar{S}_1$ and $\bar{S}_2$. In this case, in autarky, a country would produce either at $\bar{S}_1$ or $\bar{S}_2$ but would never produce both services. Trade between two identical countries would allow one country to specialize in S_1 and the other to specialize in S_2, and through trade both could reach endowment point A and thus produce X_1 of commodity X.

Two features of Figure 7.2 are of interest. Because of the symmetry, trade has resulted in the same output of X in both countries, and thus if the two countries were identical before trade they will also be identical after. Clearly both countries will gain from trade in this symmetric case. We also note that in Figure 7.2, in contrast to Figure 7.1, both countries specialize both before and after trade. Thus the gains from exchange are not due just to the fact that specialization is permitted, but rather to the combination of the possibility of specialization and the fact that through trade some of both service inputs can be obtained.

To this point we have considered only the production of X, and we now turn to the construction of the production possibility curve. The two final consumer goods are X and Y, and although both of the production functions, as given by equations (7.1) and (7.2), exhibit constant returns to scale with respect to their inputs, the fact that there are increasing returns to scale in the production of S_1 and S_2

Figure 7.2

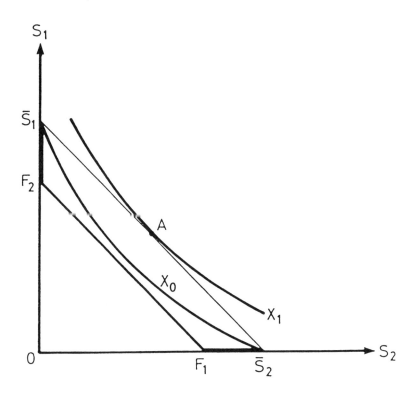

produces a production possiblility curve between X and Y that exhibits increasing returns to scale. We note, for example, that doubling the input of L to the production of S_1 and S_2 will more than double the output of the service inputs because of the existence of the fixed costs associated with F_1 and F_2. Thus the production possibility curve is as shown in Figure 7.3.[2]

This production possibility curve has three characteristics that are of interest and deserve brief comment. First, because of the increasing returns associated with the X industry, there will be some section of the PPC near the Y axis that is convex to the origin. Second, because of the fixed cost in the production of S_1 and S_2, if no X is produced, the amount of labour associated with this fixed cost can be allocated to Y, and thus the maximum Y will be Y. Thus the production possibility curve is $Y\tilde{Y}A\tilde{X}$. Third, the equilibrium commodity price ratio will not be equal to the rate of product transformation, and thus the price line will not be tangent to the production possibility curve. Thus the autarky equilibrium would be a point such as A, where the price line P is tangent to a community indifference curve.[3]

Now assume we have two economies that are identical in every respect so that Figure 7.3 represents the autarky position for both. We now suppose that trade in services only is allowed, and initially assume that we have the symmetric case shown in Figure 7.2. If Figure 7.2 represents the situation where all labour was allocated to the production of X, then X_0 corresponds to $\tilde{X}$ of Figure 7.4. Allowing trade in factor services now results in a larger maximum output of commodity X for both countries, and X_1 from Figure 7.2 gives rise to $\tilde{X}'$ in Figure 7.4. Of course a larger quantity of X can now be produced with a given amount of labour regardless of how much labour has been allocated to the X sector, and therefore the result of trade in factor services is to shift out the production possibility curve from $\tilde{Y}\tilde{X}$ to $\tilde{Y}\tilde{X}'$ as in Figure 7.4. Note that the symmetry assumption of Figure 7.2 means that the production possibility curves for both countries after trade will be identical for countries H and F.

We now want to establish where the new equilibrium for these two countries will be in the post-trade situation. First consider point B, a point on $\tilde{Y}\tilde{X}'$ with the same output of Y as point A. We recall that Y is produced under conditions of constant returns to scale, and that the two inputs in the production of Y are labour and capital. Since all of the capital in both economies is used in the production of Y, and since the production function for Y has not changed, the fact that the same amount of Y is being produced at B as at A implies that the same amount of L_y is being used to produce Y at these two positions. This further implies that the move from A to B has not changed the

Figure 7.3

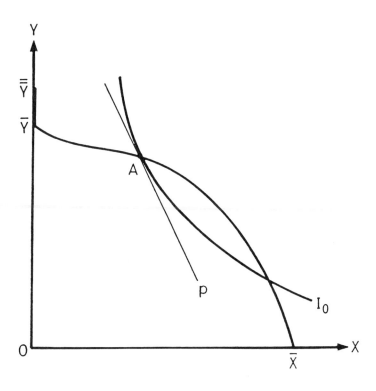

Figure 7.4

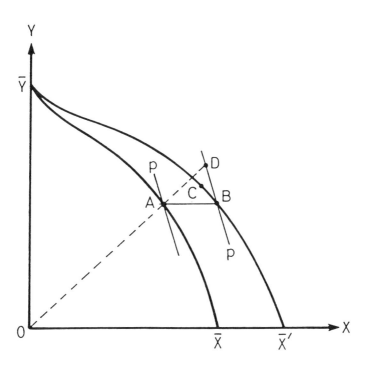

marginal product of labour in the Y industry, and thus, since $w/P_y = MPL$, the wage rate in terms of commodity Y is also unchanged. Further, since L_y is unchanged, the same amount of L must be allocated to the X industry (indirectly through the allocation to S_1 and S_2), and this in turn implies that the relative commodity price ratio has remained unchanged. Thus the commodity price line through B is identical to the commodity price through A, and this in turn implies that the slope of the production possibility curves are also the same at A and B.

Of course, given that A was an equilibrium with the commodity price ratio line tangent to a community indifference curve, and given the assumption that the set of community indifference curves is homothetic, point B could not represent an equilibrium. Indeed a community indifference curve would be tangent to the price line through B at point D on the line OAD. To find an equilibrium we must lower the relative price of X until we find a point where consumption is on the production possibility curve, and this would give a point such as C. Note that C must lie on the production possibility curve between point B and the line OD. Point C is on a higher indifference curve than A, since C is northeast of A, and since C is the new equilibrium for both economies, trade in producer services has made both countries better off. Also, because of the symmetry assumed in Figure 7.2, both countries are in equilibrium at C with the same commodity prices, and there is therefore no reason for trade in commodities X and Y. Thus, although we initially confined our attention to the situation where only S_1 and S_2 were traded, we now find that in this particular model only trade in services is required to reach the maximum welfare position for the two countries. Thus we have the following proposition:

PROPOSITION 7.2: In a symmetric world, trade in services will necessarily result in welfare improvements for both countries. Furthermore, all the gains from trade can be obtained from trade in services only.

The fact that, in the situation shown in Figure 7.4, both countries were identical after trade is a consequence of the symmetry assumptions employed in drawing Figure 7.2. If instead we consider the unsymmetric case of Figure 7.1 then several differences are found. First, we note that because the production of X is not symmetric in the two service inputs, the amount of X produced by the two countries after trade will differ. In the particular case shown in Figure 7.1, country F will have a larger output of X than will country H. This difference can be illustrated by referring to Figure 7.4, where the two production possibility curves shown are now interpreted as the two post-trade production possibility curves for the two countries. Thus $\bar{Y}\bar{X}$ is the production possibility curve for country H, while country F, with the larger amount of commodity X, has the production possibility curve $\hat{Y}\hat{X}'$.

It is easy to show that country F will enjoy a higher utility level than country H, even though both countries have exactly the same endowments of all factors and the same production functions for all commodities. Indeed the argument is exactly the same as was used to show that trade would benefit both counries for the symmetric case. Points such as A and B in Figure 7.4 show the same factor allocations to the two industries in both countries. If point A represents the new post-trade equilibrium for H, then the trading equilibrium for country F will be point C. Thus one immediate difference from the symmetric case is that the two countries, although identical in autarky in every respect, do not share equally in the gains from trade. In particular the country that produces the service that is in relatively high demand will gain relatively more. Furthermore, as we noted earlier, if demand is very biased towards one of the services, the terms of trade between S_1 and S_2 may be such that one of the two countries could be made worse by trade. We thus have the following result:

PROPOSITION 7.3: Trade in services alone can result in gains for both countries, but the trade gains need not be shared equally. In particular the country that specializes in the service that is in relatively high demand will obtain a larger share of the total gains from trade.

The fact that the service trade equilibrium of Figure 7.4 differs for the two countries produces another difference in comparison to the symmetric case considered earlier. Because relative commodity prices at points A and C are not equal, international trade in commodities X and Y will now take place if trade is allowed in both services and goods. As was noted earlier, the commodity price line tangent to a community indifference at C will be flatter than the price line at A, indicating a relatively lower price for X in country F. This will imply that, when trade in commodities X and Y is permitted, country F will export X and country H will export Y. But in models of this kind with increasing returns to scale in only one commodity, Melvin and Markusen (1981) have shown that the country producing the constant-returns-to-scale commodity may well lose from trade. This possibility is illustrated in Figure 7.5, where points A and C are the equilibria from Figure 7.4 before trade in commodities X and Y was possible. Country F, having a comparative advantage in X, will produce more X, while country H will produce more Y, and in the free trade equilibrium we have production at Q_h and Q_f and consumption at C_h and C_f for countries H and F respectively. A balance in commodity trade requires that Q_hC_h

$= Q_f C_f$. We note that goods trade has resulted in a further increase in welfare for country F but has reduced utility for consumers in country H.[4] We thus have the following result:

PROPOSITION 7.4: In an asymmetric world, trade in services will generally result in different commodity price ratios in the two countries. The price of the increasing-returns commodity (X) will be lower in the country specializing in the high-demand service, and this country will export X if trade in goods is allowed. Welfare will be further increased for the country exporting X, but the welfare of the other country may fall.

The situation of Figure 7.5 emphasizes that it is important which service a country produces. From Figure 7.1 we saw that the country fortunate enough to specialize in F_2, the high-demand service, could produce more X in equilibrium. We subsequently found that this resulted in a higher level of utility when only services were traded. This in turn led to a lower price for X in the S_2-producing country leading to further gains. There may also be losses to the country specializing in S_1. Thus the initial choice of producing S_2 resulted in two complementary trade gains. First there is the gain associated with the larger quantity of X and second, the gain associated with the comparative advantage in the production of X which the production of S_2 provided. The choice of which service to produce may therefore be very important, and could be an important public policy issue.

7.5 The Importance of Country Size

The question of how gains from trade depend on country size is of obvious importance for a country such as Canada. As has already been observed, when trade is the result of increasing returns to scale, there is a presumption that the large country will gain the most from trade, and that the small country may even lose. We will show in this section, however, that with trade in services there is a presumption that the small country will gain relatively more than the large country, and this may more than offset other disadvantages associated with being small.

We begin by assuming two countries that have the same relative capital-labour ratios, but where one country is twice as large as the other. Thus we suppose that country F has twice as much capital and twice as much labour as country H. To facilitate our example we now suppose that there are three service industries, S_1, S_2, and S_3, and initially we assume that the three service inputs enter the production of commodity X symmetrically.

Figure 7.5

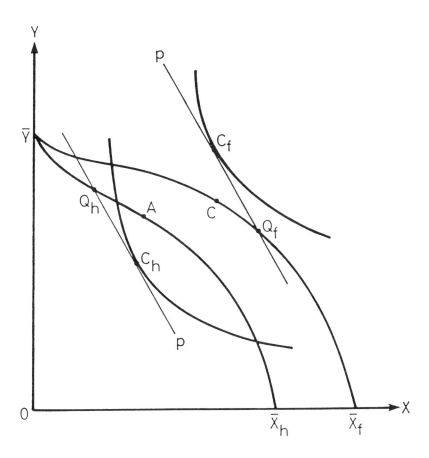

In the initial autarky situation the production possibility curve for country H is $\bar{Y}_h\bar{X}_h$ and the production possibility curve for country F is $\bar{Y}_f\bar{X}_f$ as shown in Figure 7.6. Because of the assumption that country F has twice as many resources as country H, we have $\bar{Y}_f = 2\bar{Y}_h$. Because of increasing returns to scale in the production of services we also have $\bar{X}_f > 2\bar{X}_h$. The autarky production points are A_h and A_f, and note that from our earlier discussion it must be the case that the commodity price ratio is less steep at A_f than at A_h.

We now allow trade in services, which permits the two countries to specialize in the production of S.[5] Country F, with twice as many resources as country H, would be expected to produce two of the service inputs, while country H produces the third. If the production technologies for the three services are the same, and if the large country allocates twice as much labour to the production of services as does country H, then we would find that the outputs of the three services will be identical. For concreteness suppose country F produces twelve units of S_1 and twelve units of S_2, and that country H produces twelve units of S_3. With symmetry in the production of S, prices of service inputs in the trade equilibrium will be identical, and trade will be balanced with country H exporting eight units of S_3 in exchange for four units of S_1 and four units of S_2. We note that after trade country H has four units of each of the three services, while country F has eight units of each of the three services. Thus country F has twice as much S as does country H, and consequently the maximum output of X in country F will be twice that of country H. Thus in Figure 7.5 the maximum production points for countries F and H will be $\bar{X}'_f$ and X'_h respectively, where $\bar{X}'_f = 2\,\bar{X}'_h$. The new equilibrium consumption and production points with trade in services only are A'_h and A'_f.

An interesting feature of Figure 7.6 is the fact that, while $\bar{X}_f$ is more than twice $\bar{X}_h$, $\bar{X}'_f$ is exactly twice $\bar{X}'_h$. Indeed, the new production possibility curve for country F is now exactly twice as far from the origin for any Y/X ratio as is the production possibility curve for H, and is therefore just a radial blowup of the production possibility curve for country H. Trade in services has shifted out the production possibility curve for both countries but has shifted it out proportionately more for country H.[6] Thus trade in factor services has resulted in a larger increase in welfare for country H than for country F, and thus the small country gains more than the large country when there is trade in services only. We thus have the following result:

PROPOSITION 7.5: In a world with a large and a small country, trade in services will result in gains for both countries, but the small country will gain proportionately more than the large country.

Figure 7.6

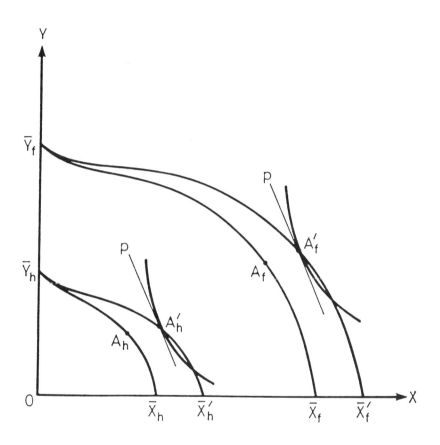

Another interesting feature of Figure 7.6 is that, because the production possibility curve for the large country is a radial blowup of the production possibility curve for the small country, and because of our assumption that tastes are identical and homothetic for the two countries, equilibrium prices at A'_h and A'_f must be the same. Note that this was not true before service trade was allowed, and in particular in the initial autarky equilibrium country F has a comparative advantage in the production of X. There is thus an interesting comparison between the effects of trade in goods and trade in services. If, in the initial autarky situation, trade in goods only is allowed, country F will export X and country H will export Y, and we could get a situation similar to that shown in Figure 7.5, except, of course, that country F would be much larger than shown. Trade in goods only will produce welfare gains for country F and there is a presumption that country H will lose. Alternatively, if, starting at the initial autarky situation, trade in services is allowed, then both countries will gain and the small country will gain proportionately more than the large country. Furthermore, in the symmetric example, trade in services exhausts all possible gains from trade and there will be no trade in goods. Note also that, while the small country gains relatively more from trade in services, both countries are better off with trade in services than with trade in goods. We thus have the following result:

PROPOSITION 7.6: In a world with a small and a large country, trade in goods only will increase welfare for the large country and may reduce welfare for the small country. Trade in services will unambiguously increase utility for both countries, and both will be better off relative to the situation of trade in goods.

If the symmetry assumption in the production of services is relaxed, then of course we would no longer expect the service-trade situation to result in identical prices in both countries, and trade in X and Y would occur. Which country will gain will depend on which country gains the advantage in producing the service that is in highest demand. Note that there is no reason to suppose that the small country will be disadvantaged. As has been shown by Markusen and Melvin (1981), a sufficient condition for gains is that trade result in a larger output of the increasing-returns commodity. This could just as easily occur for the small country as for the large country, and will depend on the allocation of service production between the two countries. This allocation could be affected by public policy.

7.6 Tariffs on Commodities Versus Tariffs on Goods

Any discussion of tariffs in this model will necessarily be complex, because in any free trade situation there are four traded commodities, the two goods and the two services, and tariffs could be levied on any of the four. Such tariffs will change production and trade patterns from the ones we have assumed. In the examples discussed above it has been implicitly assumed that services were traded for services and goods were traded for goods, and in many cases such a simplification does not restrict the generality of the results. Thus, for example, in several circumstances we found that even though trade in both goods and services was possible, only trade in services would take place. This symmetrical trade pattern, however, would not be expected to be maintained if a tariff on a service or a good were introduced. Thus in some circumstances a tariff on one service in one country might reduce trade in services and increase trade in goods, and one might have a direct exchange of services for goods. The welfare consequences of such situations will be quite complicated, and will depend on the extent to which trade in services and trade in goods are substitutes or complements. Here we will be content with some preliminary remarks on the basic differences between tariffs on goods and tariffs on services for situations where trade is symmetric.

For the case of the completely symmetric world described in Figure 7.2, we noted that in the final equilibrium there would be trade in services but no trade in goods. Obviously in this case tariffs on goods will have no effect, while prohibitive tariffs on services will substantially reduce welfare of both countries. Thus tariffs or other restrictions on the trade in services will have larger welfare consequences than tariffs on goods. If there were trade in services and trade in goods were prohibited, then a tariff on the import of a service in one country would have two effects. First it would reduce the trade in services and therefore the output of X in both countries, which would reduce welfare in both countries. The tariff could also have terms-of-trade effects, however, and these could well offset some of the welfare losses associated with the imposition of the tariff. For a country with some monopoly power in service trade there will be, as one would expect, an optimum tariff.

If one country is large relative to the other and if trade in goods is permitted but trade in services is not, then tariffs will have the usual effect found in increasing-returns-to-scale models. In the situation of Figure 7.5 a tariff imposed by the small country will generally improve welfare, since trade itself has resulted in a welfare loss. Tariffs in the large country would be expected to reduce welfare, and of course even for the small country tariffs will be a second-best solution.[7] Thus we have the following:

PROPOSITION 7.7: With trade in goods only, tariffs will reduce welfare for a large country, but may increase welfare for a small country. Tariffs will never be the first-best policy, however.

For the case with a large and a small country with trade in services, tariffs or other trade restrictions on service trade will reduce welfare for both countries, and in general would result in larger welfare losses than those associated with tariffs on goods. This is simply a consequence of the fact that, since the gains from service trade are larger than the gains from commodity trade, tariffs on service trade can cause more damage than tariffs on goods. We therefore have the following:

PROPOSITION 7.8: With trade in services and goods, trade restrictions on services will be expected to result in larger welfare losses than similar trade restrictions on goods. While, for a small country, tariffs of goods may result in welfare improvements, this will not be expected for tariffs or other trade restrictions on services.

Our discussion here of restrictions on service trade has been very general, and we have not specified exactly what these trade restrictions would be. The services traded are factor services, and thus, from the discussion in Chapter 6, trade barriers would take the form of restrictions on the repatriation of the earnings of foreigners. While such restrictions are often found, it is seldom recognized that they are, effectively, tariffs, and thus, in general, reduce domestic welfare. At the same time restrictions on repatriated earnings are not a common form of trade policy, and so there is some hope that service trade will escape the type of tariff wars that plague goods trade.

7.7 Summary and Policy Implications

This chapter began with a general discussion of the importance of increasing returns to scale in services for a trading economy. It was argued that while the traditionally internal and external economies would be observed, there may also be economies associated with space that we called economies of dispersion. Dispersion economies will result in firms operating in different locations, and could be one explanation for the phenomenon of multinational firms and international licensing arrangements. One implication of this is that, in general, multinationals and licensing franchises will reduce production costs, and therefore should be encouraged by public policy.

The major issue in the chapter was the consequences, for international trade theory, of assuming that producers services are produced under conditions of increasing returns to scale. It was assumed that services are produced using an initial fixed cost and a low constant marginal cost. Under these conditions it was shown that trade in services could result in gains for both countries, and if symmetry exists in the model, the trade in services will completely exhaust the trade gains. In a world in which economies are identical in terms of endowments and production technology, while trade in services produces gains, trade in goods does not. This result highlights the importance of free trade in services, and suggests that removing restrictions on service trade should be a high priority item in trade policy discussions.

In a world in which countries differ in size, it was shown that with trade in services, the small country would typically gain proportionately more than the large country. This is in sharp contrast to the usual international trade results where, with increasing returns to scale, the small country often loses from trade. Again this result points out, particularly for small open economies such as Canada, the crucial importance of maintaining the free flow of services across international borders.

Notes

1. The dispersion of economic activity is efficient here because the activity is specifically related to space. Our argument does *not* imply that all kinds of decentralization will be cost saving. It seems clear, for example, that many proposals to decentralize government services would not be efficient, for many such activities should be centralized. I have therefore chosen the word "dispersion" rather than "decentralization" to represent the locationally-efficient positioning of economic activity.

2. This is only one of several shapes that the production possibility curve could take. It could, for example, be everywhere convex to the origin. For a more complete discussion see Markusen and Melvin (1981).

3. For a proof see Markusen (1989a) or Markusen and Melvin (1981).

4. Even though country H produces more Y when trade is introduced, it is not necessarily the case that welfare will be reduced. The new equilibrium price line P could intersect the indifference curve through A, thus increasing welfare for both countries.

5. The countries may or may not have been specialized in services before trade is allowed. Either the situation of Figures 7.1 or 7.2 are permissible. Note, however, that symmetry in the production functions for X is assumed, so that even if both services are produced in autarky, as in Figure 7.1, service prices and the output levels of X for the two countries will be identical after trade.

6. For a more rigorous proof see Markusen (1989a). Note that the maximum output has shifted out by the same absolute amount for both countries, which in turn implies a larger proportional shift for the smaller country.

7.   We are ignoring possible terms-of-trade effects. If both countries impose tariffs then changes in the terms of trade would generally be small and unpredictable.

Chapter 8

Trade in Producer Services by the Multinational Enterprise

8.1 Introduction

In Chapter 7 we considered the effects of increasing returns to scale in the production of service inputs that could be traded. It was shown that specialization in the production of producer services could result in welfare increases for both trading economies, and that restrictions in service trade could result in substantial welfare costs. The service inputs were assumed to be produced under conditions of fixed cost and a constant marginal cost which produced internal returns to scale. For some service inputs, however, the marginal cost of providing additional units of a service input may be so small that they can be considered to be zero, in which case the service input has public good characteristics. Such public good inputs have been recognized as one possible source of scale economies associated with branch plant operations, and of particular importance are branch plants which are set up in foreign countries, these giving rise to the multinational enterprise. In this chapter we construct a simple model of a multinational enterprise to investigate how both the host and home country are affected by the formulation of the multinational enterprise. Our discussion in this chapter draws extensively from Markusen (1989b).

While there is now substantial literature on the role of the multinational enterprise, there is not yet complete consensus on why multinationals exist nor on why they have enjoyed such success in recent decades. One theory that has received a good deal of support is due to Dunning (1977, 1981), who argues that the necessary conditions for a firm to undertake direct foreign investment are advantages in ownership, location, and internalization, referred to collectively as the OLI criteria. Ownership advantage is associated with some technological advantage or the proprietary rights in some product or process. Locational advantage refers to the fact that there must be some advantages in producing locally rather than serving the market through exports. These would include the existence of tariffs, transportation costs, or the ability to access local distribution facilities or inexpensive factors of production. The internalization advantage depends on some feature of the firm that makes it more profitable to set up a foreign subsidiary rather than licensing or franchising the operation. This could relate to differences in legal or other institutional systems or to the inability to control the quality level of franchise operations.

There is not unanimous support for the view that all three of these conditions are necessary for the successful operation of multinationals. Rugman (1985, 1986) stresses the importance of internalization as the key condition for success of a multinational. Casson (1986) takes the view that ownership advantage is the most important determinant of a multinational's success. But while the discussion of the sources of advantage for a multinational are of interest, a resolution of this controversy is not necessary for our purposes. In the ensuing discussion we concentrate on the ownership advantage possessed by multinationals and argue that this can lead to the export of producer services which make the foreign branch plant more efficient than local competitors.

Ownership advantage is generally assumed to arise from knowledge-based capital possessed by the firm. It could take the form of human capital embodied in engineers or other skilled workers, and it produces an input that can be transferred among firms at very low, or perhaps zero, cost. Thus while there is a significant cost associated with obtaining the training and skills necessary to develop new processes, it may be possible to transmit this knowledge to other plants in the organization at virtually no cost. Once a new technique has been developed this new technology can be transmitted through blueprints or computer programs, and may even be transmitted electronically from the head office to various plant locations. In such circumstances this service input has public good characteristics in the sense that the use of the information by one plant does not in any way restrict the ability of other plants to take advantage of the same knowledge.

Access to this knowledge-based service input can easily bestow a significant advantage on a firm which operates in a foreign market. If one compares two firms in a local market where a domestic firm must cover all cost but where a foreign-owned subsidiary receives an important service input at a zero or very low marginal cost, then the foreign subsidiary has obvious advantages that will be reflected either in the ability to sell the product at a lower price, or in the ability to obtain pure economic profits. At the same time, as we will see subsequently, the existence of the foreign subsidiary will allow the host country to economize on resources which would otherwise have been used to cover the fixed cost of providing the service input. These resources can result in a higher level of utility for residents of the host country, depending on how the benefits of the international transmission of the service input are allocated between countries.

The plan of the paper is as follows. In Section 8.2 we construct the basic closed economy model of a multinational and the sources of advantage for a multinational operation are identified. In Section 8.3 we consider a trading world and show that the operation of a multinational will generally result in gains from trade to one or both of the two countries. Sections 8.4 and 8.5 investigate, respectively, the sources and determinants of gains from trade for the host and home countries. Section 8.6 provides some brief comments on licensing and franchising, and Section 8.7 provides the conclusions and policy implications.

8.2 The Closed-Economy Model

We assume that the economy produces two commodities, X and Y, using labour, L, as the single factor of production. Y is produced under conditions of constant returns to scale, and the units of Y are chosen so that $Y = L_y$. The total amount of labour in the economy is assumed to be fixed and fully employed in either the Y or X industries so that we have $L = L_X + L_Y$. In the Y industry it is assumed that there are two fixed costs of producing output. To produce any amount of X the firm must undergo a fixed cost F, referred to as the firm-specific fixed cost. This cost must be borne by any firm entering the Y industry, but it will not depend on the number of plants the firm operates. We can think of F as representing research and development expenditures which are associated with the ability to produce the product Y. The second fixed cost is G, the plant-specific cost. This cost is associated with setting up a new plant and will be borne at every production location.

The firm-specific cost F provides the production advantage for the multinational firm. We can think of research and development expenditures which must be undertaken before any output can be produced, but where once these expenditures have been made, the knowledge obtained can be transferred at no cost to any other plant that the firm operates. Thus once a firm is in operation it can set up a branch plant either in another part of the country or in another country at lower cost than could a single-plant firm. This advantage has been referred to as multi-plant economies of scale.

The production possibility curve for the economy is shown in Figure 8.1. If all the labour is allocated to the production of Y then quantity $\bar{Y}$ can be produced. If any amount of X is to be produced then the firm must undergo, first, the plant-specific cost G, shown as $G\bar{Y}$ and then the firm-specific cost F, shown as FG. For additional units of X it is assumed that output is increased under conditions of constant marginal cost, and if all labour is allocated to the X industry, $\bar{X}$ can be produced. Thus for the economy the production possibility curve is the line $\bar{Y}F\bar{X}$.

Because of the fixed costs in this model, it is easily shown that average cost exceeds marginal cost. Marginal cost, as we have already noted, is just the slope of $F\bar{X}$. Average cost can be found by considering any point on the production possibility surface such as A. The total cost of producing X_1 at A will just be the total cost of the labour allocated to the X industry. Because of our assumption that there is a single factor of production, this will be the amount of labour in the economy minus the amount allocated to the production of Y. In terms of commodity Y, the total amount of labour in the economy is given by $\bar{Y}$, the maximum output in the Y industry. The labour allocated to the Y industry at production point A is equal to Y_1, and thus the amount of labour used to produce X must be $\bar{Y} - Y_1$. Average cost of producing X_1 is therefore $(\bar{Y} - Y_1)/X_1$, which is just the slope of $\bar{Y}A$. In this model, because average cost always exceeds marginal cost, long run production will take place only if price exceeds marginal cost. The zero profit condition will prevail if price is equal to the slope of the average cost line $\bar{Y}A$.

In Figure 8.2 we show a situation where the firm is making positive profits. Equilibrium production is at point A where the price line P is tangent to a community indifference curve. National income in terms of commodity Y can be measured by extending the price line to the intersection with the Y axis at I. Total factor income, which here is just the returns to labour in the economy, is point $\bar{Y}$, and thus the difference $I - \bar{Y}$ will be profits in the X industry. With prices P and labour income $\bar{Y}$ the total utility of workers is at point C where the price line through $\bar{Y}$ is tangent to the highest indifference curve. In a closed economy the distribution of total income as between returns to labour and profits is of no particular interest, since all income must accrue to domestics. If international investment is allowed, however, then it is possible that a foreign multinational may be able to capture some or all of the profits $I\bar{Y}$. We turn our attention to this and other related questions in the next two sections.

Figure 8.1

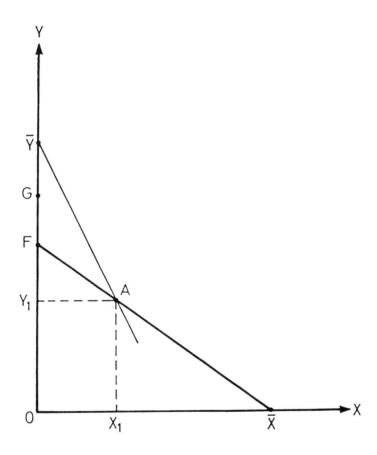

8.3 Welfare for the Host Country

We now assume that there are two countries, H, which is the host country in which the multinational firm locates a plant, and F, the foreign country that is the home of the multinational. We assume that in the foreign country the X industry has been monopolized and that the firm-specific cost F has already been incurred. We now suppose that the foreign firm sets up a plant in the host country, which it can do without incurring the firm-specific cost. Thus the relevant production possibility curve is now $\bar{Y}G\bar{X}'$ in Figure 8.3. From a purely production point of view this is a clear advantage to the host country, since the production possibility curve has been shifted out from $F\bar{X}$ to $G\bar{X}'$. In terms of commodity Y the benefit is F, the distance FG in Figure 8.3, and this can be regarded as the value of the service import associated with the multinational enterprise. We note that if this entire benefit were repatriated to the foreign country the home country would be no worse off. Whether the host country benefits from the multinational will clearly depend on who receives the value of the service imports. We can thus state the following:

PROPOSITION 8.1: The existence of a foreign multinational firm in the host country will shift out the production possibility curve and raise national income.

Figure 8.3 illustrates the case where the host country receives the imported service without making any payment. As in Figure 8.2 we suppose that the initial autarky position in H is point A with prices P. As was mentioned earlier this is the situation where the X producer is just covering average cost and is therefore making no profits. We now suppose that the host country market is opened up to foreign competitors and that the foreign multinational, because it is in competition with other potential foreign rivals, is also forced to price at average cost. This would produce an equilibrium in H at a point such as B where price line P' is tangent to a community indifference curve at B. In this situation residents of H have clearly been made better off by the operations of the multinational, for while they previously consumed at A they now consume at B on a higher community indifference curve. In this situation the foreign multinational is just covering average costs and is therefore not repatriating any profits. The entire benefit of the imported service goes to residents of H. While the foreign multinational is not making any profits, neither will it be making losses on its worldwide operation, since the export of this factor service has been costless. At the zero profit condition the foreign multinational will be indifferent as to whether or not it operates this plant in the home country. Presumably any small profits would

Figure 8.2

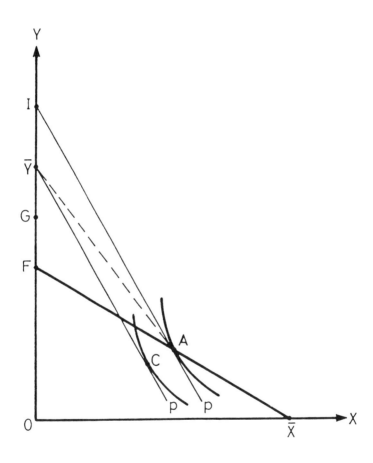

Figure 8.3

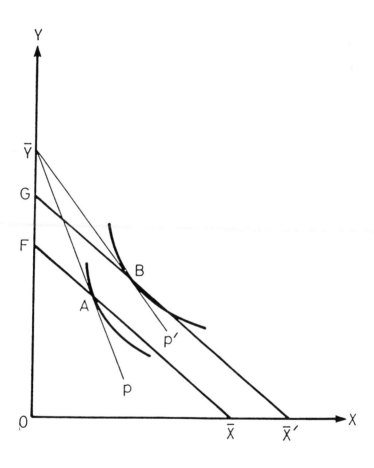

persuade the firm of the advantage of establishing this multinational plant. We thus have the following result:

PROPOSITION 8.2: If the foreign multinational is forced to sell at average cost in the host country, then all the benefits of the multinational will accrue to the host country.

Another interesting characteristic of the situation of Figure 8.3 is that, although the host country is receiving a service input that is of significant value, there are no international payments for this service, and indeed there are no international flows of goods at all. Again this is because it is costless for the foreign multinational to supply this service input and therefore, as a limiting case, zero returns are acceptable.

In Figure 8.4 we illustrate a situation where the host country pays an amount for the import services that leaves it just exactly as well off as in autarky. As in the previous diagrams the initial autarky equilibrium is at point A on price line P. As before, since P equals average cost, the domestic producer of X is making no profits, and all income accrues to labour. We will assume that in this situation the domestic producer of X is a monopolist, and that the market size is just large enough so that no profits can be earned at equilibrium. We now suppose that a foreign multinational is allowed to enter the country and we further suppose that the foreign firm is not faced with competition. This will allow the foreign firm to charge the same price as the host country firm had charged in autarky, since the demand conditions in the host country will be identical and will therefore lead to the same price for commodity X. With the same price and with consumption at point C, we have the total value of production equal to I in terms of commodity Y. Labour's income is still Y and with prices P consumption continues to take place at point A for domestic workers. The distance IŶ is the amount of domestic income repatriated to the foreign multinational, and in this situation the domestic economy is indifferent to whether or not the multinational sets up a branch plant. In this case the balance of payments accounts will show a flow of either X or Y (or both), from the host country to the foreign country in payment for the service input. We thus have the following:

PROPOSITION 8.3: If the foreign multinational can sell the product in the host country at the pre-trade average-cost price, then all profits from the multinational enterprise will be repatriated and the host country will be indifferent to the presence of the multinational firm.

Figure 8.4

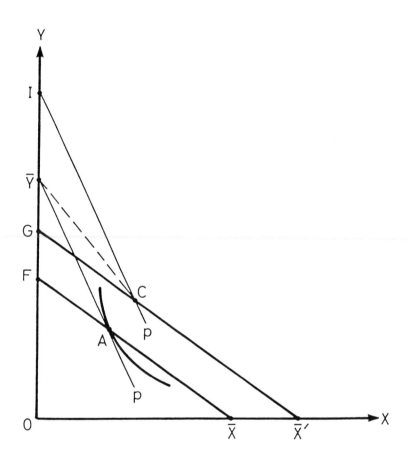

It is even possible that the host country can be made worse off when the multinational enterprise displaces the domestic producer, although the assumptions required for such a case may seem somewhat unrealistic. In Figure 8.5 we have again represented the initial autarky situation as point A with average cost ȲA equal to price P. It is again assumed that the domestic producer, because of a threat of competition, has been forced to price at average cost, resulting in a situation where marginal revenue is less than marginal cost. We now assume that the foreign multinational enters the host market and that this foreign firm, by virtue of its monopoly power, can equate marginal cost with marginal revenue. This would result in a relative price of X of P', higher than P, and this could result in an equilibrium consumption point for the host country at point C. Domestic factor payments are Ȳ and with prices P' domestic labour would consume at point C. The consumption point C is clearly on a lower indifference curve than A and thus labour in the host country has been made worse off by the introduction of the multinational. The multinational repatriates profit equal to IȲ, which is more than the firm-specific cost F. Thus in this case the multinational is able to repatriate earnings which are larger than the benefit that accrues to the host country. It is assumed that the domestic firm producing X cannot re-enter the market because it conjectures that, should it enter, the multinational would lower price to a point such that profits would be negative. We thus have the following:

PROPOSITION 8.4: **If a foreign multinational can make monopoly profits in a situation where the host country firm cannot, then the repatriation of profits may leave the host country worse off.**

In the situation of Figure 8.5 it would clearly be optimal for the host country to prevent the entry of multinationals through some type of foreign investment policy. It should be noted, however, that this situation seems very unlikely. To derive Figure 8.5 we had to assume that the domestic firm was forced to price down to average cost because of competition, but that the foreign multinational faced no such constraints and was able to charge the monopoly price. One could perhaps justify this situation by supposing that it was the domestic multinational which originally presented the threat to the host country firm and that once the foreign multinational has entered the market it does not face similar competition, perhaps because of its much larger size. Nevertheless, the special assumptions required for this result are somewhat strained, and this situation must be regarded as unlikely.

Figure 8.5

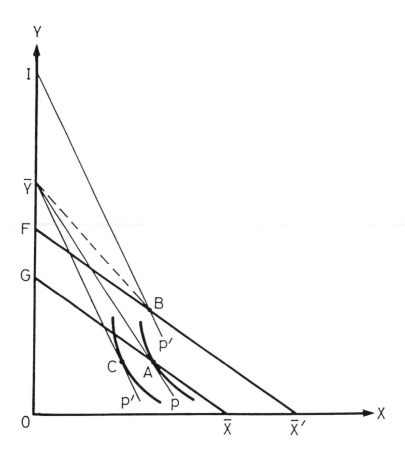

8.4 Welfare for the Foreign Country

In our simple model the analysis of the welfare gains for the foreign country, that is, the home of the multinational firm, is straightforward. To this point we have had no commodity trade as such, and the only commodity movements have represented payments for the exports of factor service from the foreign country. In Figure 8.3 we analyzed the case where the host country was able to capture the full benefit associated with the export of the factor service, and as a consequence the foreign country receives no benefit and is indifferent to whether it forms a multinational firm in the host country or not. In Figure 8.4 we analyzed the case where the entire profits associated with the multinational were repatriated to the foreign country and where the host country received no benefits. This case is clearly the mirror image of the situation of Figure 8.3 and in this case all the benefits accrue to the foreign country. In the situation of Figure 8.5 the repatriated earnings were larger than the cost savings for the host country associated with the service imports and as a consequence the foreign multinational captures more than the fixed cost F and thus gains from the export of the factor service while the host country suffers a welfare loss.

Of course many other situations are possible. In particular it is easy to construct a situation where the benefits associated with the existence of the multinational firm would be shared by both countries. Indeed this should be regarded as the most probable outcome, for otherwise there is little incentive for one or the other of the two countries to engage in the activities we have described. Indeed countries which do not gain from the existence of a multinational firm would be expected to pursue some policy which would allow them to capture some part of the overall benefit. It must be recalled that the existence of the multinational does result in larger world output. Without the international transfer of the service factor both countries must undergo the cost F, while with the multinational firm in place the firm-specific cost F need only be borne once. Thus labour is released to produce more output, and the issue is simply who benefits from this larger world output. In general the presumption would be that the gains will be shared by the two countries, although a much more detailed analysis would be required with much more specific assumptions concerning production and tastes before any statement of how the gains will be shared could be made. We thus have the following result:

PROPOSITION 8.5: If multinationals are organized because of the existence of firm-specific costs, then there is a presumption that both countries will gain from the formation of multinational enterprise.

To this point our analysis has abstracted from pure commodity trade, and the only factor flows have been payments for factor service exports. Models in which commodity trade will exist can certainly be constructed. Such an analysis would raise the issue of whether a country would find it more beneficial to export a commodity or whether it should export the factor service and reap the benefits associated with the payments for these services that we described earlier. Although a full analysis of this question is beyond the scope of the discussion here, some of the issues involved can be identified from Figure 8.6. We suppose that a country is initially at equilibrium at point A with prices P and that initially we have neither trade nor the existence of multinationals. We now assume that the firm has the option of either exporting commodity X or of setting up a branch plant in the foreign country and obtaining the earnings associated with the export of factor services. If the firm chooses to export X, then an equilibrium could be represented with production at B and domestic consumption at C. We note that the switch from autarky to trade has resulted in an increase in the production of X, the good in which increasing returns to scale exists, and it is well known that gains will be achieved by increasing the output of the increasing returns commodity in models with increasing returns to scale. In Figure 8.6 such gains are shown by the movement from consumption point A to the free trade point C.

Now suppose that rather than trade the country establishes a multinational enterprise and sets up a plant in the host country. Whether this is more or less beneficial than exports clearly depends on what profits the firm will be able to repatriate from its foreign subsidiary. As we have already seen, that will depend on the conditions in the host country and on the degree of competition, and no general statement can be made. It is possible that repatriated earnings could result in a consumption point above point C, but equally as possible that consumption would be somewhere between A and C, and could even be at A if no profits can be repatriated from the foreign subsidiary.

The trade versus foreign investment issue is further complicated by the fact that it may be possible, through trade, to generate a larger world output than is possible through the formation of a multinational enterprise. If one country specializes in Y then they need not undertake any of the fixed costs associated with producing X. If the other country specializes in X then they reap the advantages of producing the increasing returns commodity. Such a situation minimizes the fixed cost associated with producing X for the world as a whole and could well be optimal. A possible trading situation is shown in Figure 8.7 where two identical countries with production functions $\bar{Y}F\bar{X}$ are assumed to trade. Although by no means certain, it is

Figure 8.6

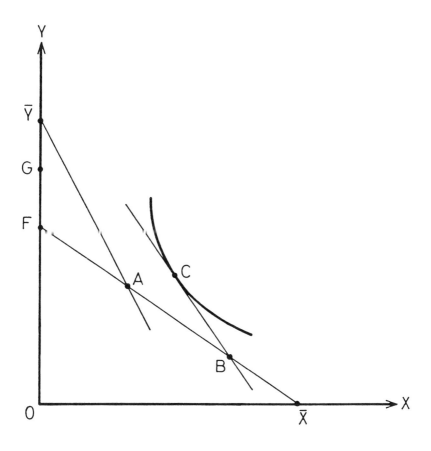

possible that the specialization and trade equilibrium shown in Figure 8.7 dominates the equilibrium associated with the existence of a multinational enterprise. Thus we have the following:

PROPOSITION 8.6: In general there can be no presumption as to whether pure commodity trade or factor service exports associated with the existence of multinational firms will yield higher utility levels either for the two countries or for the world as a whole.

8.5 Licensing and Franchising

In earlier sections we have assumed that a firm that has the ownership advantage will enter the foreign market by setting up a branch plant. There are, however, other ways in which the firm can make use of the firm-specific knowledge or skills that it possesses without undertaking direct foreign investment. Two such ways that have been discussed in the literature are licensing and franchising, both of which involve an operation in which the foreign firm is given access to the specialized information and in return makes a payment to the home firm. A variety of reasons for why franchising or licensing would be preferred to direct foreign investment have been discussed in the literature. It is possible that local firms may have an advantage in production or distribution making it more efficient to use local firms rather than to set up a branch plant. Local firms may be more familiar with customs and tastes and may be more efficient at marketing the product. In such a case it may be profitable for the firm to license the technology rather than to set up a branch plant.

A variety of other issues have been addressed in the literature on licensing and franchising. One of the problems associated with licensing is that it may be difficult for the firm to control the quality of the output produced by the firm in the foreign country. Unless the firm obtaining the license has some clear stake in the long-run operation of the plant then it may well drive down quality in the hope of reaping large short-run profits. The home firm could cancel the license but by the time it does so the damage may well have been done and the reputation of the firm may have been destroyed. In such situations it is argued that some type of profit-sharing arrangement will be required to insure that the licensing firm faces the proper incentives.

While the problems with licensing and franchising are often somewhat different than those associated with the establishment of branch plants that undertake production activities, from the point of view of our analysis there is very little difference in the final outcomes.

Figure 8.7

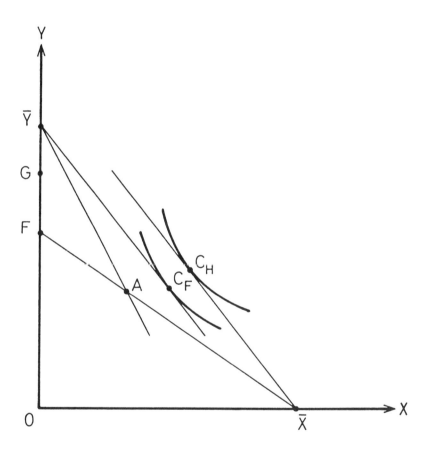

In both cases domestic factors of production will be used, and indeed in our simple models one cannot distinguish between the existence of a multinational enterprise that sets up branch plants and a firm that licenses the use of its factor service knowledge. There may, of course, be very substantial differences in terms of policy. The operations of multinational enterprises very often involve direct foreign investment whereas franchising operations need not. Concern with the level of foreign ownership and foreign control may very well prompt governments to prefer one form of activity to another. Such concerns, however, are largely beyond the scope of this analysis.

8.6 Conclusions and Policy Implications

This chapter has been concerned with the existence of economies of scale associated with the provision of a service input at low or zero marginal cost. If this input can be provided to other plants in the same firm it becomes a public good within the enterprise, and this allows a firm to set up branch plants that would have a clear production advantage over single plant operations. When these branch plants are located in foreign countries we have the phenomenon known as multinationals.

After setting up the basic model we examined the consequences of such multinationals both for the host and the home countries. It was found that the existence of a multinational will result in larger world output, and the issue then becomes how this output is shared between the two countries. Situations exist where the host country receives all the benefit and alternatively it is possible to construct situations where all the benefit accrues to the home country. It is even possible, although perhaps not very realistic, to construct situations where the host country is harmed by the formation of a multinational enterprise.

In the analysis we considered polar cases, and a more likely result is that both countries would gain when a multinational is set up. The obvious policy implication of this result is that foreign governments should be receptive to the existence of multinationals and should certainly not, as a general rule, discourage their formation. While it is possible that multinationals will result in a larger repatriation of earnings than the benefit they provide for the host country, such situations seem unlikely.

The question of whether multinational enterprises are the optimal form of organization is complicated when commodity trade is introduced. In general there can be no presumption as to whether the formation of multinationals or the existence of free trade in commodities would yield higher welfare for the two trading countries and for the world as a whole. Much more research is required before this difficult question can be resolved.

Chapter 9

Commodity Flows, Service Trade, and Investment: A Ricardo-Viner Approach

9.1 Introduction

A good deal of the discussion in earlier chapters has analyzed the consequences for the domestic economy of factor service imports. In Chapter 6, for example, we considered the case where, in a two-factor two-commodity model, one commodity and a factor service were tradable. It was argued that the non-traded commodity could be a consumer service. Trade in producer services was also analyzed extensively in Chapters 7 and 8. This concentration on the international flows of factor services is largely a consequence of the perception that most services that move across international borders are services that enter the production function of domestic firms.

While an important component of international service trade is undoubtedly in factor services, modern technological advances have resulted in a situation in which service commodities can also be traded. While contact services cannot be traded in a real sense, intermediation services certainly can, with banking, finance, and insurance being cases in point. In such industries it is possible for foreign firms to provide consumer services to domestic residents. With an efficient telecommunication system it is possible for a resident in Canada to obtain banking services or financial advice from bankers or stockbrokers in New York. Alternatively, domestics could obtain the advantages of foreign banking or finance by allowing foreign firms to set up plants in Canada and provide these services directly to domestics. The principal goal of this chapter is to compare these two alternatives.

A government, in defining economic policy, may well be faced with the alternatives of allowing residents to obtain services from foreign firms or of giving foreign firms the right of establishment to allow them to directly provide services to domestics. An important issue is which of these alternatives would be preferable from the point of view of the domestic economy. As might be expected, there is no unambiguous answer to this question, and optimal policy will depend on the parameters of the model.

In this discussion it is important to distinguish between the flows of the service factor and trade in the service product itself. When we discuss the importation of products services such as banking we refer to a situation where domestics make arrangements with foreign companies located in the foreign country to provide these services. Flows of factor services, on the other hand, involve the foreign country providing services to the domestic economy which, when combined with local factors, allows the production in the home country of the service product. This distinction is important because there is some confusion in the literature on this issue. Some discussions, of which Stalson's (1985) is an example, would consider both of these activities as the importation of banking services. As has been stressed in earlier chapters, it is important to distinguish whether commodity services or factor services are being exchanged internationally. Indeed, it is possible to imagine trade of factor services for the service commodity, although this particular case is not addressed below.

We begin our analysis in Section 9.2 with a brief description of the model and then in Section 9.3 turn to an analysis of the alternative trade flows for services described above. Significant differences in the analysis arise depending on whether factor endowments are "normal" or "extreme", and these are examined in Section 9.4. The case of free trade in both factor services and service products is considered in Section 9.5, and we conclude with the basic policy recommendations in Section 9.6.

9.2 The Model[1]

The model used in this chapter is the Viner-Ricardo or specific-factor model, which can be seen as combining some of the characteristics of the Ricardian model where a single factor of production is assumed, and the Heckscher-Ohlin model which allows free factor substitution among industries. Specifically it is assumed that the production process of each industry in the economy uses one factor that is specific to that industry and labour. Labour is completely mobile among industries, while the specific factor is not. The specific factor may be free to move between the same industries in different countries, however, and indeed in our analysis it will be assumed that all specific factors except the service factor are completely internationally mobile. It is further assumed that there is completely free trade in all non-service activities. It is assumed that the economy is a small, open, price taker both in products and factor markets, and thus all prices except the price in the service industry are exogenous to the model. Technologies are assumed to differ among countries, and in particular we consider the case where the domestic economy has a technological advantage in the service industry. Because of the openness of our model an equilibrium will have a distinctly Ricardian flavour, in that we would generally expect to find only one manufactured good produced in a domestic economy. This will be the product that, because of technological or endowment advantages, provides the highest return to domestic labour. Note that because of the assumption that all specific factors, except for those in the service industry, are internationally mobile, all specific factors in a given manufacturing sector will receive the same return regardless of where they are employed. Thus in the initial equilibrium we would expect to observe the economy producing and exporting some manufactured good, M, importing a variety of other manufactured goods, and receiving payments from abroad for the use of the exported specific factors.

In the specific factor model it can be shown that there is a positive relationship between the return to the specific factor, r_S, and the price of the service product, p_S. This relationship is illustrated in the left-hand panel of Figure 9.1. The locus BCE represents the relationship between r_S and p_S which exists in the domestic economy.

Because of the fact that technology in the home country differs from that abroad one would not expect the locus ECB to describe the tradeoff between r_S and p_S in the world economy. With the assumption that the domestic economy has a superior service industry, it can be shown that the equilibrium values of r_S and p_S in the rest of the world would give a point such as C^*. The location of C^* shown in Figure 9.1 is consistent with our technological assumption since, if the domestic economy were to pay the going world price for the factor service, given by r^*_S in Figure 9.1, domestics could provide the service product at price $p_S(B)$, a price lower than the world price p^*_S. Alternatively, we note that if the domestic product price for the services were equal to the foreign price, then domestic factor services could receive the r_S associated with point E, a value higher than r^*_S.

In the right-hand panel of Figure 9.1 the domestic demand and supply curves for the service product are illustrated. The position of these curves will be determined by such things as the endowment of the factors and the income of domestic residents, and could result in

Figure 9.1

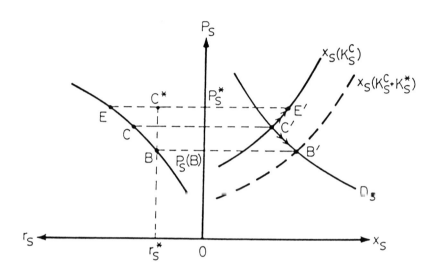

the equilibrium price for service products given by point C'. We note that at the equilibrium C' the domestic economy has a lower price for service products and a higher return for service factors than in the rest of the world.

9.3 Alternative Trade Outlets for Services

From Figure 9.1 it can be shown that the home country can gain either through trade in factor services or trade in the service product. If trade in service products is allowed, then since at C' the home price of the service product is lower than found abroad, home producers would be attracted by the foreign market and would export the service product. Output would expand along the supply curve and would move from C' to E', at which point service product prices would be equal to those abroad. It is clear that the home country would gain from such an expansion since a significant proportion of output is now being sold at higher prices, resulting in higher returns both for the specific factor and for labour.[2]

The alternative policy is for the home country to allow the entry of foreign service factors into the domestic economy where, as can be seen from the comparison of points C and B in the left-hand panel, prices are higher than abroad. An inflow of foreign factors would shift the supply curve in the right-hand panel of Figure 9.1 to the right until a new equilibrium is achieved at B', where the supply of services now depends on both domestic factor services (K^c_S) and foreign factor services (K^*_S). At this point the return to factor services in the domestic economy has been reduced to r^*_S, the rate that prevails in the rest of the world. Again it is clear that domestic welfare has been improved since the benefit associated with the service factor inflow will be larger than the marginal cost paid for this factor at the new equilibrium point.[3] Thus we have the following:

PROPOSITION 9.1: When the home country enjoys a technological advantage in the production of services, either trade in the service product or trade in the service factor will increase national income.

In the situation shown in Figure 9.1 the initial equilibrium point, C', lies midway between the two possible equilibriums associated with service flows and product service trade, that is between E' and B'. This results in a lower product service price and a higher factor service price at home than abroad, and this we will refer to as the normal case. In general it will be difficult to determine which of these two trade options is preferred by the home country, for such a determination involves comparing the welfare changes associated with the movement from C' to E' with the movement from C' to B'. It is clear, however, that had the initial equilibrium been closer to one of the two final equilibrium points, then a clear statement on an optimal policy could be made. Thus suppose that initially C' had been very close to B'. In such a case there is very little to be gained from allowing factor services to enter the domestic economy. If factor services are restricted and instead domestic producers are allowed to provide the service product to foreigners then a substantial gain can be achieved, and thus in this situation trade in service products is clearly to be preferred. Alternatively, with an initial equilibrium closer to E' allowing trade in factor services to flow will provide the larger welfare gain. In general, however, there is ambiguity in which policy is to be preferred, and a determination will require very specific knowledge about the parameters of the model, both at home and abroad. Thus, we have the following:

PROPOSITION 9.2: If, in the initial equilibrium, we observe a higher product service price and a lower factor service price in the domestic economy, an unambiguous ranking of the welfare consequences of factor trade and product trade is generally not possible.

9.4 The Case of Extreme Endowments

In the situation of Figure 9.1, initial supply and demand conditions with no service trade were such that the initial equilibrium produced a service product price that lay between the two possible trading equilibrium points represented by E' and B'. This is by no means necessary, however, and in Figure 9.2 we show situations where the initial equilibrium can lie either above E' or below B'. Again it is possible to show that either trade in service factors or trade in the service product can result in gains for the economy. In this case, however, the two options provide quite different results for the local service sector.

We first consider equilibrium C' in the right-hand panel of Figure 9.2, corresponding to point C on the left-hand side. Such an equilibrium could occur if the home country has such an abundance of the service factor, relative to the supply of labour and other specific factors, that even with the superiority in technology, the price of the service product is less than $p_S(B)$. If, starting at equilibrium C', trade is allowed in the service factor, then the outflow of the service factor will reduce the supply abundance and shift the service product supply curve to the left until a new equilibrium is achieved at B'. Here the price of the service factor is r^*_S both at home and abroad, and we have an equilibrium.

Figure 9.2

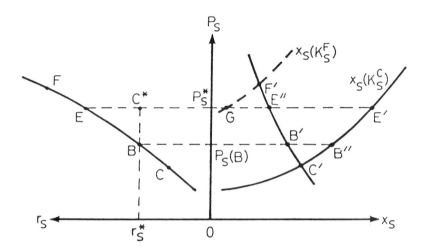

Alternatively, suppose that trade is allowed only in the service product. In this case output expands and the economy moves up the supply curve to an equilibrium at E' where product price at home and abroad has been equalized at p^*_S. It is also easy to compare the welfare changes associated with these two trading regimes. For trade in the service product, consider the movement from C' to E' to consist of the two segments C' to B" and B" to E'. At B" we note that the domestic service price is $p_S(B)$ and the service factor price is r^*_S, exactly the same as for the service factor flow that resulted in equilibrium B'. Furthermore, while trade patterns will differ at B' and B", home economy welfare cannot, since commodity prices and factor prices will be the same.[4] Thus since the welfare increase in moving from C' to E' is larger than that associated with moving from CB", which is equal to the welfare change in moving from C' to B', we have the result that trade in the factor product produces a larger welfare gain than trade in factor services. We therefore have the following:

PROPOSITION 9.3: If factor service endowments are so extreme as to result in both lower service factor prices and service product prices, then trade in either service products or service factors will increase welfare, but there will always be a larger gain from free trade in service products.

For the case of abundance of the service factor, the two trading options described above also produce quite different outcomes for the size of the service sector in the domestic economy. For trade in the service factor, factors will leave the economy and the service sector will shrink in spite of the technological advantage enjoyed by the service industry. With trade in the service product, however, output will expand and the domestic service sector will show substantial growth. Thus we have the following result:

PROPOSITION 9.4: For the case of extreme endowments, service factor trade and service product trade will have opposite effects on the size of the service sector.

An alternative situation in which endowments are extreme is represented by initial equilibrium F', where the home country's endowment of the service factor is so small that, in spite of the technological superiority in service production, both the service factor price and the service produce price are higher domestically than in the rest of the world. Again we consider the two options of trade in the service product and trade in the service factor. For trade in the service product, the domestic economy would import GE", and equilibrium would be at G with service product prices p^*_S. With trade in service factors, the higher domestic price would produce an inflow of the service factor and this would shift the supply curve $x_S(KF_S)$ to the right in Figure 9.2. Equilibrium would be reached when the demand and supply curves intersect at B' where domestic and world prices of the factor service have been equalized at $r*_S$.

The welfare effects of these alternative trade patterns are now easily compared. Again we consider the movement from F' to B' as a movement first from F' to E" followed by a movement from E" to B'. The welfare increase associated with the factor inflow that moved the equilibrium from F to E" is the same as the welfare increase associated with the importation of the service product producing point G, because both these equilibria have the same product and factor prices. The movement from E" to B' produced by the continued inflows of service factors results in a further increase in welfare, however, and thus welfare is higher at B' than at G. We thus have the following:

PROPOSITION 9.5: When service factor supplies are so scarce that both the service factor price and the service product price are higher in the home country than abroad, while trade in either the factor or the product will increase welfare, larger gains can be obtained by liberalizing trade in the service factor.

Here we note that product trade reduces the size of the service sector while factor flows increase the size of the service industry. Thus Proposition 9.4 applies here as well.

We have seen that for the two cases of extreme endowments illustrated in Figure 9.2, both trade in the service factor and trade in the service product will increase utility for the home country. Furthermore, there is no ambiguity in the welfare comparisons of these two patterns of trade. For equilibrium C', where both the factor price and the product price were lower than in the rest of the world, maximum utility is obtained by allowing trade in the service product. For an equilibrium such as F', with higher prices for both the service factor and the service product, maximum welfare is achieved by allowing free trade in the service factor. But while the optimal trade pattern is different for these two cases, there is a common element, for the higher welfare gain is associated with the largest expansion of the service sector in the home country. We thus have the following:

PROPOSITION 9.6: For extreme factor endowment, the trade policy that results in the largest welfare gain is the one that results in the largest increase in the size of the service sector.[5]

9.5 Completely Free Trade

In the previous discussion it has been assumed that the economy must make a choice of allowing trade in factor services or in the service product. If completely free trade is allowed, however, then no such decision will be required, and all factors including the specific factor in the service industry will seek their highest reward in the world. If, as has been previously assumed, the domestic economy has a superior technology for the production of services, then this would imply that the home country will specialize in service industries, and the manufacturing sector in this economy will disappear. In this model endowment comparisons no longer influence trading patterns since world prices will be equalized by trade, and factors will simply locate wherever technology provides the highest return.

The comparisons of welfare in the free trade case are also straightforward. Certainly completely free trade cannot provide a smaller increase in welfare than that associated with trade in either factor services or service products, and indeed it is easy to see that free trade will always result in a superior welfare situation for the domestic economy. In general, with trade in only service products or factor services we will not get the complete equalization of all factor and product prices that is required for a world equilibrium and thus free trade is the preferred option. Of course this does not necessarily imply that free trade is better than restricted trade, for in this model, as in most others, the possibility of an optimal tariff certainly exists if the country has some monopoly power in trade. Thus we have the following:

PROPOSITION 9.7: For a small, open economy, free trade in both the service product and the service factor will maximize welfare for the home country.

9.6 Conclusions and Policy Implications

This chapter has focused on the effects on economic welfare of two alternative options for service trade. The welfare consequences of trade at the service product level were compared to a situation where trade at the service factor level was permitted. The principal result was that trade in either the service factors or the service products will result in an unambiguous increase in welfare for the domestic economy. Which of these two alternatives is to be preferred was shown to depend on the initial circumstances, which depend on endowments and technology both at home and abroad. In the "normal" case, where, because of the technological advantage in the production of services, we observe higher factor prices and lower product prices than abroad, then unambiguous conclusions are generally not possible. For cases of extreme endowments, however, the two trade options can be ranked unambiguously. We found that if trade is allowed in the area where price divergence is larger, the utility gains will be larger. This option also produces the biggest increase in the output of the service sector. It should be noted, however, that this larger welfare gain will be associated with more structural change in the economy, and the costs of such adjustments have not been included in our analysis. Policy makers should be aware of this trade-off when considering policy options for the service sector.

It was shown that completely free trade in both service factors and service products will dominate free trade in either. There are, however, important differences depending on which path to free trade is chosen. For example, if we first open up trade in the market that has the largest price difference and subsequently open up the other market, then the output changes of the two policies will be reinforcing, while the price changes will be in opposite directions. Alternatively, if we first open for trade the market with the smaller price difference, then price changes are monotonic but quantity adjustments will be in opposite directions. This overshooting of the equilibrium price or quantity can produce short-run costs to factors of production and consumers, and policy decisions should take these costs into account.

The pattern and direction of price changes also have implications for factor returns. It can be shown, for example, that changes in the real rewards to labour are inversely related to the changes in p_S . Thus policies that produce the largest increases in p_S , and that result in the largest overall changes in welfare, also produce the largest reductions in the real return to labour. This is not an unexpected result, of course, for the same basic conclusion holds in the standard endowment model.[6] It does suggest, however, that if the gains from trade are to be widely shared in the economy, then moves to free trade must be accompanied by policies that redistribute income.

Notes

1. The analysis of this and subsequent sections of this chapter closely follows Jones and Ruane (1989).

2. For an algebraic formulation of these welfare gains see Jones and Ruane (1989).

3. For a full analysis of this gain see Jones and Ruane (1989).

4. Note that the prices of other specific factors and other products are equalized by trade.

5. Although this proposition has been shown in the context of extreme factor endowments, note that it is also true for the "normal" endowments considered earlier and illustrated in Figure 9.1.

6. In the Heckscher-Ohlin framework, the Stolper-Samuelson theorem tells us that a relative increase in the price of a commodity will reduce the real income of the factor used intensively in the other industry.

Chapter 10

Productivity in Service Industries

10.1 Introduction

The issue of the importance of productivity in service industries has received a good deal of discussion in the literature, and a number of specific examples of technological change in service industries have been considered in earlier chapters. The importance of the issue, however, would seem to warrant some further analysis of this issue. The purpose of this chapter is to provide an overview and to address some issues that have not yet been treated.

We begin, in Section 10.2, with a conceptual discussion of how productivity in services could be measured. This discussion draws heavily on the conceptual framework developed in Chapter 3. In Section 10.3 we go on to consider the issue of whether service industries could serve as an engine of economic growth. This is a particularly important question in the Canadian context for there has been a good deal of discussion about whether services can be relied on to "pick up the slack" associated with the decline of the resource industries in western Canada. We construct a general equilibrium model and demonstrate that some of the previous conclusions cannot be supported in a more general framework.

While specific examples of services have been considered throughout the book, and technological change analyzed for transportation and factor services used as inputs, very little attention has been paid to technical change in the traditional contact services that were identified in Chapter 3. In Section 10.4 we take up this special topic, and argue that while some types of contact services may well form the basis of a comparative advantage for a country or for a region, productivity changes in such industries are not to be expected. In the concluding section we summarize the results concerning productivity in services, both from this chapter and from elsewhere, and provide some comments on the policy implications.

10.2 Productivity in Services

The basic argument of this section is that productivity can best be measured by the extent to which the service sector is able to reduce price differences between producers and consumers. To present our analysis we draw heavily on the discussion of Chapter 3 and in particular on equations (3.5) and (3.6) from that chapter. These equations are reproduced here for easy reference.

(10.1) $X_c = G(X_p, K_g, L_g) + D(X_p, K_d, L_d)\, Q(d)$

(10.2) $X_c = H(X_p, K_h, L_h) + T(X_p, K_t L_t)\, Q(t)$

Recall from Chapter 3 that the terms G and H in equations (10.1) and (10.2) describe the technology for producing a unit of X_c (a unit of the good that provides utility to a consumer) from a unit of X_p (a unit of output of X). It is assumed that X_p and X_c are in contiguous locations. Thus the G and H represent the physical transformation of a commodity required to produce a unit of X_c from a unit of X_p. The second terms of (10.1) and (10.2) are associated with the actual transformation or transmission. For (10.1) this could be, for example, transportation costs, while for (10.2) could be storage costs.[1]

There has been a good deal of discussion in the literature on whether productivity in the service sector has fallen or risen and on the issue of how one should measure productivity in these industries.[2] The definition and classification of services from Chapter 3 allows us to cast some light on these questions. We first note that substitution and intermediation services dominate contact services in terms of employment and output (regardless of how output is measured) and certainly account for most of the growth in the service sector. Indeed substitution and intermediation services can be seen as technological advances that allow us to overcome the constraint of the double coincidence of time and space required by contact services. Thus technological advance in the service sector will, at least to some extent, take the form of replacing contact services with substitution and intermediation services.

Productivity changes in service industries can take place in two distinct ways. We can have technological change in the G or H components of equations (10.1) or (10.2) or in the D and T parts of these two equations. Technological progress in H or G can take the form either of a new technology or of improvements in existing technology. It seems clear that much of the technological advance that has taken place in the service industry can be attributed to the development of new technologies that previously were not available. As we have observed, many services that originally were contact services have been replaced, through the development of new technology, by substitution services. The development of the telephone, television, and modern data processing operations are obvious examples. Of course improvements in existing technology have also been important contributors to the technological advance in the service sector. Recent years have seen major advances in data transmission networks, and developments in computer technology have revolutionized data processing and data transmission systems.

One aspect of the service sector that is often discussed is the fact that while there is rapid technological change in some areas, other industries are characterized by relatively low and stable productivity. If major technological advances in service industries occur through technological improvements in terms G or H of equations (10.1) and (10.2), then we would expect to observe such differences in productivity. Such technological change converts some contact services to intermediation or substitution services and significant improvements in efficiency would be observed in these, while the unchanged contact services would be unaffected. Of course this does not imply a static technology in the production of contact services. Electric hair clippers probably increase the efficiency of barbers, and new techniques in medicine may well have increased the efficiency of certain operations. Such advances, however, are quite different than technological changes that relax the time and space constraints of what were previously contact services. Thus we have the following result:

PROPOSITION 10.1: Technological change in service industries is often difficult to identify, since it often takes the form of a new technology.

When one lists major innovations that have affected the overall course of economic development, many of them are in the service area. They would include the steam engine, the automobile, the steam locomotive and the airplane. All of these represent changes in the technology of transportation. The invention of the telephone, radio, television, and the new advances in telecommunications all represent technological changes in communications. Certainly no one would suggest that technical progress in these areas has been slow. These advances are often regarded as new products or techniques, however, rather than as advances in existing technology.

An issue that may be as important as whether technological progress has been made is how such change can be measured. The economic problem of overcoming the constraints of time and space as described in Chapter 3 was the minimization of the cost of providing services subject to the technological constraints imposed by the transformation function. The minimization of the cost of producing X_c from X_p can be seen as the minimization of the difference in price between these two forms of commodity X. Thus technological change in the service sector will be reflected in lower prices of commodity X_c. Furthermore one would expect the reduction in the price of X_p to result in an increase in the demand for the service used to provide it. For example, an improvement in the transportation system will mean that existing customers will find that the price of X_c has fallen, and sectors of the market previously deprived of the commodity because of high prices can now be served. One would therefore not be surprised to find that technological advances in such service industries result in a larger quantity of this service being provided. This, of course, is exactly the phenomenon we discussed at some length in Chapter 5.

If technological improvements result in more use of the service, then the total cost of providing such services may rise. In attempting to measure productivity in the service sector some researchers have compared the value of the output of the service industries with the labour inputs required to produce them, and have found that productivity so measured has fallen or at least has not increased. The difficulty, of course, is that this is not the appropriate measure of productivity for a service industry. A reduction in the price of X_c could certainly be consistent with an increase in the labour cost of providing such services. As a simple example consider a neutral technological advance in a transportation sector that reduces the average cost of transporting a commodity between two locations. With neutral technological progress the capital-labour ratio can be assumed unchanged. Further suppose that the reduction in the price of X_c results in an increase in demand such that the total expenditure on the transportation service is exactly what it was previously. With the total value of output the same, and because of the fact that technological change has been assumed to be neutral, the same amount of capital and labour will be employed as was the case before the change took place. Thus a measure of productivity that compares the value of output to the input of labour will indicate that no technological progress has been made, or at least that the productivity of labour has remained unchanged. Of course real productivity has risen as evidenced by the fact that consumers of X_c pay less than previously for a unit of output. Thus we have:

PROPOSITION 10.2: The appropriate measure of technological change in services is the calculation of whether and by how much the gap between consumer prices and producer prices has been reduced.

As another example consider two groups of consumers separated by some natural or artificial barrier that prevents exchange between the two groups. Now suppose a technological change reduces this barrier and permits trade to take place. Even though commodity prices are not completely equalized by trade, the observation that exchange takes place implies that gains from trade are being enjoyed by both groups. This is a simple consequence of the familiar gains-from-trade theorem. These gains will exist even though one would observe resources being used to produce the transportation service— resources that were previously employed to produce commodities.[3] Furthermore, subsequent improvements in the technology of transportation would generally increase the volume of trade and the total cost of transportation, and could quite conceivably increase the transportation cost per unit of labour employed in the transportation sector. Nevertheless it is clear that the change in transportation technology has been beneficial to both groups of consumers.

There has never been any question about the gains associated with trade either among nations or among individuals. Such trades, whether they be interspatial or intertemporal, are facilitated by the service sector, and in a competitive model the fact that trades take place is *prima facia* evidence that consumers are made better off. Trade is made possible by services, and the gains-from-trade theorem therefore can be seen as capturing some of the aspects of economic gains associated with the provision of services. There is therefore a gains-from-services theorem which goes as follows:

PROPOSITION 10.3: Gains from Services: In a competitive world the introduction of a new technology in the service area that increases trade among economic units will be beneficial to all traders. This will be true even though the service uses resources previously employed for producing consumption goods.

The gains-from-trade theorem is one of the most important propositions in economic theory, and the gains from international trade are considered to be very substantial. The gains-from-services theorem subsumes the gains from international trade, but also includes the internal domestic gains from intranational and inter-temporal exchanges that are facilitated by the service sector. Relative to the gains from international trade, the gains from trade due to services must be enormous.

10.3 Services as an Engine of Economic Growth

One aspect of productivity in services that has become important in Canadian public policy debate is the issue of whether growth in service productivity could form the basis of regional economic expansion. In discussing the problems faced by Western Canada in overcoming slowdowns associated with weak foreign markets for resources, the Economic Council of Canada (1984) has argued that services could become an engine of economic growth. This is obviously an important issue in the services area, and we will discuss the question in some detail. We concentrate our attention on a summary version of the argument contained in Swan (1985).

While the question of what constitutes an "engine of economic growth" is obviously central to a discussion of whether services can promote economic growth, there does not seem to be complete agreement on a definition. Swan (1985, p. 344) is very clear on this issue, and defines an engine of economic growth as "...any change in economic conditions that contributes to raising per capita living standards in that year." As Mansell (1985) has argued, this is a somewhat weaker definition of an engine of growth than is usually assumed, and would not correspond to the conditions for a growth pole as described, for example, by Perroux (1955). While I tend to agree with Mansell, researchers are free to use whatever definitions they prefer, and even if such definitions are somewhat misleading when compared to common usage, Swan's research deserves to be evaluated in terms of his own assumptions and definitions.

Given Swan's rather modest requirements, it is clear that technological improvement in any sector could serve as such an engine of growth, and certainly productivity improvements in the service sector will be no exception to this statement. There remains the question, however, of what the effects of such technological improvement will be on such parameters as commodity outputs, commodity prices, and factor rewards. We begin our discussion by considering, in Figure 10.1, a small open region producing a service Y and a good X, using capital and labour as factors of production. We assume that both the service and the good are tradable, not because this is necessarily the most realistic case but rather because it is the easiest to analyze. The tradable services could be commodities such as communications, banking and finance, or insurance. It is assumed that commodity X is a good such as food or manufactured products, and we will assume that both commodities are produced under conditions of constant returns to scale. Initially we assume that Y, the service commodity, is capital intensive relative to commodity X. In the initial situation we have production at point Q and consumption at point C, with the region exporting good X and importing the service Y.

We now assume an improvement in technology in the production of commodity Y, and for simplicity we assume that the technological change is neutral, implying that for a given ratio of factor prices the same proportion of capital and labour will be used in the Y industry both before and after the technological change. The effect of such technological improvement is most easily demonstrated by considering the unit value isoquants of Figure 10.2. Here X_0 and Y_0 are two isoquants which, given the prices P_0 shown in Figure 10.1, produce the same total revenue. With a neutral improvement in technology in the Y industry, the old isoquant Y_0 must now represent a higher output of Y, which implies that $P_y Y_0 > P_x X_0$, so that the situation with wage-rental ratio w_0 cannot be an equilibrium. To re-establish equilibrium we must find a new Y isoquant such that the value of output in the X and Y industries is again the same. Such an isoquant could be Y_1 with a new wage rental ratio w_1. We note that the equilibrium capital-labour ratio has fallen from k_y to k'_y in industry Y and from k_x to k'_x in industry X.

To illustrate how this technological change in industry Y will affect the outputs of the two industries we consider Figure 10.3, which shows the Edgeworth-Bowley box for the region. Corresponding to the equilibrium shown in Figure 10.1 with production at Q, and the corresponding equilibrium of Figure 10.2 with wage rental ratio w_0, we have equilibrium point A in Figure 10.3. From Figure 10.2 we saw that a technological improvement in industry Y would result in a reduction in the capital-labour ratio in both industries, and this will give rise to a new production point such as B in Figure 10.3. Note that because of our assumption that technological change has been neutral, so that the only change required for industry Y is a renumbering of the isoquants, the production contract curve $O_x A O_y$ of Figure 10.3 is unchanged by the technological progress.

From Figure 10.3 it is clear that the move from A to B has resulted in a reduction in the output of commodity X, since B is clearly on a lower isoquant than is A. For Y, not only is point B on a higher isoquant than A, but, because of the technological improvement, the new isoquant through A also represents a higher level of output than previously. Thus, in Figure 10.1, given the same commodity prices, production would be at a point such as Q' and consumption at point C'. We note that C' represents a higher level of utility than C, and thus the technological improvement has unambiguously made the residents in this region better off, in the sense that with an appropriate redistribution of income all consumers could enjoy more consumption of both commodities.

Figure 10.1

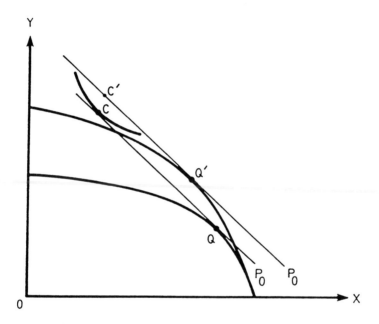

Figure 10.2

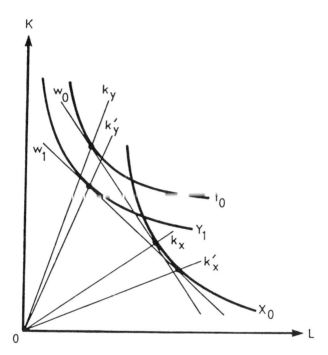

But while aggregate consumption will necessarily be higher after the technological change, it is clear from both Figures 10.2 and 10.3 that the wage-rental ratio will have been reduced in going from A to B. From Figure 10.3, because of the homogeneity of the production functions, the wage rental ratio at B is equal to the slope of the X isoquant at E, which is clearly less than the slope at A. Thus the technological improvement in the service sector has made workers worse off relative to capital owners.

Of more importance than labour's relative position is the fact that, in the example just constructed, labour will be made absolutely worse off by the technological change. This can be seen from Figure 10.3 where we note that the movement from A to B has resulted in a reduction in the capital labour ratio in industry X, which in turn means that the marginal product of labour in the X industry has fallen. A condition for profit-maximization in production is that firms are paid the value of their marginal product, which implies that the real return to labour has been reduced. Further we note that in equilibrium $w = P_xMPL_x = P_yMPL_y$. With perfect labour mobility, labour must receive the same return in both industries, and consequently labour will be worse off with respect to either commodity X or commodity Y. At the same time capital owners will be made absolutely better off, for not only will the relative return of capital rise but the return to capital measured in terms of either commodity X or commodity Y will have increased.[4] We can conclude, then, that in the example with technological improvement in the capital intensive service sector, and with fixed commodity prices, labour will be made unambiguously worse off and capital unambiguously better off. This is in sharp contrast to Swan (1985), who argues that an improvement in the service sector will increase the wage rate.

Of course the result that labour will be made worse off by technological advance in the Y industry depends on the assumption that the service industry is capital intensive. Had we assumed that the service sector was labour intensive, then a technological improvement in the service sector would result in a real and relative increase in the wage rate and a real and relative fall in the return to capital. The point is that the effect on factor returns depends crucially on the factor intensities assumed for the two industries. We thus have the following result:

PROPOSITION 10.4: For a small region, technological improvement in a traded service will result in overall gains, but will reduce the real income of the factor used intensively in the other industry.

Figure 10.3

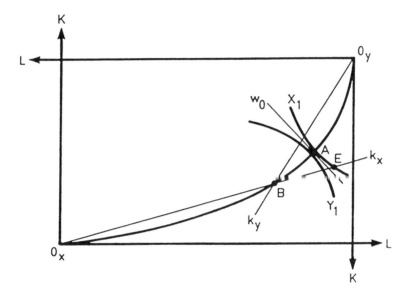

For simplicity we have assumed a small open region that trades both the service output Y and the good X. As has already been noted, for many service sectors, output can be traded only with difficulty, and thus we now turn to the case where commodity Y cannot be traded. In the simple example of Figure 10.1 this leads to another extreme case, for now trade is not possible, and we are left to consider the case of a closed region. We could suppose, for example, that point Q represents both the production and consumption point in the initial equilibrium. We now assume the same technological change in the Y industry, and assume initially that prices remain at P_0. With homogeneous preferences, and because the output of Y has risen and the output of X has fallen, there will be excess supply of Y and excess demand for commodity X. This will lead to a relative increase in the price of X moving production down the production possibility curve from Q'. In Figure 10.2 this will mean that the wage-rental ratio will increase, and this in turn will imply that labour will be made better off both relatively and absolutely in comparison to the case where commodity prices were fixed.

Whether labour will be better off than in the initial situation at Q is unclear, and will depend on the exact nature of the production functions and on preferences. The possibility that labour could be made better off with technological change in Y can be seen by supposing that preferences are Leontief, or in other words that there is zero elasticity of substitution in consumption. This implies that the two goods will be consumed in the same proportion regardless of prices and income. This being the case it is clear that after the technological change a larger quantity of both X and Y will be consumed by consumers, which in Figure 10.3 will imply equilibrium at some point on the production contract curve between A and O_y. Any such point implies an increase in the capital-labour ratio as compared to A, and consequently an increase in the real and relative return to labour. Of course, because both production functions have been assumed to be homogeneous of the first degree, if labour is made better off capital must necessarily be worse off. Alternatively, if there is a high degree of substitution in consumption, then in Figure 10.1 the new consumption point would be close to Q'. This implies a reduction in the output of X, and in Figure 10.3 would result in an equilibrium point on the segment AB of the production contract curve. In this range the real and relative returns to labour have fallen and the real and relative returns to capital have risen, and thus in a closed economy the effect of technological change on factor rewards is ambiguous. Thus labour may be better or worse off even when technological change occurs in the capital intensive service sector. Analogous but opposite results apply to the case where the service sector is assumed to be labour intensive. Thus effects of technological change on factor rewards will be ambiguous, although there is a presumption that technological improvement will be beneficial to the factor that is used intensively in the service sector; that is, in the sector in which the technological progress takes place. Thus we have:

PROPOSITION 10.5: In a closed economy where services are not traded, a technological improvement will produce aggregate welfare gains, but the effect on real factor rewards is ambiguous. There is a presumption that the real return of the factor used intensively in services will rise, however.

When we initially considered Figure 10.1 it was assumed that there was trade in both commodities X and Y and that the improvement in technology had no effect on prices faced by the region. Now suppose this region trades primarily with other regions in the economy, where all regions are assumed to be large enough to affect equilibrium commodity prices. An improvement in technology in one region would now be expected to change the equilibrium terms of trade, and this situation is shown in Figure 10.4. Here T_WG_W is the production possibility curve for region W, assumed to be the same region as shown in Figure 10.1. T_EG_E is the production possibility curve for region E, so that in the initial equilibrium region E produces at Q_E and consumes at C_E while region W produces at Q_W and consumes at C_W. The trade vectors Q_EC_E and C_WQ_W are equal indicating that trade is balanced between these two regions.

We now suppose that the technological change analyzed in Figure 10.1 takes place in region W so that production becomes Q'_W and consumption C'_W. The length of the trade vector for region W has clearly been reduced and consequently there is now an excess supply of commodity Y and an excess demand for commodity X. Thus the relative price of X will rise in both regions resulting in an increase in the output of X and a reduction in the output of Y in both regions. A new equilibrium will be achieved (not shown) with a relatively higher price of X, and this will result in the same change in relative factor rewards as analyzed for the situation of the closed economy. While the initial improvement in technology in the Y industry will reduce the real and relative return for labour in region W and increase the real and relative return for capital, the improvement in the terms of trade associated with the increase in the relative price of X will tend to offset the initial changes, and the final effect on the returns to the factors is indeterminant. Note also that the improvement in the terms of trade will result in a further welfare increase for region W, since the new equilibrium point will necesssarily be on a higher community indifference curve than point C'_W of Figure 10.4.

Figure 10.4

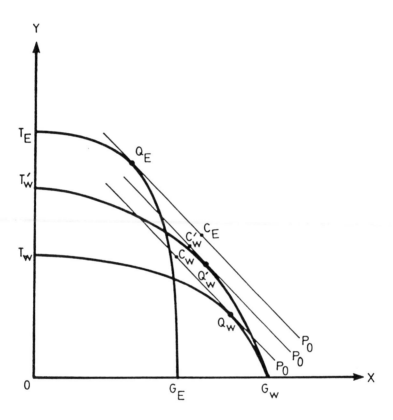

Just the opposite effects are occurring in region E. The deterioration in the terms of trade will reduce the overall consumption level and make the region worse off. At the same time, because of the shift in production towards more X and less Y, labour's real income will rise and capital's real income will fall.

The specific results just derived depend crucially on the assumptions made about the capital intensities of the two industries and on the initial trading pattern assumed. For example, had the technological improvement in industry Y taken place in region E, the initial effects on the real and relative returns to factors would be the same as found for region W, but the effect on the terms of trade would be the opposite. In particular, the larger increase in the output of Y and the smaller output of commodity X in region E would result in a deterioration in the terms of trade for E, and it is even possible that region E would be made worse off relative to consumption point C_E by the terms of trade deterioration associated with the technological change. This is an example of immiserizing growth, and simply illustrates the fact that we cannot assume that a technological advance in a region will necessarily make consumers in that region better off. Thus we have:

PROPOSITION 10.6: If regions (or countries) have some monopoly power in trade, then it is possible that a technological improvement will lower aggregate real income. The effects on real factor returns are ambiguous.

We have shown that, in an open region where equilibrium prices are determined by the interplay of domestic demand and supply conditions, technological improvement in a service industry, or any other industry for that matter, need not necessarily be an engine of economic growth. Technological improvement can leave a region worse off in the sense that average per capita income would be lower than before the technological change took place. Of course this possibility is a consequence of the fact that trade in both commodities is possible. For a closed economy, technological change will always increase average per capita income, for the production possibility curve after the technological advance will always dominate the original production possibility curve. This is the result identified in Proposition 10.5.

With technological change in one industry in only one region we necessarily have a situation where the wage-rental ratios between the two regions will differ. If both regions are small and face an externally given terms of trade, then Figure 10.2 could represent the equilibrium factor prices in the two regions after the technological change has taken place. With no technological change in region E, w_0 would remain the wage-rental ratio for that region, while w_1 becomes the factor-price ratio for region W. Now even if prices adjust so that factor prices change in both regions, there must remain a difference in the slopes of the wage-rental ratio lines in the two regions as long as both regions continue to produce both commodities.   Thus even if commodity prices change, the final equilibrium will be similar to that shown in Figure 10.2.

The fact that factor prices are unequal between regions in the final equilibrium means that there will be a tendency for factors to move from one region to the other.   In particular labour will leave region W and move to region E while capital will be encouraged to relocate from E to W.   Furthermore this migration of factors will not, by itself, equalize the wage-rental ratios between the two regions. Because the technological change has resulted in different production functions for the two regions, no amount of factor flows will equate wage rental ratios unless we have complete specialization in one or both regions.   And of course the direction of factor flows depends crucially on the assumptions made about which industry is capital intensive. Had it been assumed that the service sector was labour intensive, then with technological improvement in the service industry, labour would have migrated to region W and capital would have moved from region W to region E.   Thus, whether the factor movements associated with technological change will make the factor endowments of the two regions more or less similar will depend on the assumptions about the factor intensities of the two industries. We can now state the following:

PROPOSITION 10.7: Technological change in one region only will produce interregional factor price differences and will produce interregional factor migration. These factor flows can either increase or decrease the differences in relative factor endowments among regions.

The two-sector model is somewhat restrictive when technological change in the service sector is to be considered, for either one must assume that services are traded or assume that there is no trade at all. Certainly the simple models we have considered in this chapter do not capture all the interesting characteristics of the service sector.   It would be reasonably straightforward to extend the models to allow for the presence of a non-traded commodity.   The three-good two-commodity model discussed by Melvin (1968), for example, could easily be adapted for this purpose.   Alternatively one could assume three commodities and three factors and analyze technological change in terms of the three outputs.

Increasing the complexity of the models, however, would certainly not make the analysis of technological change in the service sector any easier, nor would it produce more definitive conclusions. We have already seen that the welfare effects of technological improvement will depend on whether the region is small, and in which commodity the region has a comparative advantage. The effects on the returns to factors will depend on whether the service industry is capital intensive or labour intensive, and on whether the output of the service sector is imported, exported, or not traded at all. Furthermore we have considered only a single type of service industry, namely a service that is directly purchased by consumers. Further complications arise when one considers producer services or intermediation services such as transportation. Some of these models were discussed in earlier chapters. The point is that no general conclusions can be reached concerning the welfare effects nor the effects on the returns to factors when technological change in the service sector is assumed. Definitive conclusions are possible only when the kind of service being considered is specified precisely and only when knowledge of the technological conditions under which services are produced is available. The argument that services can serve as an engine of economic growth and can result in an increase in the returns to labour may hold in some circumstances, but is not a generally true proposition. Definitive conclusions depend on knowledge of both the nature of the service industries and on the role that services can play in a trading economy.

10.4 Technological Change in Contact Services

It was argued in Section 10.3 that the role of services, and the importance of technological change in service industries for regional development, will depend crucially on the type of service being considered. In this section we will consider the possible effects that technological change in contact services could have on regional development and trade.

While many of the traditional contact services such as retailing, haircutting, and repair and maintenance, would not be expected to have any substantial effect on regional development and trade, some service industries may. One example is tourism, and there can be no doubt that regions such as Atlantic Canada have benefited substantially from their export of tourism. Other tourist related industries that can be used to produce exports would include activities such as legalized gambling and prostitution. States such as Nevada and cities such as Atlantic City have been able to increase economic activity substantially by legalizing casino gambling. Some cities, such as Rochester Minnesota, Montreal, and London Ontario, have developed expertise in certain medical practices that have resulted in a substantial export of medical services. One could also include university towns such as Ann Arbor Michigan and Madison Wisconsin as examples of areas which, through the provision of a contact service, have generated economic growth and development.

While there can be no doubt that the contact services described above can be important export industries that can generate regional income, it is less clear that technological progress will result in their becoming engines of economic growth. With regard to natural tourist attractions such as Cavendish Beach or Niagara Falls, regions either have them or they do not, and although their attractiveness can be enhanced, endogenous technological progress seems unlikley. Tourist attractions such as legalized gambling and prostitution can certainly be introduced, and there is no doubt that provinces such as P.E.I. could substantially increase the tourist trade by such activities. However, the fact that provinces have not taken advantage of such options suggests that the citizens regard the negative externalities of such activities as outweighing any positive benefits the additional tourist trade might have. Such contact services also suffer from the disadvantage of being ephemeral, as was pointed out earlier. Las Vegas is an important gambling centre and a significant tourist attraction largely because other nearby jurisdictions do not allow such activities. Legalized gambling throughout the United States would almost certainly reduce the comparative advantage enjoyed by Nevada. But in any case, even though these services provide a substantial amount of income and employment, it is difficult to imagine them as important engines of regional economic growth. Similar arguments would apply to contact services such as medical facilities or universities. The comparative advantage in these activities is ephemeral and depends on the ability of the city or region to train, hire, and keep the expert personnel required to provide the services. And even when this is successfully accomplished the prospects for substantial economic growth would seem to be very limited. We can thus conclude the following:

PROPOSITION 10.8: Although traditional contact services can be an important source of income, they seem unlikely to become engines of economic growth for regions or countries.

10.5 Summary and Policy Implications

There has been a great deal of discussion of the issue of productivity in the service industries, and some economists have been concerned about the possibility that slow growth in services would result in a slowdown of economic activity in general. In earlier chapters, and in particular in the discussion of transportation in Chapter 5, it was shown that technological change in services could substantially increase the welfare of the community, even if it resulted in a reduction in the production of consumer goods. Furthermore, it is clear that many of the significant advances that have occurred in technology have been in service industries, and would include such things as the invention of the telephone, the radio, the steam engine and the airplane. Obviously technological changes such as these have had a tremendous effect, both on growth and on economic welfare in general. Indeed, because of the effect that technological improvements can have on the overall level of economic activity, and in particular on consumer welfare, every effort should be made to encourage technical progress in the service areas.

An additional difficulty that arises in service industries is that productivity is typically very difficult to measure. Measures such as the productivity of labour tend to be misleading, particularly when it is often very difficult to measure output accurately. In Section 10.2 we argued that the appropriate measure of productivity for many service industries is the extent to which the difference between producer and consumer prices is reduced by the technological change. This approach emphasizes the importance that improvements in service technology can have for an economy, and makes it clear that all of the gains associated with trade, and this includes both domestic and international trade, can be attributed to the service sector. Gains from services are clearly very substantial. If public policy is interested in increasing the gains from trade, then it should be even more interested in increasing the gains associated with technological improvements in the service sector.

In Section 10.3 we analyzed the issue of whether, in terms of regional development, services could serve as an engine of economic growth. While services can be as important for increasing national income as any other sector, and indeed we have already argued that significant welfare increases can be associated with advances in service technology, the effects on such things as factor returns are not as clear. It was shown that changes in the real income of factors associated with technological change in services will depend on a variety of things, including the factor intensity of services, whether services can be traded, and whether the region or country has monopoly power in trade. In general very little can be said about how the real returns to factors of production will be affected by a technological improvement in services.

In Section 10.4 we turned our attention to the question of whether contact services could serve as growth poles for a region or country. It was argued that although contact services can often be an important source of income, there would not seem to be much scope for technological improvement in most of the services that fall in this classification. If services are to be relied on to provide an engine of economic growth, then the more technological advanced areas would certainly seem to hold the most promise.

Notes

1.   For a more complete discussion of equations (10.1) and (10.2) see Section 3.5 of Chapter 3.

2.   Early classical writers such as Smith took the view that services were unproductive activities. Communist countries, following Marx, still do not include personal services in their measure of GNP.

3.   For a more detailed discussion see Chapter 5.

4.   These results are straightforward applications of the well-known Stolper-Samuelson theorem.

Chapter 11

Policy Conclusions

11.1 Introduction

Concluding chapters in volumes such as this typically begin with a review of the principal results and then go on to discuss the major policy implications. Throughout our discussion we have highlighted the principal findings in propositions, and a summary of our results would therefore essentialy be a restatement or a relisting of all these propositions. This seems unnecessary, however, since the propositions are easily found either by scanning the text or by referring to the table of contents. A summary of the results will therefore not be provided, and instead we will concentrate our attention on a discussion of the policy implications that arise from the analysis.

We will focus our attention on several major themes that have arisen during the discussion, and in each case we will draw on the analysis from the various chapters to elucidate and support a number of policy recommendations. These policy recommendations will be identified in the same way that the principal results were identified as propositions throughout the body of the text. We begin, in Section 11.2, with the basic issue of comparative advantage in services, paying particular attention to the ways in which comparative advantage in the models we have discussed differs from the traditional trade analysis. Transportation has been a recurring theme throughout our analysis, and issues and recommendations concerning this important service sector will be taken up in Section 11.3. Factor services have been emphasized as one of the important service flows from an

173

international trade point of view and these will be examined in Section 11.4. Section 11.5 will provide some recommendations regarding multinationals and the final section will provide some brief concluding remarks.

Before proceeding with this discussion, however, a caveat is in order. Our entire analysis has been theoretical, and policy recommendations which derive entirely from theory must always be suspect to some extent. Theoretical conclusions, by definition, are a consequence of the underlying assumptions that have been made, and in this as in any area there can be substantial disagreement as to which assumptions are the appropriate ones. As is well known from international trade theory, results concerning the effects of trade on such things as factor price changes very much depend on the particular assumptions made about production conditions, and in many cases seemingly modest changes in the assumed technology can result in quite different theoretical results.

The theoretical difficulties are exacerbated by the fact that there is virtually no empirical literature that addresses the specific policy issues with which we are here concerned. Not only does this produce a certain amount of uncertainty about which of the theoretical models are more appropriate, it also produces a situation in which it is difficult to establish whether some results are more important than others. The present state of empirical analysis in the service area does not even provide us with reliable information on such basic questions as which services are most important in international trade. Nevertheless, while mindful of the difficulties associated with providing policy recommendation from a theoretical study of an area still very much in its infancy, we do feel that the analysis points quite clearly to several significant policy recommendations. It is to these recommendations that we now turn.

11.2 Comparative Advantage in Services

Chapter 3 provided some background material on the discussion of comparative advantage in services, and in Chapter 4 the issue of comparative advantage in services was considered in more detail. The question of what gives rise to comparative advantage has a long and well-known history in the international trade literature, and indeed much of traditional trade theory is concerned with the issue of why trade takes place. Standard trade models attribute comparative advantage to such things as endowment differences, returns to scale, differences in tastes, and differences in technologies, and it seems clear that service trade, just as is true for goods trade, could be caused by any such difference among countries. But while substantial similarities between the determinants of service trade and goods trade were identified, the principal result of Chapter 3 was that sources of comparative advantage in services often do seem to differ from those of traditional trade theory. In particular, in many of the models considered, comparative advantage in services is seen to depend on human capital. Thus in Chapters 6 and 7, which addressed various aspects of trade in factor services, trade in services involved the international provision of information, engineering skills, management skills, or other special forms of human capital.

An important characteristic of comparative advantage based on human capital is the fact that the producers of these services typically are footloose. Thus the comparative advantage that a country might enjoy, and which is embodied in a group of architects, physicians, or specialized managers, could easily disappear if these individuals migrated elsewhere. Thus maintaining a comparative advantage in such activities may involve providing an economic and social climate that is attractive to the professionals involved. As the production of services becomes a more and more important component of economic activity it will become increasingly important to provide an economic, social, and physical environment that professionals and entrepreneurs find amenable. We thus have our first recommendation.

RECOMMENDATION 1: If services are to become an important export sector, social policy must provide an economic climate that professionals and entrepreneurs find appealing.

Comparative advantage in services is ephemeral not only because individuals possessing human capital can move, but also because the skills associated with certain kinds of service activities can often be learned by others. The comparative advantage associated with a certain technique or with certain skills will be lost if other countries, through education and training, are able to produce equally skilled individuals. Furthermore, comparative advantage in services that is based on human capital is not a static condition, but depends on continuous progress in education, research and development. Much of this education and training is seen to have public good characteristics and is therefore provided by some level of government. But whatever the source of the funding, education and training seem crucial to the maintenance of a population with the prerequisite skills. From this it follows that a country should expect to maintain a comparative advantage in services associated with human capital only if it is prepared to spend substantial amounts on education, skill training, and research and development. This provides us with our next recommendation.

RECOMMENDATION 2: High levels of expenditure on education and research and development are essential if service industries are to become important export industries.

Recommendation 2 seems particularly important in the Canadian context, for in recent years there has been a reduction in education expenditures, relative to other social programs, by almost all levels of government. In the area of research and development, expenditures in Canada are small by almost any standards. A continuation of underfunding in these two important areas could have catastrophic consequences for Canadian service industries in the future.

In a country such as Canada, which has distinct and well-defined regions, the ephemeral nature of human capital is a particular problem. Provincial goverments may be reluctant to spend large sums on higher education if the individuals trained are unable to find satisfactory employment locally and therefore move to other jurisdictions. Alternatively, some provinces might feel that educated and skilled people can be attracted from other provinces, and thus they may allocate less than the optimal amount of resources to their own education systems. These are examples of the free-rider problem, and it is well known that in such circumstances less than the optimal amount of a public good, in this case education, will be provided. There would seem to be two sources of this difficulty. The first is the fact that higher education is provided largely by the state, and the second is that education is under provincial rather than federal jurisdiction. Note that if individuals were required to pay for their own education, then there would not be a problem, since institutions would arise to meet whatever demand was forthcoming. The institutions, of course, would have no interest in where the purchaser of these educational services finally decided to locate. An alternative approach to the problem would be to have higher education provided by the federal government. In principle at least, the federal government has no interest in where individuals for whom it has provided education and training locate within the country. And while there is, of course, the possibility that Canadians, having received an education in Canada, will move to other countries, international migration is insignificant when compared to the potential for interregional factor movements. The appropriate provision of education and skilled training would therefore seem to require the following:

RECOMMENDATION 3: The provision of higher education should be substantially privatized, and whatever public funding is required should be provided by the federal government.

11.3 The Transportation Sector

The importance of the transportation sector has been evident throughout our analysis, and this important service industry was discussed in some detail in Chapter 5. A principal feature of our analysis was the argument that transportation should be seen as arising endogenously within an economy from the desire of individuals to obtain commodities that they do not themselves produce. When production is associated with particular resources, and when these resources are separated by substantial distance, the importance of an efficient transportation system becomes obvious. In a country like Canada, where distance is one of the principal constraints that must be overcome in market-clearing activities, efficient transportation systems for overcoming the constraints of space become of paramount importance.

It was also argued that the appropriate way of analyzing international transportation is to consider it as a logical extension of the domestic transportation industry. This is not the approach that is typically taken when transportation is introduced into the analysis of international trade. Indeed, most traditional models assume that transportation is only required if international trade takes place. This approach to transportation is not only logically inappropriate, but also misses one of the important features of trade in transportation services. To be successful in the international transportation industry, a country must develop a comparative advantage, and in many circumstances such a comparative advantage will develop from the need to provide domestic transportation.

The provision of an efficient domestic transportation and communication system therefore has two clear advantages. First it permits efficient exchange among domestic consumers, and this, as was shown in Chapter 5, can result in substantial welfare improvements for the residents of the economy. Indeed, technological change in the transportation sector could have a larger effect on domestic welfare than an equal technological advance in the goods-producing sector. Second, the development of an efficient domestic transportation service can provide the economy with a comparative advantage that will result in that service being exported to foreign countries. This brings us to the next recommendation.

RECOMMENDATION 4: The provision of an efficient domestic transportation system is essential to the welfare of an economy such as Canada, not only because it facilitates domestic exchange but also because it could lead to an international comparative advantage in the transportation industry.

The provision of an efficient transportation system is of particular importance from a public policy point of view, for transportation has a very clear public goods component. The maintenance of an efficient road system and the provision of efficient and adequate air terminals will probably remain the responsibility of governments, for it is not clear that the private sector could provide such facilities efficiently. There is a good deal of evidence that expenditure on transportation facilities in Canada has fallen as a proportion of the total budget, and if this were to continue it could have significant consequences for the transportation industry, and eventually for the overall welfare of Canadians.

Of course an efficient transportation network requires more than just the provision of public goods such as roads and airports. Regulations that impede the interprovincial flows of goods and services can be as important a detriment to the transportation system as poor facilities. Historically, for example, interprovincial regulations on trucking have been a hodgepodge of measures that have made it difficult for firms to run an efficient interprovincial trucking system. Certainly Canada has not gone as far as the United States in removing restrictions on the transportation system, and as a consequence Canada is perceived to have a competitive disadvantage in areas such as trucking. This leads to our next recommendation.

RECOMMENDATION 5: The deregulation of the transportation system will be an important first step in producing a transportation system in Canada that is able to compete in world markets.

One of the interesting results that developed from the discussion of an endogenous transportation system in Chapter 5 was the possibility of an economy purchasing its transportation from a foreign country and paying for these imports by exporting goods. It was shown that, if an economy has an inefficient transportation system, a substantial increase in domestic welfare could be achieved by allowing foreign firms to provide domestic transportation. In general both countries would gain from such an exchange, but it was of interest to note that small countries would generally have an advantage in terms of the distribution of the free-trade gains. This leads to the following recommendation:

RECOMMENDATION 6: Free trade in transportation can provide substantial welfare gains for participating countries, and thus every attempt should be made to remove restrictions on the international flow of transportation services.

One of the characteristics of the model in which a country buys transportation services from another country and pays for them with exports is that in such a situation the country importing the transportation services will necessarily experience a merchandise trade deficit. Indeed, in the simple symmetric model described in Chapter 5, goods will flow only in one direction. A similar situation arose in Chapter 6 where factor services were considered, where it was found that the export of management services in exchange for commodities could also result in a merchandise trade deficit. Indeed, this would seem to be a fairly general proposition. If a country is substantially involved in the export of services, since these services are typically not counted in merchandise trade, and since they must be paid for by goods, a merchandise trade imbalance must necessarily arise. The point is that this is a logical consequence of the pattern of trade when services are involved, and this, in turn, is a natural consequence of the comparative advantages that the countries enjoy. In such circumstances concerns about such deficits are clearly misplaced, and any attempt to artificially eliminate these deficits can only result in a reduction in the utility of all participants. Thus we have the following:

RECOMMENDATION 7: A merchandise trade deficit is a necessary consequence of service trade, and should not be the focus of commercial policy action.

In connection with Recommendation 7 it should be noted that, if service trade is an important component of international transactions, a deficit in goods is of no more significance than a deficit in automobiles or a deficit in French wine. It makes no more sense to insist on a balance in commodity trade than it would to insist that Canada export as much wine to France as we import from that country.

In some situations Canadian government policy also acts to reduce the international competitiveness of the domestic transportation system. One example is the gasoline tax imposed both by the federal and provincial governments. When gasoline taxes were first introduced they were seen as a method of financing the construction and maintenance of the Canadian road system. For many years there was a rough balance between the taxes collected from gasoline sales and the expenditure on the highway system. In recent years, however, both the federal government and provincial governments have seen gasoline taxes as a general tax revenue, and there is no longer any relationship between expenditures on highways and tax collected from gasoline and other fuel sales.

The high Canadian fuel taxes, particularly when compared with the tax levels in the United States, produce a significant disadvantage for Canadian transportation, particularly trucking. One immediate effect is to widen the cost differences which presently exist between east-west transportation and north-south transportation. North-south transportation between many trading centres in North America is cheaper for two reasons. First, the distances are typically shorter, since Canadian markets are often closer to U.S. markets than to alternative markets within Canada. Second, trucking to or from the United States allows firms to take advantage of low fuel costs south of the border. When one adds to these the lower level of regulation that exists in the United States one finds that the Canadian trucking industry is at a significant disadvantage compared to its counterpart in the United States.

It is easy to think of several reasons why the gasoline tax has become such a popular revenue source in Canada in recent years. One reason is that the gasoline tax is a good source of revenue since the demand for gasoline tends to be quite inelastic, at least in the short run. The switch from gallons to litres has also made it easier for the governments to raise gasoline taxes without a public outcry. The recent federal tax increase of 1 cent a litre does not seem like much and does not raise much controversy, even though it will probably be magnified to approximately a 2 cent increase at the pumps. This tax increase denominated in terms of gallons is 4 1/2 cents, which will probably result in a 9 or 10 cent increase per gallon to the final consumer. One suspects that a proposal to increase the consumer cost of gasoline by 10 cents a gallon would have received a lot more attention.

The petroleum price increases of the last two decades has also been a factor in encouraging higher gasoline taxes. The real or perceived gasoline shortages prompted a great deal of interest in conservation, and one long-run method of reducing quantity demanded was to increase the price. Higher taxes have thus been seen as a conservation measure. It is difficult, however, to think of any persuasive argument to support forced conservation as a welfare increasing policy. The higher market prices associated with market conditions would, themselves, do the job. It would seem difficult to defend the current levels of gasoline taxes, and we have the following:

RECOMMENDATION 8: As a measure of insuring competitiveness in the transportation sector, every effort should be made to reduce the government's reliance on fuel taxes as a source of revenue. An appropriate policy would be to match government expenditures on highways and roads to highway fuel tax revenues.

11.4 Factor Services

Trade in factor services is one of the most important service trade items, and seems likely to become of increasing significance in years to come. The analysis of trade in factor services is complex, for factor services occur in many different forms, and the characteristics of the services are quite varied. One complication is the fact that many services are produced under conditions of increasing returns to scale. This topic was taken up extensively in Chapter 7.

In the discussion of Chapter 6 we found several instances where the introduction of trade in services necessitated some rather fundamental reinterpretations of traditional trade theory. Trade patterns, for example, are not always what one would expect from the observation of a country's relative factor endowments. Thus it is quite possible to observe a country that is well endowed with capital importing capital-intensive goods if they are also exporting factor services. It also was shown that traditional commercial policy measures such as tariffs and quotas may not have the expected results on relative commodity prices. Thus a tariff on an import of a commodity may actually lower the relative price of that good and could result in an increase in the output of both goods. Of course these differences are not a reflection of the fact that traditional trade theory is incorrect, but rather arise when service trade, which we have assumed to be a flow of capital services, is a substitute for commodity trade. The result is that attention should focus on rates of exchange between factor services and commodities, and not on the terms of trades between goods traditionally considered in international trade discussions. Thus if service trade is an important component of a country's international transactions, a good deal of care must be taken in formulating policies that attempt to adjust domestic production patterns. This leads to the following recommendation:

RECOMMENDATION 9: If service trade is an important component of international transactions, then tariffs and quotas should not be relied on as a method of adjusting domestic production and employment patterns.

Another important feature of trade in factor services is that services may be either substitutes or complements for trade in goods. This issue has arisen in several places throughout our earlier discussion. It can be shown that where services and goods are substitutes in trade patterns, commercial policy instruments such as tariffs or quotas may have very little influence on domestic welfare, even though they may substantially alter trade flows. Thus, in a situation where one has trade both in goods and in factor services, restrictions on the imports of a good may simply result in a larger quantity of factor services entering the country. This result confirms the widely-held view that Canadian tariff policy has, at least to some extent, resulted in substantial foreign investment in Canada. By the same token, restrictions on foreign investment, if goods are free to move, will simply result in a larger trade volume with only very modest effects on domestic welfare. Of course, as with any distortion, whatever welfare consequences there are will be negative. Thus we have the following:

RECOMMENDATION 10: When both goods and services are free to move internationally, policy makers should recognize the fact that traditional commercial policy measures may be ineffective in producing changes in domestic welfare.

But goods and services are not always substitutes in international trade. Indeed, as was shown in Chapter 7, in many circumstances services and goods are close complements, and in such situations the implications for trade are very different indeed. An obvious example of such complementarity occurs with goods such as computers or other technical equipment that requires servicing by expert technicians, or which necessitates training of local operators before the equipment can be efficiently utilized. In such circumstances the good cannot be used efficiently unless the required service can be provided. If the service requires specialized knowledge or training available only where the good is produced, then obviously the efficient utilization of the product requires that both the service and the good be allowed access to the foreign market. In such circumstances restrictions on service trade will also effectively eliminate the trade in goods, and there could be significant welfare consequences.

Even in less severe circumstances where services and goods are not such close complements, it was shown in Chapter 7 that restrictions on service trade may have much more profound effects than restrictions on trade in goods. Indeed, in some circumstances, service trade replaces the need for trade in goods, and in fact goods trade alone would not occur if service trade is not permitted. Note that this situation is very different from the substitute case discussed above. The fact that trade in some producer services eliminates the need for trade in goods is quite different from the case where they are substitutes, and where trade in either will produce the same welfare effect. In the present case service trade is a requirement for any gains from international trade. Again we find that restrictions on service flows may have much more significant consequences for the economy than tariffs on goods. We thus have the following:

RECOMMENDATION 11: In many circumstances restrictions on service trade will have much more severe consequences for the domestic economy than tariffs on goods, and thus trade restrictions on services should be avoided.

An issue that was taken up in Chapter 6 was the effect of domestic taxes on the trade patterns when there is trade in both goods and services. It was shown that the traditional results, namely that commodity taxes can have exactly the same effect on trade flows as tariffs, required substantial modification. Although there are domestic tax measures that would duplicate the effects of tariffs, these typically would involve restrictions on foreign-earned income. Governments typically do not impose restrictions on foreign-earned income as part of a commercial policy, but the discussion of Chapter 6 does point to the importance of such measures as a determinant of trade patterns. In particular, discriminatory treatment of any factor of production, whether domestic or foreign, could have substantial impacts on international trade flows. To avoid such distortions one should aim for a neutral tax system, and one should not permit the tax treatment of domestics to vary significantly from the tax treatment afforded comparable individuals who reside in countries that are major trading partners. Of equal importance, perhaps, is the attempt to assure that individuals in different regions are treated equally by the tax system. Substantial differences among regional tax systems can result in distortions in domestic trade, and can also affect international trade patterns. We thus have the following:

RECOMMENDATION 12: If service trade is an important component of international transactions, then it is important, both for domestic and international efficiency, to maintain a neutral tax treatment for mobile factors. In particular, the harmonization of the tax treatment of capital, both domestically and internationally, should be a policy goal.

11.5 Multinationals and Foreign Investment

The possibility that services may give rise to the formation of multinationals and the introduction of international franchising operations was introduced in Chapter 3 and discussed in detail in Chapter 8. The principal result from this discussion is that, to some extent at least, multinationals arise because of economies of scale in the provision of some services internal to the firm. Producer services that are produced with high fixed and very low marginal cost can be provided to two or more plants almost as cheaply as to one. In particular, the average and marginal cost of producing a commodity in a two-plant firm will be less than if two independent firms existed to produce this product. The principal result is that, since the existence of multinationals lowers cost, economic welfare will generally be increased by their existence.

The fact that multinationals increase efficiency, however, is not the end of the story. Because the economies of scale are internal to the firm, one would expect some type of imperfect competition to develop. Firms can typically make pure economic profits, and in this case the distribution of welfare will very much depend on where the owners of the multinational firms reside. It is certainly possible that a substantial share of the gains associated with the high level of efficiency will be transferred to foreign countries if the multinationals are foreign owned. Even with this proviso, however, it was shown that it will generally be true that both the host and donor countries will gain from the existence of multinational firms.

Some of the same characteristics are true for franchising operations. Franchises typically arise when there are economies of scale, either in advertising, promotion, or in the purchasing of inputs. In general, the ability of such firms to capture these economies of scale will result in welfare gains, although as was the case with multinationals, it is not always clear to whom these gains will accrue. On balance, however, and particularly since multinationals are not domiciled in a single country, general welfare gains to society are to be expected from the operation of such companies. We thus have the following result:

RECOMMENDATION 13: Multinationals and franchise operations typically result in an increase in economic efficiency, and public policy should not discourage this type of economic activity.

A discussion of multinationals cannot be logically separated from a discussion of foreign investment, and thus our conclusion that public policy should not discriminate against multinationals also suggests that one should not discriminate against foreign capital in general. A caveat must be added, however. Burgess (1989) has argued that in a world with foreign ownership and a variety of restrictions on the flow of goods and factors, one cannot assume that the liberalization of factor service flows will necessarily increase domestic welfare. In a world with many distortions we have a second-best situation, and as is well known, definitive results are difficult to formulate. Thus one must not automatically assume that service trade liberalization will necessarily increase domestic welfare if this liberalization takes place in a situation where a variety of other distortionary policies are in place.

In some circumstances economic policy makers may be faced with a choice of allowing trade in a service product, or of granting rights of establishment to foreign firms, which may require the importation of service factors. Thus, for example, we may have the choice between allowing domestics to buy banking services from foreigners, or alternatively of allowing foreign banks to bring their expertise to Canada and set up branches that will directly serve domestics. These options were addressed in Chapter 9, and it was found that an unambiguous ranking is not possible unless endowments at home were "extreme". One general result shown was that there is always a positive relationship between the size of the welfare gain and the expansion of the service industry. This provides a convenient and simple rule for policy formation, and leads to our next recommendation:

RECOMMENDATION 14: Larger welfare gains are associated with increases in the size of the service sector in the domestic economy and thus policy should be formulated on the basis of how the size of the industry will be affected.

An important issue related to investment in the service industries is the question of how productivity can be measured and whether technical change in services can form the basis of sustained economic growth. Methods of measuring technical change in services have proven to be elusive, due partly to the fact that new technologies in this area are often markedly different than the old, making comparisons difficult. At the same time it is clear that many of the really important technological advances throughout history have occurred in service industries, and have facilitated trade and communications. Indeed, any trade requires transportation services, and thus gains from trade are really gains from services, and this includes *all* trade, not just international trade. This suggests the following:

RECOMMENDATION 15: Technological advances in service industries, particularly in transportation and communication, can provide enormous benefits to society, and thus social policy should encourage research in these important areas.

While we have argued that, in general, technological advances in services can produce significant welfare gains for society, it does not necessarily follow that regions within a country should count on the service sector becoming an engine of economic growth. Major technological advances in services will have widespread effects and there seems to be no reason to expect them to affect regional disparities in one way or another. It is unlikely that a disproportionate share of the benefits could be captured by a region or even by a country. Furthermore, technological change in services, just as technological change in any sector, will generally increase the returns to some factors and reduce the returns to others. The direction of the changes will depend on many factors including the capital intensities of the industries involved, and such changes could just as easily increase regional differences as reduce them. This leads to the following:

RECOMMENDATION 16: Public policy should not rely on technological advance in service industries to correct regional economic disparities.

11.6 Conclusions

The purpose of this study has been to investigate the importance of the existence of a significant services industry for an economy that is heavily involved in international trade. The principal conclusions have been highlighted as propositions throughout the analysis, and our major policy recommendations have been presented in earlier sections of this chapter. In conclusion it seems important to recognize that the research reported here is still at a very preliminary stage, and should be thought of simply as the starting point for what will undoubtedly become a significant research area in the future. The theoretical results we have reported must be regarded as preliminary, and undoubtedly many important topics have been omitted. As was mentioned earlier, the lack of information on exactly which services are most important for international trade makes it difficult to be sure that we have focused attention on issues of major importance. Thus our discussion has been very general, and future research will undoubtedly show that some of the issues we have considered are not as important as others. Nevertheless, it is hoped that the theoretical research presented here will prove useful for subsequent researchers interested in the area of international trade in services.

Bibliography

Aukrust, O. (1977), "Inflation in the Open Economy: The Norwegian Model," in Krause, L. and W.S. Salant (eds.), *World Wide Inflation*, Brookings Institute, Washington, 107-153.

Baumol, W.J. (1967), "Macroeconomics of Economic Growth," *American Economic Review* 57, 415-426.

Baumol, W.J. (1985), "Productivity Policy and the Service Sector," in R.P. Inman (ed.), *Managing the Service Economy: Prospects and Problems*, Cambridge University Press, Cambridge.

Benz, S.F. (1985), "Trade Liberalization and the Global Service Economy," *Journal of World Trade Law* 19, 95-102.

Bhagwati, J.N. (1985), "Trade in Services and Developing Countries," Xth Annual Geneva Lecture delivered at the London School of Economics, November 28.

Brander, J. and P. Krugman (1983), "A Reciprocal Dumping Model of International Trade," *Journal of International Economics* 13.

Brander, J. and B. Spencer (1984), "Tariff Protection and Imperfect Competition in the Presence of Oligopoly over Economies of

Scale," in Kierzkowski (ed.), *Monopolistic Competition and International Trade*, Oxford University Press, Oxford, 313-321.

Burgess, D.F. (1989), "A Specific Factors Model on Trade in Services," *International Economic Review* (forthcoming).

Calvo, G. and S. Wellisz (1983), "International Factor Mobility and the National Advantage," *Journal of International Economics* 13, 103-104.

Casas, F.R. (1983), "International Trade with Produced Transport Services," *Oxford Economic Papers (New Series)*, Vol. 35, No. 1 (March), 89-109.

Cassing, J. (1978), "Transport Costs in International Trade Theory: A Comparison with the Analysis of Non-Traded Goods," *Quarterly Journal of Economics* (November), 535-550.

Casson, Mark (1986), "General Theories of the Multinational Enterprise" A Critical Examination", Chapter 2 of Mark Casson, *The Firm and the Market: Studies on Transactions Cost and the Strategy of the Firm* (in mimeo).

Deardorff, A. (1985), "Comparative Advantage and International Trade and Investment in Services," in Robert M. Stern (ed.), *Trade and Investment in Services: Canada/U.S. Perspectives* (Toronto: Ontario Economic Council), 39-71.

Deardorff, A. (1987), "Notes on the Gains from Trade in the Presence of Domestic Distortions," The University of Michigan Working Paper.

Dixit, A.L. and V. Norman (1980), *Theory of International Trade*, Cambridge University Press.

Dornbusch, R. (1980), *Open Economy Macroeconomics*, Basic Books, New York.

Dunning, John H. (1977), "Trade, Location of Economic Activity and MNE: A Search for an Eclectic Approach", in Ohlin, Hesselborn, and Wijkman (eds.), *The International Allocation of Economic Activity* (London: Macmillan).

Dunning, John H. (1981), *International Production and the Multinational Enterprise* (London: George Allen and Unwin).

Economic Council of Canada (1984), *Western Transition* (Ottawa: Supply and Services Canada).

Ethier, Wilfred (1979), "Internationally Decreasing Cost and World Trade," *Journal of International Economics* 9, 1-24.

Ethier, Wilfred (1982), "National and International Returns to Scale in the Modern Theory of International Trade," *American Economic Review* 72, 389-405.

Ewing, A.F. (1985), "Why Freer Trade in Services is in the Interest of Developing Countries," *Journal of World Trade Law* 19, 121-135.

Falvey, R. (1976), Transportation Costs in the Pure Theory of International Trade," *Economic Journal* (September), 536-550.

Findlay, R. and H. Kierzkowski (1983), "International Trade and Human Capital: A Simple General Equilibrium Model," *Journal of Political Economy* 91 (December), 957-978.

Fuchs, V.R. (1968), "The Service Economy," National Bureau of Economic Research, New York.

Gershuny, J.I., and I.D. Mills (1983), *The New Service Economy*, Frances Pinter Publishers, London.

Helpman, Elhanan (1981), "International Trade in the Presence of Product Differentiation, Economies of Scale and Monopolistic Competition. A Chamberlinian-Heckscher-Ohlin Approach," *Journal of International Economics* 11, 304-340.

Herberg, H. (1970), "Economic Growth and International Trade with Transport Costs," *Zeitschrift fur die Gesamte Staatswissenschaft* (October), 577-600.

Herberg, H. and M.C. Kemp (1969), "Some Implications of Variable Returns to Scale," *Canadian Journal of Economics* II, 403-415.

Hill, T.P. (1977), "On Goods and Services," *The Review of Income and Wealth* 23, 315-338.

Hindley, B. and A. Smith (1984), "Comparative Advantage and Trade in Services," *The World Economy* 7, 369-390.

Inman, Robert P. (1985), "Introduction and Overview," in R.P. Inman (ed.), *Managing the Service Economy,* Cambridge University Press, Cambridge.

Jones, R.W. (1965), "The Structure of Simple General Equilibrium Models," *Journal of Political Economy* LXXIII, 557-572.

Jones, R.W., (1971), "A Three-Factor Model in Theory, Trade, and History," in J.N. Bhagwati et al. (eds.), *Trade, Balance of Payments, and Growth: Essays in Honor of Charles P. Kindleberger,* North Holland, Amsterdam, 3-21.

Jones, R.W., I. Coelho, and S.T. Easton (1986), "The Theory of International Factor Flows: The Basic Model," *Journal of International Economics* 20, 313-327.

Jones, Ronald W. and Henryk Kierzkowski (1989), "The Role of Services in Production and International Trade: A Theoretical Framework," in *The Political Economy of International Trade,* edited by Ronald W. Jones and Anne O. Krueger, Part I (Basil Blackwell Publishers), forthcoming.

Jones, R.W. and F. Ruane (1989), "Options for International Trade in Services: A Specific Factors Framework," *Economica* (forthcoming).

Kierzkowski, Henryk (1984), "Services in the Development Process and the Theory of International Trade," *Discussion Paper in International Economics,* No. 8405 (Geneva: Graduate Institute of International Studies).

Kierzkowski, H. (1986), "Modelling International Transportation Services," I.M.F. Research Paper, DM/86/35.

Kierzkowski, H. (1987), "Recent Advances in International Trade Theory: A Selective Survey," *Oxford Review of Economic Policy,* Vol.3, No. 1.

Kravis, I.B. (1983), "The Share of Services in Economic Growth," in F.G. Adams and G. Hickman (eds.), *Global Econometrics: Essays in Honor of Lawrence R. Klien,* Cambridge, Massachusetts.

Krugman, Paul (1979), "Increasing Returns, Monopolistic Competition and International Trade," *Journal of International Economics* 9, 469-479.

Kuhn, P. and I. Wooton (1987), "International Factor Movements in the Presence of a Fixed Factor," *Journal of International Economics* 22, 123-140.

Kuznets, S. (1972), *Modern Economic Growth*, Yale University Press, New Haven.

Lancaster, K. (1957), "The Heckscher-Ohlin Trade Model: A Geometric Treatment," *Economica* 19-39.

Lancaster, K. (1966), "A New Approach to Consumer Theory," *Journal of Political Economy* 74, 132-157.

Lancaster, K. (1980), "Intra-Industry Trade under Perfect Monopolistic Competition," *Journal of International Economics*, 10, 151-175.

Leveson, I. (1985), "Services in the U.S. Economy," in R.P. Inman (ed.), *Managing the Service Economy: Prospects and Problems*, Cambridge University Press, Cambridge.

Mansell, R.L. (1985), "The Service Sector and Western Economic Growth," *Canadian Public Policy* XI Supplement, 354-360.

Markusen, James R. (1983), "Factor Movements and Commodity Trade as Complements", *Journal of International Economics* 13, 341-356.

Markusen, J.R. (1988), "Production, Trade and Migration with Differentiated Skilled Workers," *Canadian Journal of Economics* 21 (August), 492-506.

Markusen, J.R. (1989a), "Trade in Producer Services and in Other Specialized Intermediate Inputs," *American Economic Review* (March), 85-95.

Markusen, J.R. (1989b), "Service Trade by the Multinational Enterprise," in Peter Enderwick (ed.), *Multinational Service Firms*, Routledge, 35-60.

Markusen, J.R. and J.R. Melvin (1981), "Trade, Factor Prices, and the Gains from Trade with Increasing Returns to Scale," *Canadian Journal of Economics* XIV, 450-469.

Markusen, J.R. and J.R. Melvin (1988), "Trade in Goods and Producer Services as Substitutes and Complements," Institute for Research on Public Policy, Victoria, B.C..

Melvin, J.R. (1968), "Production and Trade with Two Factors and Three Goods," *American Economic Review* LVIII (December), 1249-1268.

Melvin, J.R. (1969), "Increasing Returns to Scale as a Determinant of Trade," *Canadian Journal of Economics* II (August), 389-402.

Melvin, J.R. (1970), "Commodity Taxation as a Determinant of Trade," *Canadian Journal of Economics* III, 62-78.

Melvin, J.R. (1985a), "Domestic Taste Differences, Transportation Costs and International Trade," *Journal of International Economics* 18, 65-82.

Melvin, J.R. (1985b), "The Regional Economic Consequences of Tariffs and Domestic Transportation Costs," *Canadian Journal of Economics* 18, 237-257.

Melvin, J.R. (1987a), "Services: Dimensionality and Intermediation in Economic Analysis," Working Paper, Institute for Research on Public Policy, Victoria, B.C.

Melvin, James R. (1987b), "The Role of Services in a Small, Open Regional Economy," Working Paper, Institute for Research on Public Policy, Victoria, B.C.

Melvin, J.R. (1989), "Trade in Producer Services: A Heckscher-Ohlin Approach", *Journal of Political Economy* (forthcoming).

Mundell, Robert A. (1957a), "International Trade and Factor Mobility," *American Economic Review* 47, 321-335.

Mundell, Robert A. (1957b), "A Geometry of Transport Costs in International Trade Theory," *Canadian Journal of Economics and Political Science* (August), 331-348.

Nordhaus, W. (1972), "The Recent Productivity Slowdown," Brookings Economic Papers, No. 3, 493-596.

Perroux, F. (1955), "Note on the Concept of 'Growth Poles'," in McKee, D.L., R.D. Dean and W.H. Leahy (eds.), *Regional Economics: Theory and Practice*, The Free Press, New York (1970).

Ramaswami, V.K. (1968), "International Factor Movements and the National Advantage," *Economica* 35, 309-310.

Rugman, Alan M. (1985), "Internalization is Still a General Theory of Foreign Direct Investment", *Weltwirtschaftliches Archiv*.

Rugman, Alan M. (1986), "A Transactions Approach to Trade in Services," Paper Presented at the Annual Meetings of the A.E.A. at New Orleans, December.

Ryan, Cillian (1987), "Trade in the Presence of Endogenous Intermediation in an Asymmetric World," Working Paper, Institute for Research on Public Policy, Victoria, B.C.

Ryan, Cillian (1988), "Trade in Services: An Introductory Survey," *Economic and Social Review* 20, No. 1 (October).

Sampson, G. and R. Snape (1985), "Identifying the Issues in Trade and Services," *The World Economy* 8 (June), 171-182.

Samuelson, P.A. (1954), "The Transfer Problem and Transport Costs: An Analysis of Effects of Trade Impediments," *Economic Journal* (June), 264-269.

Samuelson, P.A. (1971), "Ohlin was Right," *Swedish Journal of Economics* 73, 365-384.

Sapir, A. (1985), "North-South Issues in Trade in Services," *The World Economy* 8, 27-42.

Sapir, A. and E. Lutz (1981), "Trade in Services: Economic Determinants and Development Related Issues," World Bank Staff Working Paper, World Bank, Washington.

Saxonhouse, G.R. (1985), "Services in the Japanese Economy," in R.P. Inman (ed.), *Managing the Service Economy: Prospects and Problems*, Cambridge University Press, Cambridge.

Shelp, R.K. (1981), *Beyond Industrialization: Ascendancy of the Global Service Economy*, Praeger Publishers, New York.

Stalson, H. (1985), *U.S. Services Exports and Foreign Barriers: An Agenda for Negotiations*, National Planning Association, Washington, D.C.

Summers, R.M. (1985), "Services in the International Economy," in R.P. Inman (ed.), *Managing the Service Economy: Prospects and Problems*, Cambridge University Press, Cambridge.

Swan, N.M. (1985), "The Service Sector: Engine of Growth?" *Canadian Public Policy* XI Supplement, 344-350.

Thurow, L. (1979), "The U.S. Productivity Problem," *Data Resources Review* (August).

Wolff, F.N. (1981), "The Composition of Output and the Productivity Growth Slowdown of 1967-76," mimeo.

Zweifel, P. (1986), "On the Tradeability of Services," Paper Presented to the Progress Seminar on the Service Economy (June 2/3).

Related Publications

Order Address

The Institute for Research on Public Policy
P.O. Box 3670 South
Halifax, Nova Scotia
B3J 3K6

1-800-565-0659 (toll free)

James J. McRae and Martine M. Desbois, eds. *Traded and Non-traded Services: Theory, Measurement and Policy.* 1988 $22.00
ISBN 0-88645-066-7

Roger Verreault et Mario Polèse *L'exportation de services par les firmes canadiennes de génie-conseil : évolution récente et avantages concurrentiels.* 1989 19,95 $
ISBN 0-88645-078-0

PLUS: Some 40 overview and discussion papers are also available. Discussion papers cost $7.50 each, or $200.00 for the set. Overviews cost $15.00 each. A complete set of papers and overviews is available for $250.00. For the complete list, please write to the address shown above.